D0280764

Sex Offenders in the Community

ON REFERENCE

DISCARD

Cambridge Criminal Justice Series

Published in association with the Institute of Criminology, University of Cambridge

Published titles

Community Penalties: Change and Challenges, edited by Anthony Bottoms, Loraine Gelsthorpe and Sue Rex

Ideology, Crime and Criminal Justice: A Symposium in Honour of Sir Leon Radzinowicz, edited by Anthony Bottoms and Michael Tonry

Reform and Punishment: The Future of Sentencing, edited by Sue Rex and Michael Tonry

Confronting Crime: Crime Control Policy under New Labour, edited by Michael Tonry

Sex Offenders in the Community: Managing and Reducing the Risks, edited by Amanda Matravers

Sex Offenders in the Community

Managing and reducing the risks

edited by

Amanda Matravers

WILLAN
PUBLISHING

Published in association with the Institute of Criminology, University of Cambridge, by

Willan Publishing
Culmcott House
Mill Street, Uffculme
Cullompton, Devon
EX15 3AT, UK
Tel: +44(0)1884 840337
Fax: +44(0)1884 840251
e-mail: info@willanpublishing.co.uk
Website: www.willanpublishing.co.uk

Published simultaneously in the USA and Canada by

Willan Publishing
c/o ISBS, 920 NE 58th Ave, Suite 300,
Portland, Oregon 97213-3786, USA
Tel: +001(0)503 287 3093
Fax: +001(0)503 280 8832
Website: www.isbs.com

First published 2003
Reprinted 2005, 2006, 2007, 2008

ISBN 10: 1-84392-120-0
ISBN 13: 978-1-84392-120-2

British Library Cataloguing-in-Publication Data
A catalogue record for this book is available from the British Library

Project management by Deer Park Productions, Tavistock, Devon
Typeset by TW Typesetting, Plymouth, Devon
Printed and bound by TJI Digital, Trecerus Industrial Estate, Padstow, Cornwall

Contents

List of abbreviations

ACPC	Area Child Protection Committee
ACPO	Association of Chief Police Officers
ASBO	Anti-social behaviour order
ATSA	Association for the Treatment of Sexual Abusers
BPS	British Psychological Society
CA	Court of Appeal
CDA	Crime and Disorder Act 1998
CJCSA 2000	Criminal Justice and Courts Services Act 2000
DPA	Data Protection Act 1998
ECHR	European Commission on Human Rights
HDC	Home Detention Curfew
HMYOI	Her Majesty's Youth Offending Institution
HRA	Human Rights Act 1998
LSI-R	Level of Service Inventory Revised
MAPPA	Multi-Agency Public Protection Arrangements
MAPPP	Multi-Agency Public Protection Panel
MST	Multi-systemic therapy
NAS	National Academies of Sciences
NO	Notification Order
NPD	National Probation Directorate
NSPCC	National Society for the Prevention of Cruelty to Children
OASys	Offender Assessment System
OGRS	Offender Group Reconviction Scale
PACE 1984	Police and Criminal Evidence Act 1984
PCL-R	Psychopathy Checklist Revised
PPG	Penile Plethysmograph

PPU	Public Protection Unit
RO	Restraining Order
RSHO	Risk of Sexual Harm Order
RSO	Registered sex offender
SMB	Strategic Management Board
SONAR	Sex Offender Need Assessment Rating
SOO	Sex Offender Order
SOPO	Sexual Offences Prevention Order
SOTEP	Sex Offender Treatment Evaluation Project
ViSOR	Violent and Sex Offender Register
YOI	Youth offending institution
YOT	Youth offending team

List of figures

List of tables

Notes on contributors

Detective Chief Inspector **Tim Bryan** currently works in the Public Protection Unit of the National Probation Directorate on a three-year secondment from the Metropolitan Police Service. He has been directly involved in the development of national policy and guidance for multi-agency public protection arrangements and has facilitated the management of a number of high-profile/high-risk cases. A police Fulbright Fellow in 1998, he is an ordained priest in the Church of England and has for a number of years been a child protection adviser to the Bishop of Southwark.

Cathy Cobley, a former police officer, graduated from University College, Cardiff in 1988. She has been a lecturer at Cardiff Law School since 1989, where she now lectures on the undergraduate degree programmes in criminal law, contract law and the law of evidence, and contributes to postgraduate teaching on the Legal Aspects of Medical Practice degree scheme. Her research interests include sex offenders and child abuse. She is the author of *Sex Offenders: law, policy and practice* (2000) (Jordans), and has contributed to the third edition of Lyons (2003) *Child Abuse* (Jordans).

Rowland Coombes is a Senior Clinical Therapist with the Lucy Faithfull Foundation. Having specialised in the field of sexual crime several years ago, he is currently working with young people (aged 15–21) who sexually abuse. This project, funded by the Probation Directorate, delivers assessment and treatment to young people in juvenile detention centres and young offender institutions. He also provides training and consultancy on young sex abusers in the community to probation and youth offender teams in London and elsewhere.

Paddy Doyle has worked in the criminal justice system for 25 years, specialising for the last 10 years in the management of work with sexual and dangerous offenders. He completed four years in the Public Protection Unit of the National Probation Directorate as an Assistant Chief Officer in January 2003. During that time he co-wrote the national guidance for the Multi Agency Public Protection Arrangements (MAPPA) in England and Wales. He is now a freelance consultant specialising in public protection and offender risk management.

Don Grubin is Professor of Forensic Psychiatry, University of Newcastle upon Tyne and (Hon) Consultant Forensic Psychiatrist, Newcastle, North Tyneside and Northumberland Mental Health Trust. Research interests include the assessment, treatment and management of sex offenders.

Hazel Kemshall is currently Professor of Community and Criminal Justice at DeMontfort University. She has research interests in risk assessment and management of offenders, effective work in multi-agency public protection, and implementing effective practice with offenders. She has recently completed a literature review on risk assessment tools for violent and dangerous offenders and an evaluation of multi-agency public protection panels for the Home Office and Scottish Executive, an audit of risk tools in Scotland with Professor Gill McIvor, and work (with Yates) on dangerous young offenders for the Youth Justice Board. She is currently investigating pathways into and out of crime for young people under the ESRC network (with Boeck and Fleming) and has recently completed work on attrition from accredited programmes for the National Probation Service.

Roxanne Lieb is the Director of the Washington State Institute for Public Policy, a research organization that conducts studies at the request of the Washington State Legislature. She was a fellow at the University of Cambridge Institute of Criminology in 2001–2002, thanks to support from the Atlantic Fellowship in Public Policy, a US/UK partnership administered by the British Council.

Mike Maguire is Professor of Criminology and Criminal Justice at Cardiff University. He was previously a senior research fellow at the Oxford University Centre for Criminological Research. He has managed and conducted numerous major research projects in a range of crime and justice areas, including residential burglary, victim support, policing, prisons, restorative justice, parole and resettlement. He was part of a research team that examined the multi-agency arrangements for the risk assessment and management of sexual and other dangerous offenders, and has written several articles on related topics. He has more than one hundred publications to his name, including co-editing the *The Oxford Handbook of Criminology* (Oxford University Press, third edition 2002). He is an ex-member of the Parole Board, and a member of the Correctional Services Accreditation Panel.

Amanda Matravers is a Lecturer in Criminology at the University of Cambridge Institute of Criminology, and Director of the Institute's Diploma/Master of Studies in Applied Criminology and Police Management. Her research interests are sex offending, policing and policy. She has completed research for the Home Office and the Police and Probation Services. She has also worked as an associate trainer for HM Prison Service, and run group work with offenders in prison and on probation.

Helen Power is a Principal Lecturer at the University of Glamorgan. Her current research interests relate primarily to sexual offences law, and to the legal regime within which sex offenders are managed post-release. She also researches in the field of human rights law, particularly as it relates to issues arising out of sexual orientation. She has published numerous articles in all these areas, primarily in legal journals.

Michael Seto is a psychologist with the Law and Mental Health Program at the Centre for Addiction and Mental Health in Toronto. He is also an Assistant Professor in Psychiatry and Criminology at the University of Toronto. His research interests are sexual offending and other forms of serious antisocial behaviour; the accurate assessment of risk for re-offence and criminogenic needs; sexual preferences, particularly the paraphilias; and programme evaluation.

Keith Soothill is Professor of Social Research in the Department of Applied Social Science, Lancaster University. His current research interests are in the areas of homicide, sex offending, criminal careers and crime and the media. He has taught criminology for over 30 years with well over 100 publications. He wants criminologists to appreciate the links with other disciplines and not to be too narrowly focused. He recently co-authored the book, *Making Sense of Criminology* (Cambridge: Polity Press, 2002) and the monograph, *Murder and Serious Sexual Assault: what criminal histories can reveal about future serious offending* (London: Home Office, 2002).

Preface

The management of sex offenders is a subject that raises hackles and hits headlines, but is all too seldom debated in a thoughtful and productive way. In a political climate in which the protection of the public is an overriding concern, 'management' has become a euphemism for the determination of risk, while the term 'sex offender' is used to refer to a small number of dangerous offenders convicted of serious sexual offences. Despite their rarity, the existence of these predatory individuals has been used to drive an increasingly punitive criminal justice agenda, with significant implications for the agencies charged with the task of securing public protection in the community.

There are many good reasons to regret the dominance of the dangerous predator in popular and political thought. Firstly, as many commentators have pointed out, the majority of sex offences are committed by individuals who are known by, and often related to, their victims. Secondly, at a time when we know more than ever about sex offender characteristics and responses to treatment, the focus on risk assessment overshadows the range of strategies currently available to policy-makers and practitioners. Thirdly, the punitive, populist policies introduced to counter public fears are at odds with the government's broader community safety agenda, with its emphasis on the involvement of a range of organisations, groups and individuals in the task of crime prevention.

The aim of this book is to provide a counterweight to this narrow, risk-focused agenda. It brings together experts from a range of backgrounds: criminology, social science, law, offender treatment, prisons, probation, police and policy. The breadth of their expertise takes in theoretical issues, the legal context, risk assessment and management, new treatment strategies, multi-agency work, and law enforcement. In common with many of those who work in the field of sex offending, the authors aim to illuminate an issue that is obscured by strong emotions and misinformation. Their contributions do not simply analyse existing practices and dilemmas, but explore new and developing strategies, and suggest alternative approaches to the problem of sexual violence.

The first drafts of all the chapters in this collection were prepared for the 27th Cropwood Round Table Conference 'Managing Sex Offenders in the Community', held at the University of Cambridge in November 2002. The Conference was organised by the editor with Roxanne Lieb, then a Visiting Fellow at the University of Cambridge Institute of Criminology. It was attended by some 25 participants, including senior practitioners, policy-makers and academics.

Although the Cropwood Conferences are always notable for the breadth and expertise of participants, we were extremely privileged to assemble the group who agreed to take part in this 27th meeting. Cropwood Conferences are unusual and rather special events, at which those who make up the audience add as much to the debates as those who prepare and give papers. Given the location of the Conference, we were particularly proud that our attendees included among their number no less than four past and present directors of the Institute of Criminology. The full list of participants was as follows:

Mr Andrew Bates (Forensic Psychologist, Thames Valley Project)
Mr Ian Blakeman (HM Prison Service)
Professor Sir Anthony Bottoms (University of Cambridge Institute of Criminology)
Mr Tim Bryan (Public Protection Unit, National Probation Directorate)
Ms Cathy Cobley (Law School, University of Cardiff)
Mr Rowland Coombes (National Probation Service)
Mr Paddy Doyle (Public Protection Unit, National Probation Directorate)
Chief Constable Terence Grange (Dyfed Powys Police)
Professor Don Grubin (Department of Psychiatry, Royal Victoria Infirmary, Newcastle-upon-Tyne)
Ms Jo Hebb (Kneesworth House Hospital, Hertfordshire)
Ms Liz Hill (Head of Public Protection, National Probation Directorate)
Mr Jonathan Hopkinson (National Probation Service)
Dr Gareth Hughes (Kneesworth House Hospital, Hertfordshire)
Professor Hazel Kemshall (Community and Criminal Justice Division, De Montfort University)

Ms Roxanne Lieb (Visiting Fellow, University of Cambridge
Institute of Criminology, and Director, Washington State Institute
for Public Policy, Olympia, USA)
Professor Mike Maguire (School of Social Sciences, Cardiff
University)
Dr Amanda Matravers (University of Cambridge Institute of
Criminology)
Mrs Nicky Padfield (University of Cambridge Institute of
Criminology)
Ms Helen Power (Law School, University of Glamorgan)
Dr Michael Seto (Centre for Addiction and Mental Health, Ontario,
Canada)
Professor Keith Soothill (Department of Applied Social Science,
Lancaster University)
Dr David Thornton (Sand Ridge Treatment Center, Mauston, USA)
Professor Michael Tonry (University of Cambridge Institute of
Criminology)
Professor Nigel Walker (University of Cambridge Institute of
Criminology)
Professor Donald West (University of Cambridge Institute of
Criminology)

Our first thanks go to those participants and to our principal speakers. The Conference – even if we say it ourselves – was exceptionally successful and enjoyable. The topic engendered some heartfelt and at times heated debates, but we never ran short of good humour. The draft papers submitted by our speakers were of a high standard even before being revised for publication. They appear here complete with revisions in the light of discussions and conversations that took place during the Conference, and as such constitute a fitting memorial to an invigorating and enjoyable two days.

The University's Institute of Criminology has received support from the Barrow Cadbury Trust to run the Cropwood Conference Series since 1968. The Institute is extremely grateful to the Barrow Cadbury Trust and to Eric Adams and Mrs Sukhvinder Stubbs from Barrow Cadbury, for their continuing support.

Thanks are due to the team at the Institute who helped to prepare the papers for publication. Helen Griffiths as Cropwood Secretary managed the Conference and co-ordinated the editing of the papers. Further editorial assistance was ably provided by Helen's successor, Nicola Eaton, and by Catherine Byfield and Sara Harrop, who completed the production of the manuscript with characteristic efficiency. Roxanne Lieb and Amanda Matravers would also like to thank Sue Rex, Director of the

Institute's Cropwood Programme, for her enthusiasm and advice in the early stages of the project.

The rationale for the Conference and for this book was to increase the quality of the debate in this difficult and important policy area. Readers will decide for themselves whether this has been achieved.

Amanda Matravers
Cambridge
October 2003

Chapter 1

Setting some boundaries: rethinking responses to sex offenders

Amanda Matravers

Modern penality itself is no longer seen as sufficient to control crime or adequately assure a vociferous public with its punishment prospectus. The boundaries that it set for the limits of punishment now have to be breached in a variety of ways.

(Pratt 2000: 141–2)

The criminal law sets the boundaries for what is culpable and deserving of punishment including sexual activity . . . In producing a set of recommendations which demonstrate a balance between protection, deterrence, the rights of the individual and society's expectation of acceptable behaviour, the review was set a difficult and challenging task to achieve.

(Home Office 2000: 1, 6)

Introduction

In Philip K. Dick's 1956 short story 'Minority Report' (Dick 2002), the Department of Precrime solves the problem of violent crime by the simple expedient of looking into the future, arresting potential criminals, and punishing them before they commit their offences. Had Dick shared the clairvoyant capabilities of his characters, he might have found material for a sequel in current responses to the problem of sex offending. For some dozen or so years, sex crime has been a recurring theme in criminal justice policy. A range of legislation has been introduced, providing for extended custodial sentences and community strategies including registration, supervision and surveillance. Many of these provisions have significant implications for the post-release environment of sex offenders as well as for their civil rights. They allow us to place conditions on the behaviour, activities and lifestyles of individuals convicted of sex offences and, in true Precrime style, on those we think may commit such offences in the future.

Where we diverge from the fictional Precrime system is in the rationale we offer for our arrangements. While both systems are concerned with crime prevention, the Precrime Department is unashamedly committed to the punishment of would-be criminals in a world in which crime commission has become a matter of 'absolute metaphysics'. Our own system conceptualises its use of sanctions against unconvicted and released offenders not as punishment, but as 'public protection'. The assumption is that regular penal measures don't offer sufficient protection from this offender group; only through lengthy detention in custody and constant vigilance outside it can the danger they present be ameliorated. While maintaining a broad commitment to traditional notions of due process and proportionate punishment, we reserve the right to distinguish sex offenders even from other violent offenders, extending the boundaries of punishment and of culpable behaviour.

In this chapter I try to explain why, when it comes to sex offenders, we feel justified in breaching the boundaries of punishment as far and as frequently as we do. One reason might be that sex offending presents an increasing problem, indicating that existing provisions are ineffective and revealing an urgent need for alternative, if extreme, solutions. However, the empirical evidence tells us that this is not the case. Another reason might be that the government is simply acting cynically, deliberately manipulating public fears and taking a strong line against an already-unpopular group of offenders in order to increase support for their policies and distract attention from more divisive policy areas. This is an explanation favoured by a number of commentators, but it doesn't tell the whole story. A more convincing answer is that current policy responses to sex offenders both reflect and shape a view of these offenders that is a product of our own particular culture and time. As such, these responses reveal the concerns and anxieties that preoccupy us. As such, they are also open to change, however immutable they may seem to us now.

To what extent can we anticipate a change in our thinking about sex offenders, and to what extent is this desirable? Objections to the current framework take two main forms: ethical and utilitarian. Ethical objections focus on the erosion of individual rights and conventional understandings of justice that result from preventive sentencing and post-release provisions such as registration and surveillance. At the same time, the unreliability of risk assessment leaves sex offenders vulnerable to over-prediction of their propensity for future offending (see Pratt 1997; Power 1999; von Hirsch 2003). Utilitarian objections concern the mismatch between policy and empirical knowledge about sex offenders. The popular and political preoccupation with predatory strangers means that much current policy is simply misdirected. Far from answering the need for greater protection, this leaves many victims at risk from abusers who don't fit the stereotype. Children and adults who have prior relationships with those who offend against them are liable to be treated less seriously, if not entirely overlooked by the criminal justice system (see Grubin 1998; Jenkins 1998; Simon 2003).

In spite of the variety of recently-introduced sanctions, the demonisation of sex offenders has generated a narrow range of responses dominated by incarceration and tracking. In the community, sex offender management has been focused on registration and risk assessment, with treatment and rehabilitative measures taking a back seat. Although there is now a statutory framework for multi-agency co-operation in the local management of sex offenders, the high-profile nature of this work suggests that practitioners are likely to focus their attention on making defensive (as apposed to 'defensible') decisions about risk rather than optimising the circumstances for the reintegration of offenders (see Lieb, Chapter 11 of this volume). Meanwhile, the public's interest in sex offenders is circumscribed by their belief that obtaining information about convicted sex offenders in their community is the best way to protect their children.

So what's the alternative? Society has little to gain from the exclusion of sex offenders from the possibility of reform. A shift in our thinking about sex offenders – to recognise that many of them are not demons but ordinary people and responsible agents – would allow us to develop a more holistic and contextualised approach to the problem. It would also allow for the deployment of resources into primary prevention, treatment and rehabilitative measures.

The rest of this chapter is divided into four sections. In the first, I examine the empirical evidence for a distinct and severe approach to sex offending and suggest that there is very little of it. Sex offending is not increasing, nor does it seem that the majority of serious offenders serve sentences that would widely be regarded as too lenient. On the other hand, little political effort seems to have been devoted to informing the public about the comparative success of existing measures such as the registration process. In the second section I focus on sociological explanations of our exceptionally punitive response to sex offenders. These explanations relate changing conceptions of sex offenders to the wider social context, and in particular to social and economic developments that have fostered feelings of insecurity and mistrust – feelings that find a focus in the archetype of the dangerous stranger. The third section looks at the way that legislation during the 1990s both reflected and shaped a view of sex offenders as violent predators who represent a constant threat to public safety. The final section assesses the most recent legislation in this area for evidence of a shift in the way sex offenders are conceptualised. Although there is little sign of major change, some of the policy documents reveal a renewal of interest in the balance between the rights of victims and offenders and a concern with an extended range of problems and potential solutions. If we wanted to move towards a new cycle of thinking about sex offenders, these would provide us with a reasonable foundation.

The lack of empirical evidence support for punitive responses

The view of sex offenders that supports the sorts of punitive responses that have prevailed in the last decade rests on a range of myths about their character, ubiquity, and patterns of offending. Many people – influenced, it must be said, by tabloid newspaper headlines and political rhetoric – suppose sex offenders to be more numerous, dangerous and prone to re-offending than the empirical evidence suggests. There is also a widespread perception that even the most serious offenders serve very short prison sentences that don't meet the requirements of retribution and public protection.

Popular views often fail to take into account the variety of behaviours collected under the umbrella label of 'sex offences'. These include behaviours that do not involve contact, such as voyeurism and exhibitionism, as well as intrusive and sadistic violent abuse. Common sex offences include behaviours that are consensual as well as ones that are violent and coercive.[1] Although many of these offences involve exploitation and abuse, only a very small proportion are in accordance with the predatory, compulsive, sexually sadistic offences that – understandably – preoccupy the public imagination.

The other important point about the range of behaviours that qualify as sex offences is that it changes over time. What is regarded as sexual deviance in one era may be seen as acceptable in another, and vice versa. This is one reason why it is difficult to make simple statements about the extent of sex offending on the basis of official statistics. A drop in recorded rates of an offence such as unlawful sexual intercourse (that is, sex with a girl under 16) is more likely to reflect increased social tolerance rather than a real reduction in this form of behaviour.

Similarly, significant increases in reported rapes (which have doubled since 1987) are generally attributed to changes in perceptions about sexual assault that have led the police to treat victims more sensitively and encouraged more victims to come forward (Harris and Grace 1999).

Another reason for the difficulty in extrapolating from criminal statistics is that conviction data dramatically underestimate the prevalence of sexual offending, particularly against children (Cobley 2000). The stigma attached to the crime, together with the fact that many offences are carried out in private and by perpetrators who are relatives of or intimate with their victims, results in considerable under-reporting. Studies of the prevalence of child sexual abuse (that is, experience of victimisation within a population) are generally assumed to provide more accurate information about abuse patterns. While the prevalence rates reported by these surveys tend to vary considerably (as a result of a range of factors including the definition of sexual abuse and data collection methods employed), they indicate firstly that sexual victimisation is more extensive than official statistics suggest, and secondly, that significant numbers of victims fail to disclose their abuse experiences (see Baker and Duncan, 1985; Kelly, Regan and Burton 1991; Finkelhor 1994).

In recent decades, victim surveys and the work of researchers and advocates have shown child sexual abuse and sexual assault to be more prevalent than was previously realised. However, this is not the same as saying that offence rates are increasing. In fact, the number of cautions or convictions for sexual offences has been declining steadily for over a decade (HMSO 2001). More particularly, the number of offences involving the murder of children by sexual predators has shown virtually no change since 1970.[2]

The current preoccupation with predatory violent sex offenders cannot therefore be explained by reference to their increasing numbers. Although, in popular parlance, the word 'paedophile' has become synonymous with 'sex offender', the term is a clinical one that describes a compulsive and recurrent sexual attraction to sexually immature children and applies to a minority of offenders. The majority of sexual offences against children (some 80 per cent) are carried out not by strangers but by known adults (Grubin 1998). While it's true that the criminal statistics conceal the crimes of a significant number of sex offenders, these are less likely to be carried out by anonymous strangers than by offenders who are acquainted with, and not infrequently loved by, their victims.

Another myth about sex offenders relates to their general proclivity for re-offending. Again, official statistics are somewhat treacherous: reconviction is not the same as re-offending, and, as discussed above, many sex offences are not reported. However, recidivism studies indicate that among offenders against children, under 20 per cent will go on to commit a further, similar offence (Hanson and Bussiere 1998). Rather than being a characteristic of all sex offenders, recidivism is associated with a sub-group of offenders who present a greater and longer-term risk to the community than do the majority. Significant time and resources are dedicated to distinguishing offenders who belong to this sub-group in the form of risk prediction and management. However, the predictive accuracy of current risk assessment tools is notoriously limited, particularly in relation to offenders with no known history of sexual offending (Grubin 1997).

A separate point concerns the efficacy of existing legislation. Further punitive measures might be justified if it was believed that these would deter offenders, or if it could be shown that the current framework was failing in a significant and amendable way to punish those who commit sex offences. The argument concerning deterrence is not one that is generally made in relation to sex offenders, whose behaviour is popularly (though not accurately – see Morse 2003) seen as beyond their control. Rather, the assumed incorrigibility of these offenders is the rationale for the emphasis on public protection in recent policy documents, together with the claim that the sentencing system is 'muddled' and allows sexual and other serious offenders to 'get off lightly' (Home Office 2002a: 86).

The empirical evidence suggests that sex offenders who get off lightly are the exception rather than the rule. The probability and severity of sentencing for sexual offences have increased significantly in the last decade and a half. In his review of the sentencing framework (Home Office 2001), Halliday notes that the percentage of sex offenders receiving a custodial sentence rose 31 per cent between 1989 and 1999, from 35 to 66 per cent (p. 80). The average sentence length increased by some 25 per cent during the same period. Beyond custody, there is now a formal framework for multi agency public protection arrangements (MAPPA), and a raft of measures aimed at enhancing public protection, including extended post-release supervision, registration and surveillance in the community, and multi-agency public protection panels (MAPPPs) charged with the risk assessment and management of the 'critical few' offenders adjudged to pose the highest risk.

Although it is too soon too evaluate the effectiveness of MAPPA, the first round of annual reports published in 2002 contained many confident assertions about the progress of 'protection through partnership'. The same note of optimism is sounded in the annual reports for 2002–2003: 'It is clear that in the last year . . . the multi agency public protection arrangements . . . continued to play an important role in what remains one of this government's highest priorities – the protection of the public from dangerous offenders (Minister's foreword, MAPPA Annual Reports 2002–2003).

A more cautiously optimistic tone has been expressed in relation to sex offender registration, the crime prevention effects of which are difficult to discern. However, in its core task of keeping track of sex offenders, the provision must be accorded a success, achieving a national compliance rate of approximately 97 per cent (Home Office 2002b). This figure is well in excess of that achieved by registration arrangements in the US, where a recent survey found that states on average were unable to account for some 24 per cent of offenders required to be on databases.[3]

If the problem of sex offending is not getting worse, and methods of managing it are getting better, how can we account for the continuing political and public preoccupation with these offenders? It could be argued that even if people are mistaken in their beliefs about sex offenders, the fact that they hold such beliefs explains their punitive attitudes. But this simply prompts the question of why people hold such beliefs at this particular time, and with such intensity. Clearly, the existence of a group – however small – of predatory sex offenders is a genuine cause for concern. But it's not a new cause. What is new is the instantiation of the sexual predator as a constant and central threat to children and communities. In part, this is the result of a circular process in which popular fears give rise to populist policies that respond to and thereby reinforce popular fears. What governments have done and ought to do is discussed in the next section. I continue here by exploring another explanation for the current panic about dangerous sex offenders: namely, that this does not constitute a straightforward response to a real problem, but is rather an interpretation of a problem through the lens of a particular historical period, and, as such, acts as a focus for the broader social concerns and anxieties of its time.

The social construction of sex offenders

What we do about crime problems depends on how we think about them. We tend to assume that current understandings of particular social problems are the correct ones, natural successors to the faulty, less sophisticated conceptions of the past. In reality, such understandings are social constructions that reflect particular historical moments and, more often than not, recycle rather than reject previous orthodoxies (see Tonry 1999). In a study of changing concepts of child molesters in North America, Jenkins (1998) concludes that the last 60 years have seen these come full circle, back to a 'sexual predator' model that was prominent during the 1940s, via swings towards liberality in the 1960s and a 'revolution' in the 1980s rooted in revelations about the extent of abuse perpetrated by fathers and family members.

The US is often used as a model for the UK in ways that fail to take account of the differences between the two countries. However, with a few years' slippage, policy responses to sex offenders in England and America display a remarkable degree of similarity (see Lieb 2000). From the late 1980s, both legislatures have introduced a range of stringent provisions including lengthy prison sentences and monitoring in the community; measures that are clearly aimed at, but not restricted to, serious career sex offenders. In both countries, too, these increasingly punitive responses have been galvanised by single, harrowing crimes involving the sexual murder of a child by a previously convicted offender. In the US, the murder of seven-year-old Megan Kanka led to the enactment of federal legislation mandating the release of information to communities regarding sex offenders thought to be at high risk of re-offending. In 2000, calls for a similar law in the UK followed the abduction and murder of eight-year-old Sarah Payne by a registered sex offender.

The genuinely tragic and anxiety-producing nature of such crimes goes some way to explaining the moral panics that follow in their wake. Similarly, the emotive nature of the child protection issue lends it a political appeal that makes its periodic absence from the centre of political debate more puzzling than its presence. Yet it is possible to identify ebbs and flows in concerns about sex crime in general and the threat posed by external predatory offenders in particular. Previous attempts to introduce civil commitment and preventive sentencing in the US and the UK were accompanied by vociferous debate among professionals and academics and ultimately superseded by concerns about psychiatric abuses and the prevalence of sexual abuse within the family (see Jenkins 1998; Nash 1999). The question is, what is it about our own era that has generated a 'flow' of such intensity, uniformity and relative longevity?

It is now practically orthodoxy to associate contemporary crime control with the development of a 'late modern society' characterised by uncertainty and a lack of confidence in our ability to understand and control our world through the application of science and rationality. The positive benefits of rapid social and economic change, such as increased wealth and mobility, have their concomitants in extended criminal opportunities and the erosion of social cohesion, particularly in relation to family and community ties. Feelings of insecurity are understood to be further undermined by the destabilisation of traditional institutions and an accompanying scepticism about authority and the status of expert knowledge. The late modern world is a place in which social order can no longer be taken for granted, but must be deliberately constructed and worried about; managing the risks unleashed by social change is a constant preoccupation for individuals and institutions alike. In relation to crime control in particular, the late modern period is associated with an emphasis, not on the reform of offenders who have committed offences in the past, but on the risk management of those who may go on to commit offences in the future.

The 'late modernity risk thesis' has been used by a number of commentators as the context for discussions about changes in criminological thought, policy and practice. In the main, these accounts of late modern penality are sombre ones that turn on the acknowledgement of crime as a normal part of life, something that must be tolerated rather than eliminated. In this climate of lowered expectations, the key purpose of criminal justice is no longer rehabilitation but administration, leading to the replacement of clinical judgement and attempts at reform by statistical calculations of risk and the limitation of penal goals to retribution, incapacitation and control (Feeley and Simon 1992).

The rise of this 'actuarial justice' clearly explains some aspects of current responses to sex offenders; in particular the rapid development of risk assessment and management systems, and the marginalisation of treatment. However, in order to account for other aspects of recent policy-making in this area – the speed with which new legislation has been introduced; the emotional tone that has accompanied it; and the lack of opposition or objection to measures that are by any standards extreme and carry implications for the civil liberties of suspects and offenders – we need a more sophisticated analysis of the links between social order, criminal justice and the public.

The most obvious disjuncture between the above account and our 'late modern' response to sex offenders is the construction of crime – and by implication, criminals – as 'normal': an everyday risk to be tolerated and managed. Sex offenders, by contrast, are widely regarded as abnormal and as presenting an intolerable risk to children and communities. At the same time, they are increasingly subject to the paraphernalia of late modern penality in the form of incapacitative sentencing, risk management techniques and surveillance. These contradictions are less difficult to understand if we set them in a complex social context in which the more limited, rational, managerialist agenda described above co-exists with its opposite: a criminology that re-emphasises the state's power to punish, reactivates an archetype of the offender as abnormal, and responds to popular fears via the swift introduction of exclusionary and often costly policies.

The contradictory nature of contemporary crime control is analysed by Garland (2001), who suggests that diverging policies and practices are underpinned by the polarised criminological frameworks outlined above: what he calls a 'criminology of the self', that sees offenders as rational and like ourselves, and a 'criminology of the other', that characterises them as pathological and threatening outsiders. This 'schizophrenia' is the result of the state's attempt to deal with its failure to solve the problem of crime by variously adapting to that failure, avoiding it, and denying it (see Garland 2001, chapter 5). Adaptation strategies generate pragmatic policies that recognise the wisdom of transferring some of the responsibility for crime prevention to the community via organisations and individuals beyond the formal criminal justice system. Avoidance and denial generate punitive, populist policies designed to increase support for state punishment via the exclusion and incarceration of demonised groups.

While many of the so-called 'get tough' policies of the 1990s fit into this latter category, Garland saves his most trenchant criticisms for various aspects of sex offender legislation, the key function of which, he maintains, is not to effect crime control but to express the feelings of an insecure and distrustful public. Questions about the counterproductive nature of such stigmatisation, the unreliability of risk prediction and the erosion of offender's rights are, Garland suggests 'the hesitations of a more innocent time' (2001: 137). So, too, are questions about the harm posed to children by offenders closer to home, and by structural factors such as poverty and environmental damage.

These excursions into the sociology of punishment lead us to the model or social construction of the sex offender that underpins current and developing legislative frameworks. It is a model dominated by the spectre of the unreformable, predatory paedophile; a figure whose ubiquity is reified by the requirement on a wide range of offenders to register their whereabouts with the police.

According to Jenkins' (1998) cyclical model of responses to sex crime outlined above, a more liberal climate is somewhat overdue. But Jenkins himself is pessimistic about the advent of a 'new era of indifference' (p. 232). The institutionalisation of the concept of child protection and abuse in welfare agencies, healthcare, therapy and academia has created a range of interest groups and claims-makers with a stake in the maintenance of concern about sex crime, effectively silencing the dissenting voices who challenged defective and unprincipled legislation in earlier times. As a result, Jenkins suggests, the cycle has been broken, and '. . . child abuse has become part of our enduring cultural landscape, a metanarrative with the potential for explaining all social and personal ills' (p. 232).

Clearly, the prevailing social climate lends considerable support to Jenkins' rather dismal thesis. Meanwhile, current legislative responses allow politicians to have their punitive cake and eat it, simultaneously suggesting that sex offenders are by definition 'dangerous' (hence the widespread registration and monitoring) and that this description applies to a limited group of offenders who can be identified and 'managed' via draconian but effective penal strategies. If, as Jenkins believes, there is no going back, we may cheerfully anticipate the extension of exceptional penalties to an ever-larger percentage of sex offenders, perhaps even to other groups of unpopular offenders who appear impervious to existing measures.

Jenkins is right to suggest that the institutionalisation and politicisation of sexual crime endows modern (or 'late modern') concepts of the sex offender with a durability that their predecessors lacked. However, it's also possible to argue that current and developing responses to sex offenders are characterised by some of the contradictions that Garland associates with contemporary responses to crime in general. A more optimistic reading might see in these contradictions the possibility of a new cycle of thinking about sex crime that would place more emphasis on its variety and reduce its status to one of a number of harms that may threaten the young and vulnerable.

The following sections consider the evolution of legislation in this area and the extent to which it reflects and diverges from a 'late modern' model of the sex offender as predatory stranger.

Policies and politicians 1991–2000

The literature on policy approaches to sex offending contains some strong criticisms of politicians. While crime policy-making in general has become politicised, sex offender policy seems to have an especially knee-jerk quality, reflecting a primary concern with public opinion and displaying a fine disregard for adverse side effects such as over-inclusiveness and the erosion of offenders' rights. The emotional tone has been heightened by the association of new legislation with high-profile cases involving the sexual murder of children by offenders with previous convictions for sex crime.

With the introduction of an indeterminate sentence for 'public protection', the government may have gone as far as it can along the path of exceptional custodial sentences for sex offenders (Criminal Justice Bill 2002). In any event, the research tells us, firstly, that dangerousness remains difficult to predict,[4] and, secondly, that many sex offenders are not known to statutory agencies (Cobley 2000). Responses centred around itinerant, homicidal sex offenders are therefore based on a false understanding of the nature of sex crime against children. Any government with a genuine interest in the protection of the public would therefore be wise to steer away from the current focus on extreme cases and to develop a policy agenda that is empirically not media-led.

Although public opposition to legislative arrangements for sex offenders has been non-existent, academic commentators have been highly critical of what they see as a cynically populist policy agenda (Soothill and Francis 1998; Nash 1999; West 2000). Some of these critiques are so strongly worded as to rival the rhetorical style employed by politicians in defence of the policies under discussion. Thus Garland (2001) criticises aspects of recent legislation which, he asserts, 'involve public safety considerations of doubtful efficacy and a barely sublimated punitiveness that suggests a complete disregard for the rights or humanity of those being sanctioned' (p. 133).

How did we reach a point at which such criticisms could be levelled at government policy? The legislative isolation of sex offenders has its roots in the Criminal Justice Act 1991. This Act allowed for the imposition of a custodial sentence longer than is commensurate with the seriousness of the offence in cases where this is deemed necessary to protect the public from serious harm from the offender (section 2[2][b]). In addition, in a move that had wide-ranging implications for the probation service, the Act introduced compulsory probation supervision on release for all offenders who received prison sentences of 12 months or more. This provision was intended to address concerns about sexual and violent offenders who were considered too risky for parole and who, prior to the Act, would therefore have been released unsupervised at the end of their sentence.

The assumptions underpinning these provisions – firstly, that sex offenders may justly be exempted from the principle of proportionality on which the sentencing framework rests, and secondly, that they may with equal justification be subject to monitoring and other prohibitions after completing their sentence – have governed subsequent legislative provisions. The justification for exemption from proportionality lies in the perceived 'dangerousness' of these offenders. This effectively re-verses the usual formula according to which sanctions chiefly reflect the seriousness of the current crime, by making them dependent upon forecasts of the seriousness of future crime (based, to a great extent, upon information about previous offending).

In addition to worrying about the fairness of departing from propor-tionality in general, critics have pointed to the difficulty of predicting dangerousness using existing methods (von Hirsch and Ashworth 1996). In order to ascertain whether the criteria should be applied, risk prediction must address not only the anticipated seriousness of any subsequent offending, but also the likelihood of such offending. The tendency to over-prediction is consistently reported by research (Floud 1982; Quinsey, Harris, Rice and Cormier 1998). While the current framework places increasing stress on the isolation of offenders who present an unacceptable risk to the public, the question of what constitutes an unacceptable risk will be determined less by predictive accuracy than by the social context in which assessment is being conducted. In a 'late modern' climate governed by insecurity and a preoccupation with predatory offenders, an existing liability towards overprediction will undoubtedly be intensified.

The charge of over-inclusiveness has also been levelled at the registration requirement introduced under the Sex Offenders Act 1997. The provision applies to all offenders convicted or cautioned in respect of an offence outlined in Schedule 1 to the Act, and requires them to notify the police of their address and any subsequent moves. Underlying the compilation of a register was the assumption that a widespread failure to keep adequate records had facilitated the re-offending of convicted sex offenders (Hebenton and Thomas 1996).[5] Although popularly regarded as a 'paedophile register', the database has a wide-ranging application, currently incorporating offences such as indecency between men, causing or encouraging prostitution of a girl under 16, and taking indecent photographs of children: crimes that stretch the bounds of what might be considered 'dangerous'. It also applies to children, although the registration periods are halved for offenders under the age of 18. The inclusion of cautioned offenders means that registration is not contingent on the test of court proceedings (Soothill and Francis 1998). This is particularly significant given the likelihood that registration will function as the threshold for the application of subsequent legislative provisions.[6]

The Sex Offenders Act illustrates the iterative process through which legislative responses to the problem of sex offenders in the community tend to generate problems that require additional legislative responses. While some critics suggested that the Act required too many offenders to register, other commentators noted that the failure to make the provision retrospective placed many thousands of sex offenders cautioned or convicted prior to the implementation of the legislation beyond its reach (Marshall 1997, Thomas 2000). This gap was closed by the introduction of the Sex Offender Order (Crime and Disorder Act 1998), a civil penalty breach of which attracts a custodial sentence of up to five years. In addition to requiring the offender to register under the Sex Offenders Act, conditions may be attached to an Order prohibiting the offender from engaging in specific behaviours, such as communicating with potential victims or visiting particular places. Although this provision has a lower public profile than registration, it has significant implications for the rights of offenders and has been subject to legal challenge (see Power 1999).

The Sex Offenders Act also raised questions about what being on the register entailed. Although registration was conceived as a way to enhance public protection, it was not obvious how the collection of a list of sex offenders' names and addresses would enable the police to achieve this aim. Subsequent Home Office guidance emphasised the proactive nature of the registration process, focusing on the central role of information exchange between the police and other agencies and encouraging the development of inter-agency protocols for the joint management of sex offenders (Home Office 1997). The guidance also directed the police, in consultation with the probation service, to carry out risk assessments and develop risk management plans for higher-risk offenders. This prompted the organisation of a range of inter-agency working panels that varied considerably both in structure and in quality (Maguire, Kemshall, Noaks and Wincup 2001).

The Criminal Justice and Courts Services Act 2000 (CJCSA 2000) placed these informal arrangements on a statutory footing, designating the police and probation services as a joint 'responsible authority' with a duty to establish multi-agency arrangements for the risk assessment and management of sexual and violent offenders who may cause serious harm to the public (section 67, CJCSA 2000).[7] Multi-agency public protection arrangements (MAPPA) are chiefly concerned with the management of cases that require exchange of information and collaborative work between a range of agencies. Risk assessment procedures place offenders at one of four levels (low, medium, high and very high). While lower-risk offenders are managed through normal agency procedures (primarily by the police and probation services), the 'critical few' offenders assessed as very high risk are referred to a multi-agency public protection panel (MAPPP). At this point, the offender may be subject to a range of management measures including police monitoring and surveillance, electronic tagging, curfew, prohibitions on where they go and whom they contact, restrictions on living arrangements and types of employment, and participation in treatment programmes.

The increasingly stringent nature of responses to released sex offenders has been mirrored in the sentencing framework. The Crime (Sentences) Act 1997 imposes a mandatory life sentence on a second conviction for a serious sexual offence such as rape or unlawful sexual intercourse with a girl under 13. The Crime and Disorder Act 1998 introduced extended sentences for serious sexual and violent offences; in the case of sex offenders this empowered courts to impose supervision on release for up to ten years. This comes on top of the normal period of supervision and is double the extension that can be imposed on violent offenders.

The most significant features of these more recent provisions are the primacy of predictions of future offending, and the increasingly intrusive nature of the measures to which released sex offenders may be subjected. Its civil law status means that the Sex Offender Order cannot justly be imposed as an additional punishment, but only in the name of public protection. Human rights considerations ensured that the government could impose only negative conditions on offenders, prohibiting them, for example, from going to a certain area.[8] The list of the range of measures available to MAPPPs given above includes positive obligations such as a condition to attend a treatment programme. A recent inspection of MAPPA reported 'good use' of additional requirements in case records, including participation in treatment programmes and residence in approved probation premises (Department of Health 2002).

At the end of the last century, then, sex offenders could be made subject to extended and exceptional sentences of various kinds, as well as lengthy periods of post-release supervision and monitoring that could include negative and positive obligations relating to their lifestyle and activities. Previously convicted offenders not caught by the registration requirement in the Sex Offenders Act 1997 could be made subject to it and to other prohibitions via a Sex Offender Order if their behaviour appeared on the balance of probabilities to indicate an intention to cause serious harm. To get to this point, we have had to swallow a number of principles – including innocence until proven guilty, proportionate sentencing, the avoidance of double jeopardy, and the balance of individual and community rights – that continue to define our responses to offenders who escape the 'dangerous' label. The failure of academics and experts to develop a robust liberal counter-discourse has doubtless contributed to the durability of this punitive ideological stance. However, its primary support has been the apparent willingness of successive governments to endorse a populist, tabloid-driven agenda even where this conflicts with their own policies.[9]

Setting some boundaries: the future of sex offender management

To assess the evidence for progression to a new cycle of thinking about sex offenders, I turn now to two sets of recent policy documents that characterise diverging approaches to this issue. In each case, a review produced a set of recommendations that fed into a White Paper and subsequently into a Bill. The first set, which I call the criminal justice set, includes Halliday's review of the sentencing framework, *Making Punishments Work* (Home Office 2001), the White Paper *Justice for All* (Home Office 2002a) and the Criminal Justice Bill 2002. The second set, which I call the sex offences set, consists of the review of the law on sex offences *Setting the Boundaries* (Home Office 2000), the White Paper *Protecting the Public* (Home Office 2002b) and the Sex Offences Bill 2003.

While the tone and content of the former reflect a populist approach based around the paradigm of the dangerous, predatory, unreformable sex offender, the latter present a more mixed picture that combines a concern with paedophile offenders and their propensity for future offending with a recognition that the vulnerable need protecting from offenders closer to home – or, indeed, within it. More promisingly still, the sex offences review *Setting the Boundaries* addresses itself not only to the need to provide protection for the public and 'appropriate punishment' for abusers, but also to 'be fair and non-discriminatory in accordance with the ECHR and Human Rights Act' within its terms of reference (Home Office 2000).

It would require not optimism so much as a wholesale triumph of hope over experience to regard this as the dawn of a new era of tolerance of sex offenders. However, the necessity of reconciling increasingly 'tough' measures with human rights legislation, together with a pragmatic need to limit the number of sex offenders who fall into the resource-intensive 'very high risk' category, may incline decision-makers by default towards a less populist, more principled, and potentially more effective approach.

The perils of populism

The limitations of a political strategy that allows atypical cases to shape policy was decisively demonstrated in the summer of 2000. Following the abduction and murder of eight-year-old Sarah Payne, public concerns about predatory paedophiles found expression in the tabloid-led campaign to 'name and shame' convicted sex offenders. The tragic nature of the crime would have ensured it a place in the public's memory at any time. However, the failure of a decade of decision-makers to counter populist interpretations of the sex offender problem as a problem of dangerous predators allowed the case to become a symbol of political inertia; an ironic conclusion given the extent of legislative activity in this area during the 1990s.[10] In a quintessentially late modern rejection of the capacity of government and other experts to protect them from crime, a vocal section of the public demanded the right to secure their own safety via a policy of community notification on the US model.

At this point the government's willingness to align itself with a populist agenda began to evaporate a little. The rationale for community notification is that an informed public will be in a position to protect itself by taking evasive action against sex offenders in their area. In practice, a proportion of the public adopt a rather more proactive stance, targeting attacks on suspected sex offenders. This was the chain of events in July 2000, when the publication of alleged paedophiles' names, addresses and photographs in the *News of the World* was followed by a rash of vigilante activity across the country.

Despite its ineptness (which included an attack on the home of a hapless paediatrician), this sporadic vigilantism propelled the government into another bout of legislative tinkering. In June 2000, just weeks before Sarah Payne's death, the Home Office minister Charles Clarke announced a review of the flawed Sex Offenders Act 1997. A review team including representatives from government departments, professional organisations and children's charities was appointed to identify weaknesses in the legislation and recommend improvements. In the autumn, pre-empting the work of the review team, the government announced a number of amendments to the Act in what became the CJCSA 2000. These included a reduction in the period allowed for initial registration from 14 to three days, and an increase in the maximum penalty for failure to comply to five years' imprisonment.[11] The CJCSA also introduced the restraining order, which allows restrictions to be set on sex offenders' future behaviour at the sentencing stage.

Unsurprisingly, the government did not couch its objections to community notification, as it might have done, in the language of offenders' rights, but in the more politically acceptable name of public protection. Their opposition to notification has attracted robust support from senior police officers, the probation service, child protection agencies and a range of children's charities. The prevailing wisdom is that widespread disclosure would drive sex offenders underground, decreasing compliance with registration and disrupting community treatment programmes.[12] Following the publication of the names and addresses of alleged paedophiles in the *News of the World*, the Association of Chief Officers of Probation hit back by compiling its own dossier of convicted paedophiles who had reported vigilante attacks and talked to probation officers about moving from their homes to avoid being targeted.[13]

In an effort to deflect public demands for notification, the government focused on beefing up arrangements for the risk management of sex offenders in the community, introducing the statutory framework described above and undertaking to give the public a role in the process.[14] While the campaign for 'Sarah's Law' simmered on, bolstered by the popular press and an inflammatory and highly inaccurate website (www.forsarah.com), the government remained – and remains – steadfast in its opposition to widespread community notification.[15]

Halliday, Justice for All *and the Criminal Justice Bill 2002*

In May 2000, the then home secretary Jack Straw announced a review of the sentencing framework for England and Wales. Led by a senior civil servant, John Halliday, the review team produced an impressive set of proposals that informed the 2002 White Paper on the reform of the criminal justice system (ambitiously titled *Justice for All*). The rationale for the review was the replacement of the existing framework by one that would make a greater contribution to crime prevention and public confidence (Home Office 2001: 1). The framework deemed suitable by the review team for 'present and foreseeable circumstances in England and Wales' involved the substitution of the 'muddled legacy' of the 'just deserts' approach for a modified proportionality principle that takes more account of previous and, in the case of dangerous offenders, possible future offending.

Continuing a now well-established tendency to exclude sex offenders from desert principles altogether, the Halliday report *Making Punishments Work* (2001) recommends a new 'special' sentence for violent and sexual offenders who are deemed to present a risk of serious harm to the public but who are not caught by existing legislation allowing the imposition of a life sentence. The new sentence makes release during the second half of the sentence contingent on a favourable decision by the Parole Board. Although in theory this does not alter the length of the sentence, used to its maximum extent the provision could double the length of time spent by an offender in custody. While the 'special' sentence is not limited to dangerous sex offenders, two characteristics render it 'extra special' in their case: the threshold for use, and the imposition of extended post-release supervision.

Noting the 'potentially very onerous and punitive' nature of the 'special' sentence, *Making Punishments Work* emphasises the importance of setting a threshold that will ensure its appropriate use. The rationale for divergent thresholds to be applied to sexual and violent offenders rests on the questionable assumption that 'sex offenders as a group may pose higher risks of reoffending' (p. 33, para 4.33). Somewhat inevitably, the threshold suggested for sex offenders is eligibility for registration under the Sex Offenders Act 1997.[16]

The existing framework allows the court to impose a maximum period of ten years extended supervision for sex offences and half that for violent offences. Halliday raises the question of whether a single period of ten years' should be considered for both offence types, but makes no firm recommendation pending the response of the Sex Offenders Act review. The Criminal Justice Bill 2002 maintains the distinction between violent and sexual offences, although this is not in direct response to any recommendation made by the Sex Offenders Act review team or in *Setting the Boundaries*.

Halliday's 'special' sentence is clearly in tune with a perception of sex offenders as a uniquely dangerous, high-risk group. However, in spite of their desire to develop a framework suitable for 'present and foreseeable circumstances', the review team were apparently persuaded of the need to rise above the demands of a capricious public:

Sentencing, and the framework within which it operates, need to earn and merit public confidence, but this is a complex relationship, and not one in which sentencers can simply be 'driven before the wind' of apparent public mood, regardless of the principles that need to govern sentencing.

(Home Office 2001: p. ii, para 0.5)

The criminal justice White Paper *Justice for All* (Home Office 2002a) seems by contrast to have allowed itself to be swept up and carried along by the gale of public protest that followed the murder of Sarah Payne. Although paying lip service to a proud tradition of fairness and balance, *Justice for All*'s rhetorical tone is indicative of a primary commitment to a populist agenda largely generated by the tabloid press: 'The public are sick and tired of a system that does not make sense. *They read about* dangerous, violent, sexual and other serious offenders who get off lightly, or are not in prison long enough or for the length of their sentence' (p. 86, para 5.2; emphasis added).

The assumption in *Justice for All* of the need to 'rebalance the system in favour of victims, witnesses and communities' (p. iii) reflects another prominent theme in populist crime control rhetoric: namely, the central and symbolic role of the victim. The rationale for harsh treatment lies in an assumed relationship between punitiveness towards offenders and compassion for victims. This results in a 'zero-sum policy game' (Garland 2001: 11) and a rather less inclusive distribution of justice than the White Paper's title suggests.

A further overhaul of sentencing for violent and sexual offenders is related explicitly to the Sarah Payne case and the need to counter the anxieties of parents about their children's safety (p. 95). The concession to those lobbying for community notification appears in the euphemistically titled chapter 'Enhancing the public's engagement', which praises the UK's 'strong civic tradition of public engagement in criminal justice' (p. 116). However, the restriction of lay involvement in multi-agency public protection panels to an overseeing role on strategic boards suggests that the government is learning to be cautious about engaging the public in this particular policy area.[17]

The new sentences for sex offenders in the Criminal Justice Bill currently going through Parliament propose the extended incapacitation of offenders on the basis of perceived dangerousness rather than crime seriousness. In addition to Halliday's 'special' determinate sentence, the Bill introduces an indeterminate sentence for public protection. This applies to offenders whose offences merit prison terms of ten years or over and who are assessed as dangerous. Following a minimum tariff set by the court, release will be dependent on a favourable risk assessment.

The approach to sex offenders that emerges from this set of policy documents is one that gives primacy to the protection of the public from a small group of dangerous offenders.[18] While there is nothing intrinsically wrong with including public protection among the purposes of sentencing, its dominance here is undesirable for a number of reasons. First of all, it is not clear that maximising sentences for these offenders maximises public protection. This is not only because of the vagaries of risk assessment, but also because the majority even of this highlighted group will eventually be released. Unless their extended prison terms include enhanced treatment opportunities, the risk they pose is unlikely to have altered significantly in most cases. Secondly, the current 'zero tolerance' approach implies that the right policy will totally eliminate the danger posed by dangerous sex offenders. This leaves legislators open to accusations of wholesale failure in the event of an isolated and essentially unpredictable tragedy such as the murder of Sarah Payne. It also ensures that public attention remains focused on extreme cases, exacerbating anxiety and frustration and fuelling demands for ever-more punitive responses. Finally, the increasingly familiar conflation of public protection and exceptional (now indeterminate) sentencing for sex offenders pushes at an open door in eroding their individual rights and placing them beyond the reach of justice.

Setting the Boundaries, Protecting the Public *and the Sex Offences Bill 2003*

The story so far may seem to suggest that the government has adopted a one-note response to the problem of sex offending. However, even the tub-thumping *Justice for All* acknowledges the necessity to develop provision in the community for offenders who cannot be indefinitely contained (Home Office 2002a: 112). The second set of policy documents I want to discuss doesn't detach itself from the public protection agenda, as the title of the sex offences White Paper bears out. However, its conception of the public appears to be one that incorporates offenders as well as potential victims, and if it is not free from the preoccupations of 'late modern risk society', it tempers these with a sense of the range and complexity of sex offences and offenders.

The Report of the Review of Sex Offences (Home Office 2000) commits itself to 'setting the boundaries'; not only in relation to the protection of the vulnerable from abuse, but also regarding the extent to which the law is justified in intruding into private life. Although this latter is primarily explored in relation to the unnecessary criminalisation of consensual activity between adults and under 16s, *Setting the Boundaries'* concern for the achievement of a 'safe, just and tolerant society' suggests that the review team did not see their task as part of a 'zero-sum policy game'.

From the outset, the Report establishes the 'contentious' nature of sex offence law, its 'patchwork' character and its failure in its current form to reflect what we know about sexual violence.

Published prior to the murder of Sarah Payne, *Setting the Boundaries* offers a vision of a response to this complex and disturbing problem that is not circumscribed by the spectre of the predatory paedophile. The wide-ranging perspective adopted by the Report contrasts with the narrow agenda that has shaped a decade of sex offender legislation. It covers a number of issues – sexual behaviour within the family, the definition of consent, distinguishing between juvenile and adult offenders, the difficulty of balancing protection with a concern for individual rights – that should, but seldom do, form a key part of policy debates about sex offending. Significantly, even though it lays a particular emphasis on the protection of children, the Report neither discusses nor makes recommendations relating to 'paedophile' or stranger offenders.[19]

The Review's major proposals involve the law on rape; the protection and sexual rights of vulnerable adults; and the protection of children and vulnerable others from abuse within the family and by carers and other trusted adults. The proposed offence of 'persistent sexual abuse of a child' acknowledges the long-term nature of much intra-familial sexual abuse, reflecting a course of conduct as opposed to isolated abusive acts.[20] The offence of 'familial sexual abuse' is intended to replace out-of-date incest offences with a provision that reflects the fact that many contemporary families include step-parents, adoptive parents and foster carers. However, the proposed new offence also draws attention to the neglected issue of intra-familial abuse: 'It was vital to establish that abuse within the family was one of the most serious and harmful types of abuse because of the fundamental breach of trust involved.' (p. 83, para 5.3.1).

The range of offenders envisaged by *Setting the Boundaries* stretches not only to family members and known adults, but to children too. In its consideration of child offenders, the Report is careful to distinguish between experimentation and abuse, recommending the imposition of non-criminal interventions in the former case, but stressing the need for legal remedies as well as treatment options for the latter. It also advocates consideration of the requirement for children to register under the Sex Offenders Act 1997.[21]

Another novel element in *Setting the Boundaries* is a discussion in a chapter entitled 'Further Issues' of the importance of sex offender treatment in prisons and the community. The Report recommends that assessment of need and suitability for treatment should form an integral part of any sentence for sex offenders.

The resulting White Paper on sex offences, *Protecting the Public* (Home Office 2002b), is a hybrid document, reflecting its debt to the criminal justice White Paper as well as to the Review Report. It contains echoes of the rhetoric that peppers *Justice for All*, but these are diluted by the more measured tone of *Setting the Boundaries*. The Home Secretary's Foreword acknowledges that 'we are dealing with highly complicated and sensitive issues which test the balance between the role of Government and of the individual, and of their rights to determine their own behaviour, responsibility and duty of care' (p. 5). The fact is, that when what we know about sex offenders is fed into the debate, the presence of parents, carers and children among offenders and vulnerable adults among victims renders the delivery of public protection a complex matter.

The White Paper's conception of public protection does include the p(aedophile) word, and two notable new offences aimed at predatory offenders: 'meeting a child following sexual grooming' and the 'Risk of Sexual Harm Order (RSHO)'. The sexual grooming offence targets a behaviour that has long been identified as a pre-cursor of child sexual abuse: namely, a pattern of manipulative behaviour designed to gain a victim's trust and affection. While the literature associates grooming with abuse within as well as outside the family (Salter 1988), it is linked here with the recent phenomenon of internet misuse, wherein offenders use chatrooms to deceive children about their identity and arrange meetings with them. This provides another demonstration of the way that over-emphasis on predatory strangers obscures the complexity of the issues. Although the new offence is intended to tackle grooming by offenders 'online and offline' (Home Office 2002b: 29), it isn't clear how, if at all, it would apply within the family unit.

The sexual grooming provision concerns an issue that has received considerable media attention and become a focus of public anxiety. However, like much of the legislation governing sex offending, including the new sentences introduced in the Criminal Justice Bill, it refers not to current but to potential future offending. Here, however, the issue is not whether the individual presents a risk of serious harm, but whether he intends to commit a sexual offence against a child. The same applies to the RSHO, conceived as a complementary provision, which targets those (whether previously convicted or not) whose behaviour suggests that they may present a risk of sexual harm to children. Although the Order is intended to cover a wide spectrum of behaviours, the examples given – 'explicit communication with children via email or in chatrooms or hanging around schools or playgrounds' (Home Office 2002b: 25) – are consistent with an agenda that is circumscribed by popular fears about predatory stranger offenders.

Other parts of the Sex Offences Bill more closely reflect the pre-Sarah Payne agenda of the Sex Offences Review. Clauses 28–32 focus on the sexual abuse of a child within the family, based on a recognition of the 'particular vulnerability' of children within the family. Other sections introduce offences that reflect the concern expressed in *Setting the Boundaries* about the exploitation of mentally-impaired adults.

Wisely, if belatedly, *Protecting the Public* devotes considerable space to describing protective measures that are already in place. In particular, it gives a comparatively high profile to MAPPA. Although MAPPA are replete with the trappings of late modern crime control (including a preoccupation with risk assessment and surveillance, and a downplaying of the rights of individual offenders), they are at least committed in principle to the maintenance of sex offenders outside the custodial system. Given the implications of MAPPA decisions for the rights of unconvicted as well as convicted individuals, shortfalls in consistency, accountability and regulation will need to be addressed as a matter of priority. However, in their concern with individual cases and their augmentation of actuarial assessment with professional judgement, the panels have the capability to function as a corrective to the excesses of 'risk penality' (see Maguire et al. 2000; Kemshall and Maguire 2001; and Bryan and Doyle, Chapter 10 of this volume).

The policy documents discussed above could be interpreted as evidence of a new cycle of thinking about sex offenders. Alternatively, they could be regarded as (punitive) business as usual. Sources of support for the latter include the tenacity of the predatory sex offender stereotype, and a political and public reluctance to confront the abuse of children within the family unit. Those who believe the former might cite the pragmatic need of politicians to counter popular fears when these engender public disorder and to garner support for affordable alternatives to incarceration for lower-risk offenders. The best outcome, morally and economically, would be a more holistic approach that combined imprisonment and surveillance with strategies focused on the rehabilitation and reintegration of offending individuals.

Conclusion

Changing the way we think about sex offenders is not something that can be achieved overnight; nor can it be legislated into existence. Replacing the predatory stranger stereotype with its more ubiquitous domestic counterpart requires significant effort on a range of fronts. Responsible legal strategies need to be accompanied by public information campaigns in order to counter understandable public fears and sensational media reporting. The furore over community notification and the vociferous campaign for 'Sarah's Law' may have alerted politicians to the fact that populist punitiveness can be a dangerous game. What it also revealed was the (largely untried) capability of the government to resist popular pressure and generate more imaginative solutions to the problem of community protection.

Sentencing policy is a key aspect of government responsibility in this area. For preventive sentencing to be ethically acceptable, the abandonment of proportionality it entails must clearly be demonstrated and justified. This means giving serious consideration to thresholds for eligibility and ensuring that 'special' sentences are used sparingly, as their progenitor envisaged (Home Office 2001). Beyond sentencing, government rhetoric and resources should be directed towards the support of community strategies including reintegration and treatment as well as assessment and tracking. Responsible governments need to do more than merely identify with the fears of the public; they need to invest in cost-effective and protective measures based on what we know rather than what we fear about sex offenders.

We have come as far as we can along a path that focuses popular fears on an imagined group of predatory, dangerous sex offenders and seeks by incarcerating or expelling them, to neutralise these fears. Murderously dangerous people exist, it's true, but once we have done all we can to identify and contain them, we are left with the problem of what to do with the vastly larger group of individuals whose risk of doing harm is less knowable, or very slight. This is not simply a problem for policy-makers, but also for the professionals who have to assess and manage such people, and for the public into whose communities the majority of sex offenders are returned. The failure of numerous legislative attempts to address public concerns about dangerous sex offenders would suggest that we look in vain to politicians to set our minds at rest. With provisions running the gamut from lifelong registration in the community to lifelong imprisonment outside it, it's surely time to set some boundaries for the limits of punishment for these offenders, and to explore more imaginative and integrative approaches to their management.

Notes

1   Among offenders cautioned or convicted in 2001, the four most common sex offences were indecent assault on a woman; rape of a woman; indecent assault on a man; and unlawful sexual intercourse with a girl under 16 (*Criminal Statistics England and Wales 2001*).

2   In 2001–2, 76 victims of homicide were aged under 16. Eight were known to have been killed by strangers, 43 by parents and nine by someone known to

them. There were no suspects in 16 cases as of October 2002 (*Crime in England and Wales 2001–2002: Supplementary Volume*).

3   Based on a telephone survey of 32 states carried out by the advocacy group Parents For Megan's Law (www.parentsformeganslaw.com). Florida was among the states with the best compliance rate, at 95.3 per cent; Tennessee and Massachusetts among the worst, at 63 per cent and 56 per cent respectively. The survey was prompted by an Associated Press investigation which revealed that California was unable to account for some 44 per cent of the state's registered sex offenders ('Sex Offender Registry Failing: authorities throughout the country can't find thousands despite laws', *Seattle Post-Intelligencer*, Wednesday 8 January 2003).

4   The low rate of violent recidivism and the tendency of current risk predictors to misclassify high numbers of individuals as 'dangerous' have led more than one leading commentator to suggest that the optimal way to improve risk assessment would be to predict that no one will recidivate (see Grubin 1997; Quinsey, Harris, Rice and Cormier 1998).

5   See also Soothill and Walby (1991), who identify a 'mini moral panic' over this issue in press coverage for 1985.

6   See Home Office (2001), p. 33.

7   The Criminal Justice Bill 2002 establishes the prison service as part of the 'responsible authority'.

8   Although, as Power (1999) points out, the distinction between *prohibiting* an offender from leaving his home between certain hours and *requiring* him to remain at home during certain times is largely a semantic one.

9   See Silverman and Wilson (2002) on the Home Office's ambivalent response to the *News of the World*'s naming and shaming campaign in 2001.

10 Other elements that contributed to the unusually vivid and long-lived interest the case provoked were the decision by the police to court media interest in the hope of gaining intelligence, and the high profile of the victim's parents (see Silverman and Wilson 2002).

11 The characterisation of these alterations as 'knee-jerk' measures is supported by the introduction of a further set of amendments to the legislation in the Criminal Justice Bill 2002. These are based on the recommendations of the Sex Offenders Review team which were published, somewhat belatedly, in July 2001.

12 Higher rates of non-compliance in the US suggest that community notification may have some adverse effect on registration; however, the evidence is far from conclusive (see Lovell 2001).

13 'Name and shame court threat: Probation chiefs warn *News of the World* as paedophiles go into hiding', *The Guardian*, Monday 31 July 2000.

14 So far this involvement has been restricted to oversight of, rather than participation in MAPPA. Following a pilot study involving the appointment of lay members to MAPPA strategy management boards (SMBs) in eight areas, the Criminal Justice Bill 2002 extends lay membership of SMBs across the country.

15 'Straw says no to "Sarah's Law" ', *The Guardian*, Friday 15 September 2000. 'This high compliance rate is one of the reasons why we do not feel the public

should have access to the names of people on the register. However the main reason is that evidence from across the world demonstrates that public access to this type of register drives sex offenders underground and stops them informing the police of their whereabouts' – *Protecting the Public* (Home Office 2002), p. 12.

16 And therefore includes cautioned offenders as well as those convicted of crimes ranging from exposure to rape.

17 On the narrow line between vigilance and vigilantism, see Hughes 1998 and Evans 2003.

18 Halliday makes an estimate of approximately 900 offenders based on a proportion of those serving custodial sentences of over four years and taking into account that some of these offenders will not have committed sexual or violent offences, while others who are serving shorter sentences could be classified as dangerous.

19 In fact, the Report doesn't contain one instance of the word; an increasingly rare phenomenon, as Cobley (2000) has shown.

20 This proposed new offence was rejected by the Government, on the grounds that persistence could be reflected in sentencing under existing provisions. It was also noted that the proposal would not remove the need to specify individual instances of abuse.

21 The Review of the Sex Offenders Act 1997 discussed alternatives to the current procedure, such as making child registration a matter of judicial discretion, and registering young abusers with a non-police agency. The government opted to retain registration for young offenders above the age of criminal responsibility (ten years).

References

Baker, A. and Duncan, S. (1985) 'Child Sexual Abuse: a study of prevalence in Great Britain', *Child Abuse and Neglect* 9, pp. 457–67.

Cobley, C. (2000) *Sex Offenders: law, policy and practice.* Bristol: Jordan Publishing Limited.

Department of Health (2002) *Safeguarding Children: A joint chief inspectors' report on arrangements to safeguard children.* London: Department of Health.

Dick, Philip K. (2002) 'Minority Report', in Philip K. Dick, *Minority Report.* London: Gollancz.

Evans, J. (2003) 'Vigilance and Vigilantes: thinking psychoanalytically about anti-paedophile action', *Theoretical Criminology* 7:2, pp. 163–89.

Feeley, M. and Simon, J. (1992) 'The New Penology: notes on the emerging strategy of corrections and its implications', *Criminology* 30, pp. 449–74.

Finkelhor, D. (1994) 'The International Epidemiology of Child Sexual Abuse', *Child Abuse and Neglect* 18:5, pp. 409–17.

Floud, J. (1982) 'Dangerousness and Criminal Justice', *British Journal of Criminology* 22:3, pp. 213–28.

Garland, D. (2001) *The Culture of Control: crime and social order in contemporary society.* Chicago: University of Chicago Press.

Grubin, D. (1997) 'Predictors of Risk in Serious Sex Offenders', *British Journal of Psychiatry* 170, Supplement 32, pp. 17–21.

Grubin, D. (1998) *Sex Offending Against Children: understanding the risk*, Police Research Series Paper 99. London: Home Office Research, Development and Statistics Directorate.

The Guardian (July 2000) 'Name and Shame Court Threat: probation chiefs warn *News of the World* as paedophiles go into hiding', Monday 31 July 2000.

The Guardian (September 2000), 'Straw Says No to "Sarah's Law" ', Friday 15 September 2000.

Hanson, R. and Bussiere, M. (1998) 'Predicting Relapse: a meta-analysis of sexual offender recidivism studies', *Journal of Consulting and Clinical Psychology* 66:2, pp. 348–62.

Harris, J. and Grace, S. (1999) *A Question of Evidence? Investigating and Prosecuting Rape in the 1990s*, Home Office Research Study 196. London: Home Office.

Hebenton, B. and Thomas, T. (1996) 'Sexual Offenders in the Community: reflections on problems of law, community and risk management in the USA, England and Wales', *International Journal of the Sociology of Law* 24, pp. 427–43.

Home Office (1997) *Sex Offenders Act 1997*, Home Office Circular 39/1997. London: Home Office.

Home Office (2000) *Setting the Boundaries: reforming the law on sex offences*. London: Home Office.

Home Office (2001) *Making Punishments Work: report of a review of the sentencing framework for England and Wales*. London: Home Office.

Home Office (2002a) *Justice for All*, Cm 5563. London: HMSO.

Home Office (2002b) *Protecting the Public*, Cm 5668. London: HMSO.

Hughes, G. (1998) *Understanding Crime Prevention: social control, risk and late modernity*. Buckingham: Open University Press.

Jenkins, P. (1998) *Moral Panic: changing concepts of the child molester in modern America*. New Haven: Yale University Press.

Kelly L., Regan, L. and Burton, S. (1991) *An Exploratory Study of the Prevalence of Sexual Abuse in a Sample of 1244 16–21 Year Olds. Final Report to the ESRC*. London: University of North London.

Kemshall, H. and Maguire, M. (2001) 'Public Protection, Partnership and Risk Penality: the multi-agency risk management of sexual and violent offenders', *Punishment and Society* 3:2, pp. 237–64.

Lieb, R. (2000) 'Social Policy and Sexual Offenders: contrasting United States' and European policies', *European Journal on Criminal Policy and Research* 8:4, pp. 423–40.

Lovell, E. (2001) 'Megan's Law: does it protect children? A review of evidence on the impact of community notification as legislated for through Megan's Law in the United States', *Recommendations for Policy Makers in the United Kingdom*. London: NSPCC.

Maguire, M., Kemshall, H., Noaks, L. and Wincup, E. (2001) *Risk Management of Sexual and Violent Offenders: the work of public protection panels*, Police Research Series Paper 139. London: Home Office.

Marshall, P. (1997) *The Prevalence of Convictions for Sexual Offending*, Research Findings 55. London: Home Office Research and Statistics Directorate.

Morse, S. (2003) 'Bad or Mad? Sex offenders and social control', in B. Winick and J. LaFond (eds). *Protecting Society From Sexually Dangerous Offenders: law, justice and therapy*. Washington: American Psychological Association.

Nash, M. (1999) *Police, Probation and Protecting the Public*. London: Blackstone Press.

Plotnikoff, J. and Woolfson, R. (2000) *Where Are They Now? An Evaluation of Sex Offender Registration in England and Wales*, Police Research Series Paper 126. London: Home Office.

Power, H. (1999) 'The Crime and Disorder Act 1998 (1) Sex offenders, privacy and the police', *Criminal Law Review* January, pp. 3–16.

Pratt, J. (1997) *Governing the Dangerous*. Sydney: Federation Press.

Pratt, J. (2000) 'The Return of the Wheelbarrow Men; or, the arrival of postmodern penality?', *British Journal of Criminology* 40, pp. 127–45.

Quinsey, V., Harris, G., Rice, M. and Cormier, C. (1998) *Violent Offenders: appraising and managing risk*. Washington: American Psychological Association.

Salter, A. C. (1988) *Treating Sex Offenders and Victims: a practical guide*. Newbury Park, CA: Sage Publications.

Scalora, M. and Garbin, C. (2003) 'A Multivariate Analysis of Sex Offender Recidivism', *International Journal of Offender Therapy and Comparative Criminology* 47:3, pp. 309–23.

Silverman, J. and Wilson, D. (2002) *Innocence Betrayed: paedophilia, the media and society*. Cambridge: Polity.

Simon, L. (2003) 'Matching legal policies with known offenders', In B. Winick and J. LaFond (eds) *Protecting Society From Sexually Dangerous Offenders: law, justice, and therapy*. Washington: American Psychological Association.

Soothill, K. and Walby, C. (1991) *Sex Crime in the News*. London: Routledge.

Soothill, K. and Francis, B. (1998) 'Poisoned Chalice or Just Deserts? (The Sex Offenders Act 1997)', *Journal of Forensic Psychiatry* 9:2, pp. 281–93.

Thomas, T. (2000) *Sex Crime: sex offending and society*. Cullompton, Devon: Willan Publishing.

Tonry, M. (1999) 'Rethinking Unthinkable Punishment Policies in America', *UCLA Law Review* 46:6, pp. 1751–91.

von Hirsch, A. and Ashworth, A. (1996) 'Protective Sentencing Under Section 2(2)(b): the criteria for dangerousness', *Criminal Law Review* March, pp. 175–83.

von Hirsch, A. (2003) 'Extended Sentences for Dangerous Offenders: an examination of the Bottoms-Brownsword model' (unpublished paper).

West, D. (2000) 'Paedophilia: plague or panic?' *Journal of Forensic Psychiatry* 11:3, pp. 511–31.

Winick, B. and LaFond, J. (eds) (2003) *Protecting Society From Sexually Dangerous Offenders: law, justice, and therapy*. Washington: American Psychological Association.

Chapter 2

Serious sexual assault: using history and statistics

Keith Soothill

Introduction

There is a serious neglect of history in studying sex crime and a curious reluctance to use statistical thinking beyond the calculation of risk predictions. Nevertheless, in this chapter I will attempt to make a modest contribution to the study of sex crime by embracing those two disciplines.

Certainly the current debate about sex crime has not been characterised by much discussion about the changing or persisting patterns of sex crime over time. There, are, of course, exceptions. Jane Caputi (1988), for example, boldly proclaims 'the Age of Sex Crime was first blasted into being in London, 1888, with the unprecedented crimes of Jack the Ripper. That still anonymous killer essentially invented modern sex crime' (p. 4). Certainly, the development of newspapers with wide circulations attracted new readerships, and a different relationship between the courts and its mediated audience emerged. However, few have attempted to chart the changes that have occurred over time.

Statistics have been pervasive in thinking about sex crime but in a peculiarly narrow way. There has been much about identifying factors that may predict future sex crime. Our own work (Soothill, Francis, Fligelstone and Ackerley 2002) – discussed in the next section – contributes further to this focus. However, there are other ways of using statistics. One can develop hypothetical models to assess the likely impact of a change in the societal responses to a crime – I attempt this in the second section. In the third section, I try to justify the title of this chapter by using statistics in a historical context to consider trends over time.

In brief, therefore, this chapter has three main objectives:

1. *To inform.* The aim here is to introduce some recent work on a person's previous criminal history and the likelihood of subsequent serious sexual assault.

2. *To theorise.* The aim here is to consider what is likely to happen if there is a change in the societal response to serious sexual assault – either in the reporting practices of those assaulted or in the official reaction to these crimes.

3. *To speculate.* The aim here is to develop some ideas following a systematic study of sex crime in one town, Lancaster, in the northwest of England, derived from the search of the local newspaper over a period of 120 years, 1860–1979.

In fact, it would be tempting to say that the lack of focus on history and the possible changing patterns of sex crime over time is simply because there has been little previous interest in sex crime. However, while the current interest has something of the familiar hallmarks of a moral panic (Thompson 1998), I have previously stressed how in Britain there have been concerns about sex offending in each of the decades since the Second World War (Soothill 1993). In the 1950s there was rising concern about the visibility of prostitution that eventually resulted in the Street Offences Act 1959. The move towards a partial decriminalisation of homosexuality was the focus of the 1960s and the Sexual Offences Act 1967 was the outcome, allowing homosexual acts between consenting adults in private. The new wave of the women's movement took rape as a major issue in the 1970s and, after pressure from women's lobbies, there was some recognition of the problems faced by women in the Sexual Offences (Amendment) Act 1976. While some of the focus of the 1980s was back to the visibility of prostitution with growing concern about kerb-crawling and the resulting provisions of the Sexual Offences Act 1985 enabling men to be arrested for kerb-crawling, the main concern of the 1980s was about child abuse within the family. This reached a crescendo with the Cleveland Inquiry (Butler-Sloss 1988) into the work of some paediatricians who had diagnosed sexual abuse and of the social services who took the children into care. Over the past decade or so, some debates feeding on familiar sexual themes have rumbled on. In the early 1990s there was discussion about the possible legalisation of brothels, the question of homosexuals in the armed services, the sentencing of rape cases and more inquiries about child sex abuse within the family. However, recent concern about serial sex killings and about paedophiles in the community has switched the focus from the family to strangers. Hence, in relation to sex crime, one can see that the topic has often been in the public arena and the interest is in what attracts concern at a particular time.

We will now return to our focus on why history and statistics might be of some help. The next section looks at a statistical approach in considering the relevance of a person's own criminal history when assessing the likelihood of a future serious sexual assault.

Previous criminal history and serious sexual assault

This section attempts to inform the reader about some recent work. It is in the tradition of other work that considers the factors that might identify a future sexual offender. However, most of this previous work has focused much more on the likelihood of *sexual recidivism* – that is, the likelihood of a known sexual offender going on to commit (or, more precisely, to be convicted of) further sexual offences. Our own recent work has focused on the likelihood of a person being convicted of a *serious* sexual assault *for the first time*, by considering a person's previous criminal history. The analysis focuses on male offenders. But this should not raise the ire of feminists, for it simply reflects the fact that known sex offenders are predominantly male.

The study considers the 1,057 males aged under 45 years[1] convicted *for the first time* in 1995–97 of rape or *serious* indecent assault of an adult female. The main focus of the study was on those males with previous convictions (678) who were matched to a control group of offenders with a general criminal history. Such issues as the definition of a serious sexual assault and a description of the actual statistical analysis carried out are fully addressed in the report of the study (Soothill, Francis, Fligelstone and Ackerley 2002[2]). We can, however, give something of the flavour of the findings.

In brief, a previous criminal history may be useful in helping to identify some persons who will become a danger in terms of being convicted of a serious sexual assault in the future. Perhaps more interestingly, we can begin to indicate the *relative risk* of having certain offences in one's criminal record compared with offenders who, by the same age, had not been convicted of a serious sexual assault. So, for example, we found that a conviction for a minor indecent assault of an adult female (i.e. where the sentence had been non-custodial) made the offender more than 12 times as likely to be convicted of a subsequent serious sexual assault than offenders without such a prior conviction. While many will have suspected that some kinds of less serious sexual assault are likely to be the forerunners of more serious sexual assaults, we can now put a figure on this likelihood.

However, there were also some surprises. For example, kidnapping – an unpleasant and serious offence in its own right – was shown to be a forerunner of murder on a significant number of occasions, on the one hand, and of serious sexual assault on the other. In other words, those convicted of kidnapping are four times more likely to be convicted of murder than the control group in the murder study, and four and a half times more likely to be subsequently convicted of serious sexual assault (SSA) than the control group in the SSA study. While the numbers involved in kidnapping are comparatively small, we regard kidnapping as a particularly pernicious type of behaviour where earlier intervention (that is, at the time of the kidnapping conviction) or increased surveillance (following the kidnapping conviction) may be merited.

This work has encouraged our team to consider the links between different types of serious crime. Currently there are those who study homicide, those who study violent crime, those who study serious sexual assault and so on. Such discrete studies may be too limiting and we believe that it is important to study the possible links between these various serious crimes.[3]

Another important shift that needs to be accomplished is the move from considering *relative* risk (that is, the risk compared with an appropriate control group) to considering *absolute* risk (that is, for instance, the likelihood of a male convicted of kidnapping going on to be convicted of murder). A rough estimate based on comparatively small numbers in our earlier study (Appendix B in Soothill, Francis, Fligelstone and Ackerley 2002) suggests that 1 in every 241 males convicted of kidnapping will go on to be convicted of murder. However, as mentioned above, kidnappers are also more likely to be subsequently convicted of serious sexual assault – and perhaps other unpleasant activities as well – so eventually these other possibilities must also be included in the estimates. This is future work that needs to be confronted.

Certainly the calculation of *absolute* risk is important in assessing the use of resources and their possible pay-offs. To date, this aspect does not seem to have played much part in planning a response to serious crime. In our new study we may be able to make some modest incursions down this route. Meanwhile, the point I am making is that a focus on serious crime in general may be a more useful approach rather than maintaining a somewhat narrow focus on sex crime. While moral calibrations are difficult and controversial, such crimes as murder, kidnapping, blackmail and serious sexual assault are all unpleasant, and to focus on one rather than the others – simply because of current public unease about sex crime – may help to mask the true nature of dangerousness.

Understanding the effects of changes in the societal response to serious sexual assault

This second section attempts to theorise and to consider what is likely to happen if there are changes in the societal response to serious sexual assault. For example, what happens if the reporting of rape suddenly rises as a response to a raised consciousness about the problem? What happens if there is a shift in the official reaction to such crimes? We know that such changes do take place but it is notoriously difficult to disentangle the effects. Social life is not conducted with a view to social experiments so we either have to use what is available in the social arena or to theorise the processes that underpin the changes. Here I try the latter route.

In considering the societal response to serious sexual assault, there are four basic components to recognise. At this point, for ease of presentation, I will consider these in terms of rape, as it makes clear what we are talking about. By extension, it can cover all kinds of serious sexual assault, for the logic remains the same. The four components are:

1. *The actual behaviour.* This can, of course, change over time – more people may commit rape, the definitions may change (inserting instruments into the vagina may be considered rape as much as inserting a penis; new categories of rape may be encompassed in the criminal law – since the 1990s, marital rape and male rape have been recognised as crimes). Beyond changes in definition, official reaction to rape may itself have an effect on behaviour. If all rapists were caught and convicted, it is difficult to believe that that this would not have an effect on putative perpetrators. However, in our model we will not consider changes in the actual behaviour over time. Behaviour will remain constant in our model of 1,000 rapes. Models may both simplify and distort, but the logic remains sovereign. Unlike life, models try to prevent everything happening at the same time.

2. *The reporting of rape.* This is the stage when rapes come to official notice, principally the police. Rapes may be disclosed to parents, friends or partners, but such people may advise the victim not to involve public agencies such as the police. Here we are concerned only with those rapes notified to the police. The figure of only one in ten rapes being reported to the police is a familiar proportion, so we will use that in our model. Hence, in Figure 2.1, of the 1,000 actual rapes, 100 rapes are shown as being reported to the police.

3. *Rape convictions.* It is a hazardous route from a rape being reported to a rape conviction being awarded. There are a wide variety of reasons

why the number of convictions does not equal the number of reports – the perpetrator may not be detected, the court may not believe the accusation and so on. For our model in Figure 2.1 we will assume that only one in ten reports results in a conviction. In fact, this may be a sadly optimistic figure as currently it is believed that only one in 13 reports results in a conviction. Nevertheless, in Figure 2.1 our original 'population' of 1,000 rapes is now down to 10 convictions.

4. *Offenders convicted of rape.* The number of offenders convicted of rape will relate to the number of convictions. Some offenders will be convicted of several rapes, a gang rape will involve several offenders, but mostly one offender will be convicted of one rape. In Figure 2.1, I have assumed five offenders. Rather than averaging the 10 convictions as two rapes each, I have further assumed four of the offenders have been convicted of one rape each, and one offender has been convicted of six rapes.

Figure 2.1 represents the total picture of 1,000 rapes, of which 90 per cent (or 900 rapes) are the notorious 'dark figure'; 100 rapes are reported, of which 10 per cent (or 10 rapes) successfully reach the conviction stage; and there are five offenders convicted for these ten rapes. One may challenge the numbers used but, hopefully, not the logic. While in theory one can upset the truism,[4] there are always more actual rapes than are reported, there are always more reported than are convicted, and there are usually more convictions than offenders (the alternative being that the number of convictions and the number of offenders are the same).

In life, many factors or variables change at the same time, making social science notoriously difficult to fathom. In scientific experiments, however, one attempts to change just one variable at a time. This is what I have tried to do with my model. Figure 2.2 shows two changes of conditions, shifting one variable at a time. Figure 2.2(a) – identical to Figure 2.1 – represents the starting point. Figure 2.2(b) shows the effect of doubling the reporting of rape from 100 to 200 rapes but without any changes in the proportions convicted. Figure 2.2(c) shows the effects of a change in the conviction rate.

So what does this elaborate construction tell us? First, in Figure 2.2(b) *the reporting of rape* has doubled from 100 to 200 rapes. Of course, something like this would not happen overnight. However, something like this has happened over the past two decades or so. As a result of official agencies, such as the police, providing a more sympathetic stance which, in turn, encourages parents, partners, friends and Rape Crisis Centres to suggest to the victims that they should report the offence to the police, it is not unexpected that the rate of reporting may well rise

Figure 2.1 Hypothetical model of outcome of 1,000 rapes

over a period. In our model (Figure 2.2(b)) the conviction rate remains the same and the relationship of crimes to offenders (namely, four 'single' offenders and one 'multiple' offender) also remains the same. Perhaps the main difference between this model and recent events is that

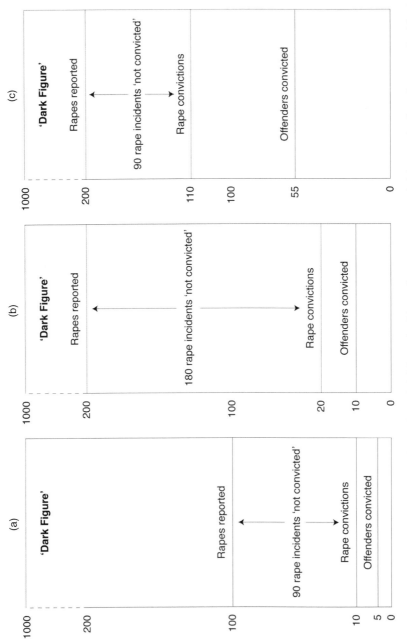

Figure 2.2 (a) Changing the hypothetical model (b) to doubling the rapes reported (c) to reducing the rape incidents 'not convicted'

the conviction rate has in reality declined, but in our model I am trying to avoid such complexities.

Comparing Figure 2.2(b) with Figure 2.2(a) provides both good and bad news. The police can show the effect of extra resources being ploughed into the problem of rape – there are now 20 rape convictions instead of 10 and 10 rape offenders have been sentenced instead of five. Using a bucket theory of rape, the bucket has been successfully lowered further into the vast reservoir of actual rapes. While on that score the advance is relatively modest, the police would expect everyone to be applauding that at least they are moving in the right direction. However, this is not the universal response.

The bad news is that now, instead of 90 reported incidents coming to nothing, there are now 180 (see Figure 2.2(b)). Proportions and percentages perhaps less impress the public and representatives of the women's movement than actual numbers. They will see (and perhaps notice in their everyday work and life – for more people are disclosing their experience of rape) a deteriorating situation, rather than being encouraged that there are actually more convictions and more rape offenders being caught. It is perhaps not surprising – as the numbers rise – that the focus increasingly moves to the low conviction rate.

It is difficult to measure a feeling that a situation is deteriorating. The present government, quite understandably, bemoans the fact that, while the actual crime rate has been falling (that is, until the most recent figures which suggest that the figures are stabilising rather than continuing to decline), a significant proportion of the population still feels that crime rates are continuing to rise.

Anyway, in the present model, it would seem a reasonable objective to get down the large figure of 180 incidents that fail to reach an outcome so that it becomes much closer to the earlier figure of 90 reported rape incidents going to waste, that is, as shown in Figures 2.2(a) and 2.2(b). This would hardly be a major victory – for the old figure of 90 raised serious concerns – but at least it should conquer the general feeling that matters are actually deteriorating.

So how much does the conviction rate need to rise just to get us back to the state it was before, with just 90 reported rapes not resulting in a conviction, and to make the public feel that fewer are getting away with rape? However, to effect this, Figure 2.2(c) shows that there must be a massive rise in the conviction rate from 10 per cent (in Figure 2.2(b)) to 55 per cent (in Figure 2.2(c)). Of course, this rise can be achieved in a variety of ways. Nevertheless, while court procedures may change so that fewer who are perhaps guilty are acquitted, this is still a tall order. Perhaps the scale of what is involved has been overlooked.

If this target were achieved, the police would – in terms of our model – now be involved in processing 55 offenders (averaging two convictions each) instead of five offenders. Also, instead of four single rapists and one multiple rapist, the pattern would now be 44 single rapists and 11 multiple rapists (involving six rapes each in our model).

The implications for police resources are, of course, enormous. Moving up from successfully processing five rapists to 55 rapists is not just an incremental rise, for as one detects more and successfully prosecutes more, each subsequent case is likely to become more difficult to process. In other words, more of the cases will be based on slender evidence as the demand to bring more offenders to justice increases. The usual tension between justice and crime control will become increasingly evident.

In the interests of scientific rigour, I have changed just one variable at a time. In reality, much else is going on and it is all much more complex than is portrayed here. Indeed, it is a familiar complaint that policy-makers tend to focus on issues in an insufficiently disaggregated way. There is a danger that this approach could face such criticism. While Figures 2.1 and 2.2, providing hypothetical models of rape outcomes, may be heuristically useful for the general point I am making, there are other factors to take into account. If it were possible to achieve a doubling in reported rapes in, say, a year, there would almost un-doubtedly be a significant change in the composition in the behaviours labelled as 'rape'. It would almost certainly be the case that the shares attributable to, for example, acquaintance rape, date rape and marital rape would grow disproportionately compared to, say, stranger rape in the thousand case increment. Each of these would have its own prior conviction base rate, so that the transition from 1,000 to 2,000 rapes would not be as straightforward as my original account suggested.[5] However, this simply underlines the point that one needs to be much more aware of the likely impact of changes.

There are societal changes that are beneficial to the police and other control agencies in meeting targets of higher conviction rates. Getting cases to court based on evidence of children in care has had mixed fortunes, but few would now deny that children in care can be raped. Prior to the 1970s it would have been virtually impossible to have a complaint of rape from a known prostitute taken seriously. Nowadays the complaint may come to court, but again with mixed fortunes. With the increased encouragement of disclosure, those committing two or more rapes on different people within family or acquaintanceship circles are perhaps less likely to remain among the 'dark figure' of rape, for one informant may encourage more reluctant others to come forward and thus help to secure a conviction.

This all brings me to my final question for this section. Where do all these 'new' convicted rapes come from? Up to now in my model, I have assumed that there are four single rapists to one multiple rapist. These are figures presented for illustration. But is this a proportion that really remains constant?

Certainly we know much more about the prevalence of rape as a result of victimisation surveys, such as the British Crime Survey; but these surveys fail to throw much light on the issue of single versus multiple rapists. In other words, the person reporting that he/she has experienced rape in the past year will not be able to say whether he/she is the only victim of the perpetrator. In fact, we know little about whether and how often rapists cross boundaries. Is the rapist in the immediate family circle also likely to commit rapes among acquaintances? Is the stranger rapist also a risk in closer relationships? In the proposed surveys about offending behaviour currently being considered by the Home Office, one suspects there will be little discovered about such matters – those committing rape are unlikely to tell those carrying clipboards what they have been up to. However, it is still a matter that needs to be confronted.

Sex crime in Lancaster, 1860–1979

The third section attempts, as promised, to speculate. It reports on some ongoing research. In fact, in developing this research, I wanted to place two strands of my own work within a more historical context. The first strand relates to sex crime and the media, where I have focused on the newspaper coverage of sex crime, principally rape (Soothill and Walby 1991, Soothill and Grover 1998). The second strand focuses on the criminal careers of sex offenders. So, for example, we took all those convicted of an indictable sex crime in 1973 – a total of 7,442 offenders – and traced their criminal careers over the next 20 years (Soothill and Francis 1997, Soothill, et al. 2000).

In studying these issues I became curious about whether contemporary sex crime problems were new, or merely old problems in new clothes. Lancaster became the location of the study, looking at sex crime in the local area over a long time-span – 120 years from 1860 to 1979. There are two major issues: detecting sex crime in the first place and monitoring sex offenders after discovery. This presentation is principally concerned with the latter issue.

Lancaster is a very old town. It received its first borough charter in 1193 – it actually became a city in May 1937 – and is known to Shakespeare lovers for its links to John of Gaunt, Duke of Lancaster, and also for its importance in the War of the Roses (White 1993). Later, Lancaster became a transit port in the slave trade – a fact not mentioned much now in polite company but local beneficiaries were responsible for some nice Georgian houses in Lancaster! In Victorian times it became important as a leading world centre for linoleum manufacture, and James Williamson (or Lord Ashton as he became known after his elevation to the peerage in 1895) became one of the richest men in Europe. Since then, Lancaster, as a manufacturing town, has been in decline. The university opened in the mid 1960s but this has not been enough to arrest a general decline. In fact, its importance as an assize town began to decline much earlier – from the 1830s when much county business began to move to Preston. Hence, during the 120 years of the study, Lancaster has had mixed fortunes. While socially maintaining its status through much of the time, there was a steady decline in its manufacturing base during the 20th century. Thus, in many respects Lancaster is a fairly typical northern town, but with some nuances of its own.

The methodology for the study was simple. A search of the local newspaper, the *Lancaster Guardian*, for all the 120 years – that is, over 6,000 editions – was carried out to identify any mention of sex offending. Hence, this study concentrates on the sex offences adjudicated by the courts *and* reported in the *Lancaster Guardian*.

The classification was broad, so included all sexual offences identified as indictable[6] (e.g. rape, indecent assault, incest) in the *Criminal Statistics: England and Wales*. In addition, appropriate non-indictable offences (notably prostitution-related offences and indecent exposure) were included. More unusually, contraventions of a local by-law and charges of 'using obscene language' were also noted. Part of the aim of including these minor offences was to try to estimate the extent to which offenders 'graduated' from minor sex crime to more serious sex crime.

While broad, the classification was not all-inclusive. There will be other crimes, not classified as sexual crime in the official statistics, that may have an underlying sexual motivation but would not be included. So, for example, theft of women's underclothes from a washing line may stem from a sexual motivation rather than being an economic crime. Similarly, murder may have a sexual component but would not be included in the present series, which is constrained by the legal category of sex crime.

Court appearances

The term 'court appearances' is important, for the focus is not simply on convicted offenders. The concern here is with those persons who came to the official notice of the courts whether they were convicted or acquitted.

Study period

1860 is the first year of microfilms of the *Lancaster Guardian* stored in the local library. Choosing 1979 as the end year not only coincided with the

Table 2.1 Timeframe of the study

Years	Periods
1860–1879	Mid-Victorian
1880–1899	Late-Victorian
1900–1919	Edwardian and the Great War
1920–1939	The inter-war years
1940–1959	Second World War and the post-war period
1960–1979	Increasing liberalisation of sex laws

start of a new era in British politics – this was the year when Margaret Thatcher first became British prime minister – but also enabled the total timeframe to be divided into six periods of 20 years (see Table 2.1).

The numbers in the series

1,791 persons have been identified as appearing on separate occasions in a court case involving a sex offence *and* reported in the *Lancaster Guardian* in the period 1860–1979. As there can be several defendants to one charge (e.g. in a gang-rape or a charge of indecency involving two consenting males), the total number of cases will be fewer, but the present analysis focuses on persons, not cases.

Table 2.2 divides the series into five major categories for each of the 20-year periods:

The 'serious non-consensual' category (which principally includes rape and indecent assault[7]) is always quite sizeable, averaging between five and eight cases per year in each period, but has the highest number of persons (bold in Table 2.2) in the last 20 years (1960–79).

Table 2.2 No. of persons appearing in a court case involving a sexual offence *and* reported in the *Lancaster Guardian* (1860–1979)

Type of sexual offence	1860–1879	1880–1899	1900–1919	1920–1939	1940–1959	1960–1979	Total
Non-consensual	97	141	106	103	148	**153**	748
Bigamy	27	23	22	49	**83**	3	207
Indecent exposure/indecency	17	55	20	11	**80**	53	236
Prostitution-type offences	5	**79**	77	—	—	—	161
Using obscene language	3	**203**	159	40	15	19	439
Total	149	**501**	384	203	326	228	1,791

Note: Bold figures show which period had the highest number of a particular offence type.

This category is particularly important, as the press reporting of 'serious non-consensual' crime perhaps informs the ethos of the times, certainly in relation to sexual offending. For each of the six periods one can calculate the proportion of the total that related to 'serious non-consensual' offences. For 1860–1879 the proportion is 65 per cent; for 1880–1899, 28 per cent; for 1900–1919, 28 per cent; for 1920–1939, 51 per cent; for 1940–1959, 45 per cent; for 1960–1979, 67 per cent. Hence, during the 1860s and 1870s, on the one hand, and 1960s and 1970s, on the other, it might have seemed that 'serious non-consensual crime' – with around two-thirds of the total cases being in this category – was an especially pressing and high-visibility problem. In contrast, during the period 1880–1920 – with only around one-quarter of the total cases – it would perhaps have appeared merely as one among many problems.[8] These, of course, are not the actual figures of sex offending but simply the numbers derived from court cases that are reported in the local newspaper. However, the reports do serve to develop the public's perception of offending. In the Victorian period the court reports were largely segregated from the rest of the paper, while since the Second World War reports of sex cases began to appear on pages throughout the newspaper (and especially on the front page for the more serious cases). Hence, these cases will make a different impact upon the reader at different periods.

As Table 2.2 shows, the number of persons charged with bigamy builds up until the peak period of 1940–59 (which coincides with the Second World War and its aftermath), but then declines quite markedly. The category, 'indecent exposure and indecency', covers a motley collection of activity. It is sometimes difficult to make precise judgments from newspaper reports. A person reported as behaving indecently may actually have been caught in consenting homosexual activity or exhibitionism (indecent exposure with intent to insult a female). On account of the lack of detail in many newspaper reports, the behaviour – which can be very different – has been grouped in one category. However, both legally and behaviourally, the activity in this category – although very annoying to innocent victims – can be adjudged as less serious than the activity which results in charges of 'serious non-consensual' offences. This category also reaches a peak in 1940–59 (bold in Table 2.2) prior to the liberalisation of the sex laws in the 1960s that decriminalised some forms of consenting homosexual activity in England and Wales.

Prostitution-type offences (which include brothel-keeping as well as prostitution) peak during the 1880–99 period and, interestingly, there are no court reports in the local newspaper of such activity since 1920 to the end of the study period. While undoubtedly there was a decline of such activity coming to official notice during the 60 years from 1920, there may also have been an editorial decision not to mention such cases in the local newspaper.

Finally, 'using obscene language' has a similar profile to 'prostitution-type' offences with a similar peak in the 1880–99 period; however, since 1920 there has been a marked decline rather than a complete absence of the reporting of this offence in the local newspaper.

Table 2.2 thus indicates how the reporting of different sexual offences peaks at different periods. The public nuisance offences of 'prostitution' and 'using obscene language' peak in the late Victorian decades (1880–99), 'bigamy' and 'indecent exposure and indecency' feature prominently during the Second World War and the aftermath, while the 'serious non-consensual' offences seem to rise from the Second World War onwards, although there have always been a sizeable number of such cases reported (particularly in the 1880–99 period).

There is always bias in newspaper reporting. At the local level it seems likely that the more serious sex crimes – that is, the non-consensual cases – will get a mention but reports on the more trivial, consensual activity (such as prostitution) or social nuisance offences (such as 'using obscene language') are less likely to be comprehensive. The exception among serious sexual offences is likely to be incest, where newspaper coverage is circumspect and often avoided.

However, the figures displayed in Table 2.2 are misleading in terms of representing sexual offending in the local area of Lancaster. Lancaster was a major assize town for most of these years and many of the more serious cases will have occurred elsewhere in the county. Furthermore, in the 19th century (before the advent of popular national newspapers) the newspaper also served a wider function – there were some cases reported from elsewhere in the country. In terms of trying to clarify what are local cases, the analysis is ongoing. However, by focusing on all those offenders having two or more separate court appearances for sex offending reported in this local newspaper in the 120 years of the study, one can consider predominantly local cases involving local people. Certainly these are the persons who continue to cause trouble in the local area. So far, 138 sexual recidivists have been identified. There will be adjustments as further refinements are made to the database. So, for instance, there are 57 juvenile offenders who have been in court for sex offences, but cannot – since 1933 – be named in the newspapers for legal reasons. Some of these may have become sexual recidivists with another court appearance for a sex offence on a later occasion. However, such adjustments are unlikely to shift the main arguments.

Elsewhere (Soothill, in press) I have shown that 49 persons – or 36 per cent of the 138 persons – had been in court for at least one *non-consensual* sexual offence among their various sexual offences. The remaining 89 (or

64 per cent of the cases) were never in court for *non-consensual* offences and probably can be regarded as social nuisances rather than a serious danger to members of the community. In brief, I am concerned here with those who appear in court for at least one *non-consensual* sexual offence together with evidence of some other illegal sexual activity in the local area.[9] With the huge benefit of hindsight, how long could those committing the more serious offences usefully have been under surveillance?

The offender whose criminal career seems to span the longest period highlights the strengths and possible weaknesses of the approach of this study. In March 1915, at the Children's Court, John Stephenson (aged 14[10]) was charged with attempting to commit a rape on a little girl of five years; after hearing the evidence the boy was sent to the Fylde Farm School, until he attained the age of 19, and his father was ordered to pay 2s. 6d. per week (*Lancaster Guardian*, 27 March 1915).

In March 1963 – 48 years later – John Stephenson (aged 62) pleaded guilty and was fined a total of £20 on four charges alleging that he indecently assaulted two girls, aged 11 and 13 years. The defence argued – and this was not rebutted in the newspaper report – that 'Stephenson was a man of previous unblemished character with a good working record as a driver for 25 years. He was not an evil or bad man, but unfortunately he had been weak and had allowed excitement to get the better of him. There was no suggestion that he had used any compulsion because the girls themselves had made no complaint.' (*Lancaster Guardian*, 22 March 1963).

Perhaps the two reports are of different men, but the names and the ages neatly match. If it is the same man, has he led a blameless life since his court appearance aged 14? Has his activity simply been undetected? Would greater surveillance have been of any help in preventing this crime nearly 50 years later?

This case, of course, is most unusual. Figure 2.3 shows – again with the benefit of hindsight – how 43 of these cases,[11] who had been in court for at least one *non-consensual* sexual offence, distribute over the 100 years (1880–1979).

The offences are shown with letters denoting different kinds of sexual activity – A = a non-consensual offence; B = bigamy and so on. When someone has appeared in court for a non-consensual offence, he is then regarded as a risk and the subsequent years – until the next court appearance for a sexual offence – are displayed as dark grey. When someone has appeared in court for another type of sexual offence, he is not regarded as a risk and the subsequent years are displayed as a patterned light grey.

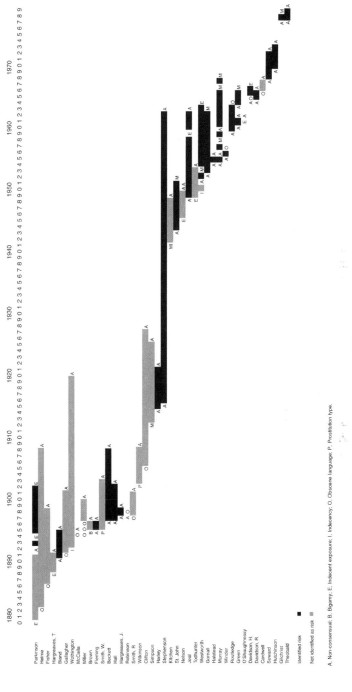

Figure 2.3 Sexual recidivists in the Lancaster area (1880–1979)

A, Non-consensual; B, Bigamy; E, Indecent exposure; I, Indecency; O, Obscene language; P, Prostitution type.

The first entry, Parkinson, appears for indecent exposure in 1880 and then again in 1892 for a non-consensual offence which changes the risk category and the colouring to dark grey. In the event he went on to appear in court for indecent exposure on two further occasions.

All those in Figure 2.3 have appeared in court at least twice for sexual offences with at least one being for a non-consensual offence. However, there are major differences between the three periods. In the 40 years from 1880 to 1919 the light grey shading predominates – showing how offenders tended to move from less serious to more serious sexual activity. In the 20 years from 1920 to 1940 there appeared to be a curious dearth of sexual recidivists in the Lancaster area. Finally, in the 40 years from 1940 to 1979, the dark grey shading predominates and the length of the official 'careers' of the offenders seems shorter. What provokes this different pattern? Why not other types of sexual activity? Perhaps there are fewer other types of sexual offences to commit in the local area during the later period – much homosexual activity has been de-criminalised, less prostitution activity in the local area and so on. Why shorter careers? Is this a result of a change of behaviour or more vigilance in reporting, detecting and bringing offenders to court? Perhaps they do not stop but more readily move on. Perhaps the surveillance is less effective in the later period and they are not caught. Clearly there is much to speculate upon.

We can identify the ages and the lengths of their 'official' criminal careers for 36 of these sexual recidivists. As Figure 2.4 shows, their 'careers' tend to be quite short, mostly starting in their 20s[12] and seemingly ending by their early 30s.

Again this phenomenon raises the question of whether they do really end their sexual offending or whether they simply move out of the area to fresh pastures. From this study we do not know the answer, but it is the sort of question for which we do need an answer.

I can provide only a glimpse of the type of questions that emerge from developing a social laboratory of this kind. It provides some 'rules of thumb'. So, for instance, it seems that of every five sexual recidivists who appear in court for at least one *non-consensual* offence, two of them will appear at least twice for *non-consensual* offences, two will have 'grad-uated' to a *non-consensual* offence after appearing for other less serious sexual offences, while one will – after the first appearance for a *non-consensual* offence – simply go on to appear in court for less serious sexual offences.[13]

Of course, we need to know much more about a local area. In what ways is its character changing? Are convicted sex offenders moving into the area? Are convicted sex offenders moving out? Essentially, however, it would be more helpful if each community could learn how to deal

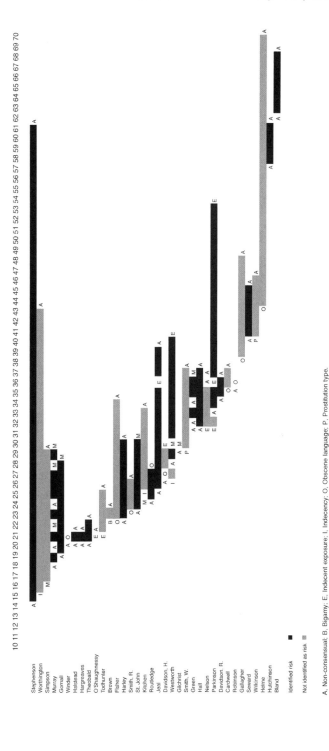

Figure 2.4 Criminal careers – in terms of ages – of sexual recidivists in the Lancaster area

A. Non-consensual; B. Bigamy; E. Indecent exposure; I. Indecency; O. Obscene language; P. Prostitution type.

with and contain its known sex offenders. The culture of NIMBY ('not in my back yard') exacerbates the problem, but that debate is beyond the scope of this chapter. This third section helps me to make the plea that we need to understand changes over time and that we can, indeed, learn from history.

Conclusion

This chapter has been a modest attempt to encourage the use of both history and statistics to greater effect in attempting to understand sex crime and formulating an appropriate reaction to the problem. Its overall theme is that studying the past may help in focusing upon both the present and the future. The first section indicates that a criminal history may provide more clues about future serious crime than perhaps has been appreciated in the past. It has long been known that evidence of routine and low tariff crime is a good predictor of future crime. In fact, the focus in predicting reconviction has been largely on the amount of crime that has been committed. Our work encourages the notion that the *type* of crime that has been committed is also important in understanding the likelihood of future serious crime.[14]

The second section encourages the notion that trying to probe the likely effect of changes of societal response to serious sexual assault by considering hypothetical models is a way forward to the challenge ahead. It demonstrates that, as the reporting of serious sexual assault increases, the conviction rate needs to rise markedly to conquer a general feeling that matters are deteriorating rather than improving. One suspects that the rise needed is much greater than most would have guessed.

The third section focuses on the possible value of developing a social laboratory in a local area to begin to understand changes over long periods of time. While the questions such work raises are not easily answerable, one should not dodge the challenge. So, for instance, are the criminal careers of most sex offenders really as short as some of this work suggests?

I have perhaps been regarded as a critic of some of the efforts with regard to the monitoring of sex offenders (Soothill and Francis 1997). I have tried to highlight the dangers of 'criminal apartheid' (Soothill and Francis 1998) and that sex offenders can be both specialised and versatile (Soothill et al. 2000). However, my position is a consistent one. We simply need more evidence. Hopefully, the three themes I have discussed demonstrate that we are gaining more knowledge about sex crime, that we need to think about the effects of changes and that there is still much to learn.

Acknowledgements

I wish to thank the Nuffield Foundation for the grant for the 'Sex Crime in Lancaster, 1860–1979' project and to Emma Robinson and Hannah Yates for their assistance in this work. I appreciate the help of many students over several years in collecting the data from the local newspaper. Also to Brian Francis for his continued support as a colleague and to Michael Tonry for his insightful comments.

Notes

1 The cut-off point of 45 years was governed by the fact that one can only obtain a full criminal history from the Offenders Index (our main data source) of those born in 1953 (and subsequent years). The Offenders Index started in 1963, by which time those born in 1953 had reached the age of criminal responsibility (10 years of age). Those born earlier than 1953 will have their criminal careers charted only since 1963, and so their records may be incomplete.

2 This work on serious sexual assault is part of a wider study that also considers murder in a similar manner.

3 This new project on 'Probing unusual serious crime', supported by the Home Office, considers 'Threats to murder', 'Procuration', 'Blackmail', 'Kidnapping', 'False accounting', 'Perjury', 'Arson', and 'Offences against the Firearms Act'.

4 False accusations could, in theory, distort the picture by producing more convictions than actual rapes, but this is not a serious issue to disturb the discussion of the model.

5 I am most grateful to Professor Michael Tonry for suggesting this point.

6 While the *Criminal Statistics: England And Wales* separate into 'indictable' and 'non-indictable' offences, the distinction is largely obsolete. Furthermore, the dividing line changes from time to time. There are certain crimes that may be tried only upon indictment, but there are a large number of indictable offences that may, in certain circumstances, be tried summarily. Conversely, there are certain summary offences that may, if the accused so wishes, be tried upon indictment.

7 Incest was also included as 'non-consensual' but sibling incest may be 'consensual'. However, newspaper reports on incest – which are quite rare – may fail to clarify this.

8 I am indebted to Professor Michael Tonry for drawing my attention to this point.

9 There are, of course, others who appear in court on one occasion for a *non-consensual* sexual assault in the local area and no evidence of any other sexual offence. Some of these could have court appearances for sexual offences in other parts of the country, but this is not the focus of this discussion.

10 The name is disclosed in the newspaper at this young age as the offence occurred before 1933 when legal restrictions on naming minors in newspaper reports were imposed.

11 Cases occurring prior to 1880 (where the evidence is sparse) and three cases with discrepant information have been omitted from this analysis.

12 As mentioned earlier, some of the 57 juvenile offenders, who have been in court for sex offences but could not be named in the newspapers for legal reasons, could become serious sexual recidivists. If so, then the average starting age for these recidivists could be reduced somewhat.

13 This 'rule of thumb' is based on Figure 2.4 where 14 of the 36 (or 39 per cent) appeared at least twice for *non-consensual* offences, 15 (or 42 per cent) 'graduated' to a *non-consensual* offence after appearing for other less serious sexual offences, while 7 (or 19 per cent) – after a first appearance for a *non-consensual* offence – went on to appear in court for less serious sexual offences.

14 A further variant of this is our work on patterns of offending over a criminal career (Soothill, Francis and Fligelstone 2002).

References

Butler-Sloss, E. (1988) *The Cleveland Report*. London: HMSO.

Caputi, J. (1988) *The Age of Sex Crime*. London: The Women's Press.

Soothill K. (1993) 'The Serial Killer Industry', *The Journal of Forensic Psychiatry* 4:2, pp. 341–54.

Soothill, K. (in press) 'Sex Crime and Recidivism in a Little English City (1860–1979)', in C. Emsley, and M. Porret (eds), *Récidive et Récidivistes: de la renaissance au XXe siècle*. Geneva: Droz.

Soothill, K. and Francis, B. (1997) 'Sexual reconvictions and the Sex Offenders Act 1997', *New Law Journal*, 147 (6806), pp. 1285–86 and 147 (6807), pp. 1324–25.

Soothill, K. and Francis, B. (1998) 'Poisoned Chalice or Just Deserts? (The Sex Offenders Act, 1997)', *Journal of Forensic Psychiatry*, 9:2, pp. 281–93.

Soothill, K., Francis, B. and Fligelstone, R. (2002) *Patterns of Offending Behaviour: a new approach*. Home Office Occasional Paper series, Home Office: London. www.homeoffice.gov.uk/rds/adhocpubs1.html

Soothill, K., Francis, B., Fligelstone, R. and Ackerley, E. (2002) *Murder and Serious Sexual Assault: what criminal histories can reveal about future offending*. Police Research Series, Paper 144. London: Home Office.

Soothill, K., Francis, B., Sanderson, B. and Ackerley, E. (2000) 'Sex Offenders: specialists, generalists – or both?' *British Journal of Criminology* 40, pp. 56–67.

Soothill, K. and Grover, C. (1998) 'The Public Portrayal of Rape Sentencing: what the public learns of rape sentencing from newspapers', *Criminal Law Review*, pp. 455–64.

Soothill, K. and Walby, S. (1991) *Sex Crime in the News*. London: Routledge.

Thompson, K. (1998) *Moral Panics*. London: Routledge.

White, A. (ed.) (1993) *A History of Lancaster, 1193–1993*. Keele: Ryburn Publishing.

Chapter 3

The legislative framework

Cathy Cobley

The increase in public and professional concern over sex offenders in recent years has been little short of phenomenal. Although sex offenders have long been treated as one of the most hated, feared and despised group of offenders, research at the beginning of the 1990s showed that sex offenders were being accorded an increasingly high profile by the media (Soothill 1991) and in 1994 it was claimed that sex offenders had been built into 'modern folk devils' by the popular press (Sampson 1994). Since then, public concern over sex offenders has continued to increase at an alarming rate and successive governments have indicated their commitment to implementing measures to improve protection of the public. There has been frantic political and legislative activity as the law struggles to construct a framework of measures to facilitate the effective management of sex offenders in the community and stem the growing public hysteria. Further reform of the criminal justice system now seems inevitable. In the wake of the horrific abduction and murder of Holly Wells and Jessica Chapman in August 2002, the government was keen to point out that it has already taken action to manage and regulate sex offenders to protect children and promised 'as we go into the next parliamentary session, we will be ratcheting up those measures even further as we learned over the last four years how best to maximise that protection' (*Daily Telegraph*, 22 August 2002).

This chapter reviews the current legislative framework and discusses its efficacy in practice and proposals for reform. The chapter also considers the substantive criminal law that determines who can be brought within the framework of control and focuses in particular on the current debate over behaviour known as 'grooming', whereby a potential offender prepares his victim for abuse.

Overview of the current legislative framework

The legislative framework developed over the last decade is firmly rooted in a policy of public protection whereby the community is protected through increased restriction, surveillance and monitoring of sex offenders in its midst (Kemshall 2001). This may be achieved through the sentences imposed following conviction for a sexual offence, and by additional control measures imposed on sex offenders living in the community.

Sentencing

The present statutory framework for sentencing is contained in the Powers of Criminal Courts (Sentencing) Act 2000 and is based on the concept of 'just deserts' – that offenders should be punished justly and suitably according to the seriousness of their offences. Those passing sentence are required to concentrate primarily on the offence or offences the offender has committed and the level of punishment commensurate with the seriousness of those offences. However, sex offenders (and those who commit violent offences) are singled out for special consideration. This may be reflected in the nature and length of sentence imposed, the release of the offender at the end of a custodial sentence and the period of supervision in the community.

Custodial sentences and release into the community

A custodial sentence may usually be imposed only if the court is of the opinion that the offence, or the combination of the offence and one or more offences associated with it, was so serious that only such a sentence can be justified. However, if the offence is a violent or sexual offence, a custodial sentence may be imposed if the court is of the opinion that only such a sentence would be adequate to protect the public from serious harm from the offender. Similarly, although the length of the sentence must usually be such as is commensurate with the seriousness of the offence, when the offence is a violent or sexual offence, the court can impose a longer term (not exceeding the maximum) as in the opinion of the court is necessary to protect the public from serious harm from the offender. Following the enactment of the Crime (Sentences) Act 1997, offenders convicted for a second time of certain serious sexual and violent offences (including rape and intercourse with a girl under the age of thirteen) are subject to mandatory life imprisonment.

Offenders sentenced to a term of imprisonment of less than 12 months will be released unconditionally after serving one-half of their sentence. The arrangements for the release of all offenders given a custodial sentence of 12 months or more include a period on licence, during which time they will be liable to be recalled to custody and will be supervised by the probation service in order to help them adjust to life in the community and to address their offending behaviour. Offenders sentenced to life imprisonment will remain on licence following release for the rest of their lives.

Offenders serving sentences of at least three months but less than four years may be eligible for early release under the Home Detention Curfew scheme (HDC), but sex offenders subject to the notification requirements of Part 1 of the Sex Offenders Act 1997 are not eligible under the scheme (s. 34A Criminal Justice Act 1991, as amended by s. 65 Criminal Justice and Court Services Act 2000).

Extended sentences
It has previously been acknowledged that there may be a need for more stringent supervision of sex offenders following their release from custody. Section 44 of the Criminal Justice Act 1991 allowed the court to direct that serious sex offenders should be supervised to the very end of their sentence, rather than to the three-quarter point which is usual for other offenders. However, in 1996 the government expressed the belief that there was a strong case for strengthening the arrangements for supervising sex offenders (Home Office 1996). Section 20 of the Crime (Sentences) Act 1997 provided for the imposition of an extended supervision period on sex offenders at the end of a custodial sentence and created a presumption that an extended period of supervision would be imposed unless there were exceptional circumstances. Such an approach was difficult to justify, as research has shown that sex offenders of different types exhibit different re-offending behaviour, and therefore that not all types of sex offenders will require the same length or type of supervision.

The relevant provisions of the 1997 Act were never brought into force and the following year the Crime and Disorder Act 1998 replaced the presumption with a discretion, allowing, but not requiring, the court to pass an extended sentence. The relevant provisions are now contained in section 85 of the Powers of Criminal Courts (Sentencing) Act 2000. If the court is satisfied that the normal period of licence to which the offender would be subject would not be adequate for the purpose of preventing the commission by him of further offences and securing his rehabilitation, it may impose an extended sentence which consists of the custodial term, followed by an extended period of supervision (up to ten years for sex offenders). During the extension period the offender will be subject to licence, and thus supervision, and will be liable to be recalled to custody at any time up to the end of the period.

Community sentences

Offenders convicted of serious sexual offences will usually receive an immediate custodial sentence and attention will be focused primarily on the length of the custodial sentence and arrangements for the supervision of the offender in the community on his release. If the offence is not sufficiently serious to justify a custodial sentence, the sentencer will then consider whether the offence is serious enough to justify a community sentence. A community rehabilitation order (formerly a probation order) may be imposed if the court is of the opinion that the supervision of the defendant is desirable in the interests of securing his rehabilitation, protecting the public from harm from him or preventing the commission by him of further offences. The order may include various requirements with which the offender must comply, including requirements as to treatment and residence, and, since June 2001, a curfew requirement may be included in the order. The order may thus be deemed suitable for those convicted of less serious sexual offences. Other community sentences include community punishment orders (formerly community service orders) and community punishment and rehabilitation orders (formerly combination orders), both of which involve the offender undertaking work in the community. The suitability of a sentence which contains no provision to address sexual offending but leaves sex offenders in the community has been questioned (Home Office 1998: para 1.11). Despite this, in 2000, 100 sex offenders received what were then referred to as community service orders and the same number received a combination order (Home Office 2001a).

Further control measures in the community

Sex offenders living in the community may be subject to controls imposed by a number of provisions which do not relate directly to their sexual offending. These provisions include anti-social behaviour orders under the Crime and Disorder Act 1998, the 'stalking' legislation contained in the Protection from Harassment Act 1997, civil law injunctions and, in cases where an individual is suffering from a mental disorder, the mental health legislation (see further Cobley 2000: para 7.35–7.73). However, specific measures have been enacted in recent years which are aimed exclusively, or in some cases primarily, at sex offenders.

The sex offender 'register'

Although the majority of convicted offenders will be required to maintain contact with the criminal justice system for a limited period of time, either through a community sentence or following release on licence after a custodial sentence, prior to the 1997 Act there was no formal way of keeping track of sex offenders in the community once their sentences had been completed. Perhaps one of the most high-profile measures in the government's response to concern over sex offenders has been the creation of the sex offender 'register', which was introduced by Part 1 of the Sex Offenders Act 1997. Although commonly called a register, the 1997 Act makes no provision for the creation of a separate register, and attempts to impose a duty on the Secretary of State to maintain such a register failed. Details of offenders were initially held on the police national computer, but the government is currently piloting a new database, known as ViSOR (violent and sex offender register) with full implementation of the database expected by the end of 2003 (Home Office 2002b). The 1997 Act requires certain categories of sex offenders to notify to the police any change of name and address during a specified period. The notification requirement applies to all those convicted or cautioned in respect of an offence listed in schedule 1 to the Act. The schedule includes offences contrary to sections 1, 5, 6, 10, 12–16 and 28 of the Sexual Offences Act 1956, section 1(1) of the Indecency with Children Act 1960, section 54 of the Criminal Law Act 1977, section 1 of the protection of Children Act 1978, section 178 of the Customs and Excise Management Act 1979 (where the prohibited goods include indecent photographs of persons who are, or appear to be, under the age of 16), section 160 of the Criminal Justice Act 1988 and section 3 of the Sexual Offences (Amendment) Act 2000. However, certain exceptions apply in the case of young offenders and consenting victims (Cobley 2000: para 7.8). The notification requirements also apply to those serving sentences at the time of commencement of the Act and to those who are found not guilty of such an offence by reason of insanity, or found to be under a disability and to have done the act charged in respect of the offence, after the commencement of the Act. Following calls for further reform, the original requirements contained in the 1997 Act were tightened by the Criminal Justice and Court Services Act 2000. The maximum penalty for failure to comply with the registration requirements has been raised from six months' to five years' imprisonment, initial registration is now required in person within 72 hours (compared to 14 days under the original requirements), the police have been given powers to photograph and fingerprint the offender on initial registration and offenders are required to give notification of foreign travel.

Multi-Agency Public Protection Panels (MAPPPs)
The police have the formal responsibility for the registration of sex offenders under the 1997 Act. However, even before the enactment of the 1997 Act, it had been common practice for the police to work closely with the probation service and other local agencies in assessing and managing

the risk posed by sex offenders and other potentially dangerous offenders in the community, and many police areas operated public protection panels to facilitate the exchange of information between agencies and the formulation of risk management plans in relation to individual offenders (Maguire et al. 2001). Section 67 of the Criminal Justice and Court Services Act 2000 now places a statutory duty on the police and probation services to establish arrangements for assessing and managing the risks posed by such offenders in the community. Strategic boards oversee the work of the panels and, in an effort to increase public confidence in the system, members of the public are now being invited to sit on strategic boards in pilot areas (Home Office 2002a).

Sex Offender Orders and Restraining Orders
Despite the implementation of the 1997 Act, concern continued to be expressed that communities were not being adequately protected against the activities of sex offenders. In an effort to meet these concerns, the Crime and Disorder Act 1998 introduced a new order – the Sex Offender Order (SOO). The order is a civil order, breach of which constitutes a criminal offence. On an application by the chief officer of police, the magistrates' court can make an order in relation to convicted sex offenders and those who fall within section 3 of the 1998 Act who have acted in such a way as to give reasonable cause to believe that an order is necessary to protect the public from serious harm from him. Although the order is a civil, injunctive order dealt with by the magistrates' court acting in its civil capacity, it now seems that the standard of proof required is the criminal standard (R (on the application of McCann) v Manchester Crown Court [2002] 4 All ER 593). The order prohibits the offender from doing any act specified in the order. However, SOOs require an offender to have acted, since the relevant conviction, in such a way as to give reasonable cause to believe that an order is necessary to protect the public from serious harm from him. Furthermore, an application must be made to the court before the order can be made and this must necessarily be some time after the relevant conviction. In order to address these shortcomings the Criminal Justice and Court Services Act 2000 amended the 1997 Act to give the Crown Court and Court of Appeal a power to impose a Restraining Order (RO) when sentencing a sex offender if satisfied that it is necessary to do so in order to protect the public in general, or any particular members of the public, from serious harm from him. As with an SOO, an RO may prohibit the individual from doing anything described in the order. Thus specific restrictions may now be imposed on an abuser when he returns to the community, without the need for his behaviour to be monitored and a further application made to the court.

Restrictions on working with children

The majority of the measures introduced to control sex offenders in the community apply to all those classified as sex offenders, regardless of the age of their victim(s). However, much of the public hysteria over sex offenders has centred on the activities of paedophiles and, in an effort to enhance child protection and allay public concern, additional control measures have been introduced to prevent paedophiles (and others deemed to be unsuitable) from working with children. The idea of preventing those who are thought to present a risk to children from having unrestricted access to children through employment, whether paid or voluntary, is not new. In the past employers had three potential sources of information which could be consulted in order to check the background of a potential employee: a criminal record check, 'List 99' and the Department of Health's Consultancy Index. Under administrative arrangements between the Home Office and the Association of Chief Police Officers (ACPO), criminal records checks could be made against those applying for work in the public sector which would give them substantial unsupervised access, on a sustained or regular basis, to children under the age of 16 or those under the age of 18 with special needs. 'List 99' was the list maintained by the Department of Education and Employment containing details of those barred from employment as a teacher or related position on medical grounds or grounds of misconduct under the Education Reform Act 1988. The Department of Health's Consultancy Index had no statutory basis but operated on an advisory basis whereby local authorities, private and voluntary organisations could check the suitability of those they proposed to employ in a childcare post.

However, concerns were expressed that the existing safeguards were not fully integrated and that there was a need for a more streamlined approach to ensure there were no loopholes. Following the recommendations of the Utting Report (Utting 1997), in 1998 the government set up an interdepartmental working group to consider the matter. The main report of the group was published in January 1999 (Home Office 1999a) and several of the report's recommendations were enacted in the Protection of Children Act 1999. Further proposals for reform were made in July 1999 (Home Office 1999b) and enacted in the Criminal Justice and Court Services Act 2000. Following these reforms childcare organisations proposing to employ an individual in a childcare setting are required to check the person through the Criminal Records Bureau, which now holds information about people included on List 99 and the Department of Health's Consultancy Index (which was placed on a statutory basis by the Protection of Children Act 1999), as well as criminal records. However, the Criminal Records Bureau does not hold information on the findings of civil courts in family cases, leading to concern that some child abusers may be 'slipping through the net' (*Daily Telegraph*, 23 August 2002).

In addition, the Secretary of State has statutory power to ban unsuitable people from working with children in the fields of education, health and social care, and the Criminal Justice and Court Services Act 2000 gives the courts a power when sentencing an offender to make an order which disqualifies the offender from working with children. The power must be exercised if the offender was over the age of 18 when the offence was committed, unless the court believes it is unlikely that he will commit a further offence against a child. If the offender was under 18, the court should impose the order only if it believes that there is a likelihood of him committing a further offence against a child. In order for the disqualification order to be made, the offender must have committed a specified sexual or violent offence against a child under the age of 18 years and must have received a qualifying sentence, which can be broadly defined as a sentence of imprisonment for 12 months or more, or a hospital or guardianship order under the Mental Health Act 1983. Provision exists for the disqualified person to apply for the order to be reviewed by a tribunal, usually after 10-year periods. The Criminal Justice and Court Services Act 2000 also created new criminal offences of knowingly applying for, offering to do, accepting or doing any work with children whilst disqualified and knowingly offering work with children to, or procuring work with children for, an individual who is disqualified, or allowing such an individual to continue in such work.

Efficacy of the current legislative framework and proposals for reform

The legislative framework created over the last decade undoubtedly provides enhanced public protection overall, but the operation of the provisions in practice can be problematic. Furthermore, it is clear that public confidence in the criminal justice system is lacking and this an issue which the government is obviously keen to address.

Sentencing and release into the community – a new framework?

During the latter part of the 1990s the current sentencing framework came under close scrutiny as it became evident that there had been a serious loss of public confidence in the system. As a result of the growing concern, in May 2000 the Home Office announced a review of the sentencing framework. The review was published in July 2001 (Home

Office 2001b) and recommended that the existing 'just deserts' philosophy should be modified by incorporating a new presumption that severity of sentence should increase when an offender had sufficient recent and relevant previous convictions. In an effort to restore public confidence and 'put the sense back into sentencing', the review also recommended a number of changes to the operation of both custodial and community sentences. Following a period of consultation, a new sentencing frame-work was set out in the White Paper of July 2002 (Home Office 2002a) and incorporated into the Criminal Justice Bill which was introduced in the House of Commons in November 2002. The proposals include the introduction of a new customised community sentence, whereby all existing community sentences would be available together in a new sentence, allowing sentencers to fit the restrictions and rehabilitation to the offender. A major overhaul of the existing framework of custodial sentences and parole is also envisaged. Under the proposals, custodial sentences of up to 12 months will be replaced by a new sentence of 'custody plus', which will consist of a maximum period of three months in custody served in full, followed by a compulsory period of supervision in the community, giving an overall sentence of up to 12 months. New sentences of 'custody minus' (a short prison sentence suspended for up to two years while the offender undertakes a community sentence) and 'intermittent custody' (a prison sentence and community sentence served intermittently) will be introduced. In the usual case, offenders sentenced to a term of imprisonment of 12 months or more will be released automatically halfway through their sentence. The remainder of the sentence will be served in the community, where the offender will follow a package of constructive activities set by the prison and probation services prior to his release. The offender will be subject to licence conditions (and supervision) until the end of the sentence.

Indeterminate sentences
More controversially, it is proposed to introduce an indeterminate sentence for offenders who commit violent or sexual offences which do not currently attract a maximum penalty of life imprisonment and who have been assessed and considered dangerous. Under the proposals, such an offender will be required to serve a minimum term and would then remain in prison beyond this time, until the Parole Board was completely satisfied that the risk he presented had sufficiently diminished for him to be released and supervised in the community. The offender will remain on licence for the rest of his life. The idea of protective sentencing, whereby a prison sentence is made longer than would otherwise be justified in order to protect the public from a risk of future harm, is certainly not new and, although difficult to justify on

ideological grounds, it is already firmly established in the current sentencing framework. However, the proposed indeterminate sentence is a radical departure from previous notions of protective sentencing and, if enacted, will inevitably be subject to challenge under the Human Rights Act 1998.

The sex offender 'register' – the third overhaul

In practice, the efficacy of the sex offender 'register' depends on two factors: first, offenders' compliance with the notification requirements and secondly the use made of that information by the agencies charged with the responsibility of assessing and managing the risk the offender presents. In relation to the former, one year after the 1997 Act came into force, the national rate of compliance with the requirement to register was said to be 94.7 per cent (Plotnikoff and Woolfson 2000). Since then the requirements have been tightened. Initially numbers were collated biannually on a national basis from the police national computer, but this arrangement has now been overtaken by guidance issued by the Home Office in respect of the statutory duty imposed on the police and probation services under the Criminal Justice and Court Services Act 2000. The guidance requires information about the number of sex offenders subject to the notification requirements in each police area to be published on an annual basis. In 2002, MAPPA annual reports indicated that there were 18,500 people subject to the notification requirements. As far as the use made of the information is concerned, it is now the function of MAPPPs to advise on the management of sex offenders, but the question of when members of the community should be informed about sex offenders living in their neighbourhood remains controversial. Calls for the public to have a right of access to the information notified to the police have been repeatedly rejected and it seems clear that the government will not be prepared to legislate on the use made of the information (see Chapter 4 in this volume).

In 2002, the government announced its intention to 'overhaul' the Sex Offenders Act 1997 (Home Office 2002b) and the proposed changes are now contained in Part 2 of the Sexual Offences Bill, which was introduced in the House of Lords on 28 January 2003. The relevant provisions of the Bill, if enacted, will require those subject to the notification requirements to notify to the police the relevant information within three days. This time period applies both to initial registration and to any changes (clauses 85 and 86). The relevant information which must be notified will include the offender's national insurance details as further safeguard against evasion. Offenders will also be required to confirm their details in person annually (clause 87). The Bill also makes provision for a new order called a Notification Order (NO) (clause 96). The police may apply to the magistrates' court for a NO in respect of an offender who has been convicted, cautioned, or had a relevant finding made against him in respect of a sexual offence in a country outside the UK, when the police believe that the offender is currently in, or is intending to come to, their police area. The effect of the order will be to subject the offender to the notification requirements, thus enabling the police to keep track of the movements of sex offenders who are known to have committed offences abroad.

Sex offender orders – a 'failed pervert law'?

The power to apply for a SOO has not been widely used, with less than 100 orders being made in the first three years following implementation of the provisions. Furthermore, it seems that the pattern of SOO applications is not uniformly distributed across the country, with six forces alone accounting for nearly half (46 per cent) of all SOOs (Knock et al. 2002). As one would expect, prosecutions for breach of a SOO are increasing over time. Three successful breach prosecutions were re-ported to have been made in 1999 and 21 during 2000. A provisional figure of 28 prosecutions has been given for the first three quarters of 2001 (HC Deb 8 May 2002, col 233W). Some offenders may be prosecuted for breaching a SOO on more than one occasion, but it nevertheless appears that action for breach is taken in respect of approximately 50 per cent of SOOs made. This casts doubt on the efficacy of the order as a deterrent from the offender's point of view, but also indicates that the order is a useful tool for controlling the activities of sex offenders in the community. Although research has found that the court sentencing for breaches is variable, of the known outcomes for breach prosecutions, 61 per cent of offenders received a custodial sentence (Knock et al. 2002).

Despite the apparent shortcomings of the SOO, the police and related agencies' response to the introduction of SOOs has been positive, with orders being seen as a practical mechanism for a multi-agency approach to the management of high-risk sex offenders which particularly strengthens the relationship between the police and the probation services (Knock et al. 2002). Interim SOOs were introduced by the Police Reform Act 2002, but more radical reform is now contained in the Sexual Offences Bill currently before Parliament.

Sexual Offences Prevention Orders

The Sexual Offences Bill contains provisions to replace the SOO and RO with a new, expanded order, called a Sexual Offences Prevention Order (SOPO) (clauses 103–09). A court will be able to make the SOPO on conviction for a relevant offence (as the current RO) or following an application by the police in respect of a person with a relevant conviction living in the community (as the current SOO). In line with existing SOOs and ROs, the order has effect for a fixed period of not less than five years and may prohibit the offender from doing anything described in the order. However, the relevant offences for a SOPO include not only sexual offences (contained in schedule 2 to the Bill), but also offences of violence (contained in schedule 3 to the Bill). The order can be made if the court is satisfied that it is necessary for the purpose of protecting the public in the UK or any particular members of the public from serious sexual harm from the offender. This is defined to mean serious physical or psychological harm, caused by the offender committing one or more relevant *sexual* offence. Thus violent offenders may be made subject to the order if there is evidence that they pose a risk of committing sexual offences causing serious physical or psychological harm in the future – the risk of such harm from further violent offences will not suffice.

Electronic monitoring – tracking by satellite?

Advances in technology have already been used to facilitate the monitoring of offenders in the community by electronic 'tagging' and it seems likely that more use will be made of this facility in the future. Indeed, calls have been made to follow the example of Florida in the USA, in which satellite surveillance technology is used to keep track of sex offenders at all times (*Daily Telegraph*, 19 September 2002). Although useful in enforcing geographical limits imposed by curfew orders and ROs or SOOs, it can be no substitute for close personal supervision, as such a system can inform the authorities only of the physical where-abouts of an offender: it cannot keep track on who the offender is with at any particular time.

Resources – who pays?

There can no doubt that the workload of many agencies involved in managing sex offenders in the community, particularly the police and the probation services, has increased dramatically in recent years. This has been brought about partly by the implementation of new responsi-bilities, such as maintaining the sex offender 'register' and the operation of MAPPPs, and partly by increased awareness of the extent of sexual offending. Without the provision of adequate resources, there is a danger that, no matter how effective the legislative framework is in theory, in practice the agencies concerned will simply be overwhelmed. One need look no further than the inability of the Criminal Records Bureau to cope with the demand for the vetting of new teachers and others working with children in the summer of 2002 to realise the implications of poor planning and inadequate resources.

There is some evidence that the government is trying to ease the pressure on individual agencies by 'spreading the load'. It has announced its intention to draw a wider range of agencies into MAPPPs, including the prison service, electronic monitoring providers, social services, housing and Jobcentre Plus (Home Office 2002a). Many of these agencies already have a significant input into the work of the panels, but, of course, widening the statutory duty to co-operate will also spread the financial burden – an aim which is implicit in the recent White Paper.

However, individual agencies will inevitably continue to find their resources stretched to the limit. In particular, advances in technology and the creation of the World Wide Web have led to a massive increase in the number of individuals viewing and exchanging child pornography on the Internet. Investigating such crimes requires a significant level of expertise which only a limited number of police officers possess. The extent of the problem, and the impact on police resources, were illustrated when the FBI reportedly passed to British police the names and addresses of 7,272 Britons who had used their credit cards to access pictures of underage children engaged in sex acts (*Daily Telegraph*, 4 August 2002). Although the number of arrests made is increasing steadily, working through the list will take a considerable amount of time and will inevitably prove to be a drain on resources which are already stretched to the limit (*Guardian*, 12 November 2002).

Ultimately, if the government is committed to providing an effective framework within which to manage sex offenders, it must be prepared to ensure that adequate resources are available.

The crucial hook – the criminal conviction

However effective the legislative framework for managing sex offenders in the community becomes in future, one fundamental issue remains: who can be subject to various control measures within the framework?

The majority of the provisions which make up the legislative framework can be used only to control and manage those convicted of sexual offences. In other words, a criminal conviction is the crucial hook on which most of the measures hang. The conviction may also serve other purposes: the sentence imposed following a conviction may go some way to satisfy the public's demands for retribution or revenge, and it can also provide a route into treatment, an option which sex offenders may be unwilling to pursue of their own volition. In the absence of a conviction, the ability to supervise or monitor an individual's movements in the community is extremely limited. Admittedly, those who have been cautioned for certain sexual offences will be subject to the notification requirements of the Sex Offender Act 1997 and may be made the subject of a SOO, and small number of offenders may be detained under the mental health legislation (see further Soothill et al. 1997). It is also now possible that mere suspicions about an individual can be disclosed if the individual seeks appointment to a sensitive position, such as one working with children. Enhanced criminal record certificates, which were introduced by the Police Act 1997, may include information which the chief officer of a police force considers relevant. There is no statutory restriction on the nature of the information provided; thus it could include details of suspicions and inconclusive police investigations. However, a criminal conviction is at the centre of society's response to the majority of sex offenders and is likely to remain so. The effective management of sex offenders within the current legislative framework therefore requires as many prosecutions and convictions for sexual offences as possible. This can be achieved in the first instance by encouraging the reporting of sexual offences, refining investigative techniques and making full use of the advent of DNA profiling, including the establishment of a national DNA database. Once a case reaches trial, the reforms made to trial procedure by the Youth Justice and Criminal Evidence Act 1999 will go a considerable way towards redressing the balance at a criminal trial in favour of the victim and thus improve the prospect of a conviction. But the one issue that is currently under consideration is the substantive criminal law relating to sexual offences.

'Setting the boundaries' – reform of the substantive criminal law

In spite of the increasing concern over sex offenders at the end of the last century, and despite the significance attached to a criminal conviction, until 1998 reform of the substantive law on sexual offences had received very little attention, either from law reform bodies or from Parliament itself. The majority of sexual offences are currently contained in the Sexual Offences Act 1956, which was a consolidating measure passed under the fast-track provisions of the Consolidation of Enactments (Procedure) Act 1949 and which was debated in Parliament for only three minutes (Bowley 1998). A small number of new offences have been created periodically over the years as lacunae in the law became apparent, and certain offences have been redefined to meet changing social conditions and advances in technology. More recently, the Sexual Offences (Amendment) Act of 2000 created a new offence of abuse of position of trust, which is committed by a person aged 18 or over who has sexual intercourse with or engages in any other sexual activity with a person under that age when they are in a position of trust in relation to the younger person.

As a result, the substantive criminal law in this area is a haphazard patchwork of provisions, many of which date back to the 19th century. In June 1998 the government announced its intention to reform the law relating to sexual offences. Following a review, the Home Office issued a Consultation Paper in July 2000 (Home Office 2000), and the government published a White Paper on sexual offences in November 2002 (Home Office 2002b). The reform proposals are now contained in the Sexual Offences Bill. The majority of offences in the Bill do not criminalise behaviour which has not hitherto been subject to the criminal law, but rather redefine existing criminal behaviour in a more consistent and coherent way. For example, the Bill contains a new offence of adult sexual abuse of a child which would cover all sexual behaviour that was wrong because it involved a child, and would complement other serious non-consensual offences (clause 9) and a new offence of sexual activity between minors (clause 14). These offences will replace existing offences which prohibit sexual activity with children, such as unlawful sexual intercourse and indecency with children. They are to be supplemented by a number of new offences, such as causing a child to engage in sexual activity (clause 10), engaging in sexual activity in the presence of a child (clause 12) and causing a child to watch a sexual act (clause 13). Overall, the provisions of Part 1 of the Bill will ensure that all inappropriate sexual activity with children falls within the remit of the criminal law – something which is not always entirely clear under the existing law. However, there is one area in which the provisions of the Bill expressly criminalise behaviour not hitherto subject to the criminal law.

Extending the criminal law – the criminalisation of 'grooming'

The Sexual Offences Bill seeks to address, for the first time, the problem of potential offenders who spend a considerable amount of time and effort 'grooming' potential victims. The concept of 'grooming' involves a potential offender making contact with potential victims (who will usually be children), either directly or through internet chatrooms, with a view to building a relationship of trust which can subsequently be exploited by engaging in sexual activity with the victim – in effect 'softening up' the victim. Although those who work with sex offenders are familiar with this type of behaviour, it is a concept which has only recently caught the attention of the public. Under the present law, whereas the actual exploitation of a position of trust will amount to a criminal offence (whether under the offence of abuse of a position of trust or by the law regulating sexual activity with minors), behaviour prior to the actual abuse will not generally be caught by criminal law. If an individual's behaviour is causing concern, the police could apply for a SOO, which would prohibit the individual behaving in a specified way with the threat of criminal sanctions if he persists. However, a previous caution or conviction for an offence listed in schedule 1 to the Sex Offenders Act 1997 is an essential prerequisite for a SOO; thus the order cannot be used to regulate the behaviour of those who have not previously been cautioned or convicted. The law of attempt will be of very limited use. Under the Criminal Attempts Act 1981, liability for attempting to commit an indictable offence is dependent upon doing acts which are 'more than merely preparatory' to the commission of the offence, which means that, in practice, the criminal justice system cannot intervene until the actual physical exploitation takes place. This had led to calls for reform which would allow intervention some considerable time *before* the physical exploitation takes place – i.e. which would criminalise the preparatory acts involved in grooming.

Grooming – the issues considered

Drafting an offence of grooming is fraught with difficulty. Although it needs to be a substantive offence in itself, as opposed to being an inchoate offence such as attempt, it will be essentially anticipatory in nature. There must be some identifiable actions by the offender which would trigger the liability, but those actions must be undertaken with a view to preparing the victim for sexual activity, whatever form that may take. Hence the *mens rea* will be a central element and the offence will be one of specific or 'further' intent – i.e. it will be incumbent on the prosecution to prove beyond all reasonable doubt that the offender was acting with the intention of initiating or facilitating sexual activity with the victim.

The definition of the behaviour involved, the offender and the victim must all be considered. Grooming may cover a wide range of conduct, the essential element being the ultimate purpose of the person engaged in the behaviour. The offence will therefore need to be drafted to reflect this and not define the behaviour so as to restrict unduly the potential range of conduct. The offence will be enacted primarily to protect minors, although other vulnerable people, such as those with a mental disability or disorder who do not have the capacity to consent to sexual activity, may also be potential victims of grooming and so arguably should be afforded the same protection. As far as the offender is concerned, on the one hand it is acknowledged that there are young people who abuse and exploit other children and who may well be engaged in grooming their victims. On the other hand, if the offence is drafted to include young persons it could become unacceptably wide and include behaviour such as a 15-year-old boy 'chatting up' a girl of the same age in the hope of encouraging her to engage in sexual activity. Therefore, in line with the offence of adult abuse of a child outlined in the consultation paper (Home Office 2000) and now contained in the Sexual Offences Bill, the offence should be restricted to those over the age of 18 who engage in grooming those under the age of 16, with further consideration perhaps being given to extending the offence to protect those over 16 who do not have the capacity to consent to sexual activity.

Grooming – taking a bold approach

Taking the above factors into consideration, a bold approach to grooming would allow intervention as soon as it became clear that the offender was acting with the necessary intention, and an offence of grooming could be drafted along the following lines:[1]

It shall be an offence for any person over the age of 18 to behave in a manner calculated to create or develop a friendship with a minor under the age of 16, or to initiate or further a relationship of trust or dependency with a minor, and to do so with the intention of rendering the minor more susceptible to being procured to engage in any activity of a sexual nature which, if carried out, would constitute a criminal offence.

Such an offence would encompass a wide range of behaviour, the crucial factor being the offender's intention in so acting. Although at first sight proving such an intent may appear to be an insurmountable hurdle, given the fact that the grooming process often involves a course of conduct over a considerable period of time, the hurdle may not be as difficult as it seems. For example, a series of increasingly explicit emails, perhaps including deliberate misrepresentations of the offender's age, combined with the suggestions of sexual activity taking place between the offender and victim, would arguably be sufficient to prove the further intent required. A statutory exception could be enacted to ensure that those delivering recognised sex education programmes or giving contraceptive advice to minors are not brought within the remit of the offence.

Grooming – a more cautious approach

The government has acknowledged the need to criminalise the behaviour involved in grooming potential victims for abuse, and has now included provisions in the Sexual Offences Bill to address the problem. However, it is evident that a rather more cautious approach than that suggested above is to be adopted. The Bill introduces a new offence of meeting a child following sexual grooming (clause 17). The offence will be committed by a person aged 18 or over (*A*) who intentionally meets, or travels with the intention of meeting, another person who is under the age of 16 (*B*), having met or communicated with *B* on at least two earlier occasions. *A* must intend to do anything to or in respect of *B*, during or after the meeting and in any part of the world, which if done will involve the commission by *A* of a relevant offence. Therefore liability will arise only when *A* actually meets *B*, or is travelling with the intention of meeting *B*, and so the potential offender who grooms a child over the internet will not commit the offence until he makes a physical move towards meeting the child. The offender must intend to commit a sexual offence involving the child, although he does not have to intend the offence to take place at the meeting – i.e. he commits the offence if he meets the child, intending to use the meeting for further grooming, with a view to committing a sexual offence in relation to the child at a subsequent meeting. For the purpose of grooming, a sexual offence is defined to include an offence under Part 1 of the Bill and will thus include offences such as causing or inciting a child to engage in sexual activity (clauses 10 and 11), so that the offender who grooms a child to prepare them for sexual activity with a third person will be liable.

The Bill makes specific provision for mistaken belief as to the age of the victim. This is an issue which has been controversial in recent years. Traditionally, it was thought that where the aim of a sexual offence was to protect a minor, liability in respect of the victim's age was strict – i.e. the offender would be liable even if he honestly and reasonably believed that the victim was over the relevant age (R v Prince (1875) LR 2 CCR 154). However, in R v K ([2001] 3 All ER 897) and B v DPP ([2001] 1 All ER 833) the House of Lords decided that, in relation to indecent assault and indecency with children, a belief that the victim was over the relevant age would entitle the offender to an acquittal. Furthermore, it was decided in both cases that the belief did not have to be based on reasonable grounds, it would be sufficient if it was honestly held. The Sexual Offences Bill takes a rather different approach. An honest belief in the victim's age will not suffice. If an offence in Part 1 of the Bill protects a victim under the age of 13 years, no specific mention is made of a mistaken belief as to the victim's age, and liability as to age will presumably be strict. Where the victim is between 13 and 16, the prosecution must prove that the offender did not reasonably believe that the victim was 16 or over. For example, clause 12 of the Bill creates an offence of engaging in sexual activity in the presence of a child. One of the essential elements of the offence is *either* that the child is under 13, *or* that the child is under 16 and the offender does not reasonably believe that the child is 16 or over. Interestingly, the offence of grooming in clause 17 makes no such distinction: the prosecution must prove that the offender did not reasonably believe that the child was 16 or over, regardless of the child's actual age. Hence children under 13 are not afforded the added protection in relation to grooming that they are given elsewhere in the Bill.

Grooming and preventative measures – Risk of Sexual Harm Orders

Although clause 17 of the Sexual Offences Bill does not criminalise behaviour prior to an actual meeting, clause 110 of the Bill provides for a new civil preventative order, the Risk of Sexual Harm Order (RSHO), which is clearly intended to address grooming behaviour prior to a meeting with the victim. The police will have the power to apply to the magistrates' court for an RSHO in respect of an adult aged 18 or over who has on at least two occasions engaged in sexually explicit conduct or communication (which may, but need not, amount to a criminal offence) with a child or children under 16 and there is reasonable cause to believe that the order is necessary to protect a child or children from harm from the adult. The order can impose prohibitions on the adult necessary to protect children generally or any child from harm from the adult. Breach of the order constitutes a criminal offence with a maximum penalty of five years' imprisonment. In many respects the proposed RSHO is an order similar to existing SOOs and ROs and to the proposed SOPOs. However, there are significant differences. Whereas SOOs and ROs require a risk of 'serious harm', and the proposed SOPOs require a risk of 'serious sexual harm', the proposed RSHO requires only a risk of 'harm'. Furthermore, unlike the existing SOOs, ROs and proposed SOPOs, there is no requirement that the adult have a previous conviction of any kind. The RSHO will admittedly be useful where the conduct of an adult is such that he is thought to present a risk to children in general. However, where an adult is grooming a particular child, given the fact that the police must presumably prove the risk of harm beyond all reasonable doubt before an order can be made (R (on the application of McCann) v Manchester Crown Court [2002] 4 All ER 593), the suggested bold approach to grooming would arguably be preferable, as it would obviate the need for further action for breach of the civil order.

Conclusion

The legislative framework has been developed and considerably expanded in recent years, and those charged with the responsibility of managing sex offenders in the community now have a comprehensive range of measures at their disposal. Further expansion of the framework is currently contained in the Sexual Offences Bill, and it seems clear that increasing reliance will be placed on the use of civil preventative orders, breach of which constitutes a criminal offence. Work will also continue in other key areas, such as assessment of the risk posed by individual offenders. Public protection has been the central focus of these developments. Despite this, spurred on by media reporting of cases of sexual offending, particularly against children, public hysteria over sex offenders continues unabated and, each time a case is reported, politicians proclaim, 'it must never happen again'. However, as one senior police officer explained, 'No system is 100 per cent effective. It doesn't matter how much legislation you put in place, you can never stop every sex offender. You can monitor him and you can reduce the risk, but you have to be realistic' (Grange 2001). The risk posed by known sex offenders can be diminished by effective management within the legislative framework, but an unknown number of sex offenders are currently beyond the reach of the legislative provisions because they have not been convicted of a sexual offence. Identifying these offenders and bringing them within the framework must now be a priority.

Note

1   My thanks to my colleague, Robert Lynn, for his helpful suggestions on the drafting of the offence.

References

Bowley, M. (1998) 'A Sexual Scandal', *The Times* 23 June 1998.

Cobley, C. (2000) *Sex Offenders: law, policy and practice*. Bristol: Jordans.

Hall, S. (2001) 'Argument rages over Sarah's Law', *The Guardian* 13 December 2001.

Home Office (1996) *Sentencing and Supervision of Sex Offenders: a consultation document*. London: HMSO.

Home Office (1998) *Exercising Constant Vigilance: the role of the Probation Service in protecting the public from sex offenders*. London: Home Office.

Home Office (1999a) *Report of the Interdepartmental Working Group on Preventing Unsuitable Persons from Working with Children and Abuse of Trust*. London: Home Office.

Home Office (1999b) *Report of the Interdepartmental Working Group on Preventing Unsuitable Persons from Working with Children and Abuse of Trust: update*. London: Home Office.

Home Office (2000) *Setting the Boundaries: reforming the law on sex offences*. London: Home Office.

Home Office (2001a) *Cautions, Court Proceedings and Sentencing, England and Wales 2000*. London: Home Office.

Home Office (2001b) *Making Punishments Work: report of a review of the sentencing framework for England and Wales*. London: Home Office.

Home Office (2002a) *Justice for All*, Cm 5563. London: HMSO.

Home Office (2002b) *Protecting the Public*, Cm 5668. London: HMSO.

Jones, G. (2002) 'Ministers to tighten laws protecting children', *Daily Telegraph*, 22 August 2002.

Kemshall, H. (2001) 'Risk Assessment and Management of Known Sexual and Violent Offenders: a review of current issues', Police Research Series Paper 140. London: Home Office.

Knock, K., Schlesinger, P., Boyle, R. and Magor, M. (2002) 'The Police Perspective on Sex Offender Orders: a preliminary review of policy and practice', Police Research Series Paper 155. London: Home Office.

Maguire, M., Kemshall, H., Noakes, L., Wincup, E. and Sharpe, K. (2001) 'Risk Management of Sexual and Violent Offenders: the work of public protection panels', Police Research Series Paper 13. London: Home Office.

Plotnikoff, J. and Woolfson, R. (2000) 'Where are they now? An evaluation of sex offender registration in England and Wales', Police Research Series Paper 126. London: Home Office.

Sampson, A. (1994) *Acts of Abuse: sex offenders and the criminal justice system*. London: Routledge.

Soothill, K. and Walby, S. (1991) *Sex Crimes in the News*. London: Routledge.

Soothill, K., Francis, B. and Sanderson, B. (1997) 'A Cautionary Tale: the Sex Offenders Act 1997, the police and cautions', *Criminal Law Review* 1997, pp. 482–90.

Utting, Sir W. (1997) *Report of the Review of Safeguards for Children Living Away from Home*. London: HMSO.

Chapter 4

Disclosing information on sex offenders: the human rights implications

Helen Power

Introduction

The criminal justice system is in the grip of a 'public protection' agenda, at the heart of which is multi-agency co-operation. Such co-operation is most obviously manifested in the development of Multi-Agency Public Protection Arrangements (MAPPAs) for the risk assessment and management of dangerous and sex offenders in the community via Multi-Agency Public Protection Panels (MAPPPs), on which sit representatives of the police, probation and prison services (as well as those from social services and healthcare agencies).[1] The growth of multi-agency co-operation is said to provide evidence of a shift away from post-war 'penal welfarism' toward a new 'risk penology'. The thesis, as summarised by Kemshall and Maguire, is that the movement towards risk penology is

> fuelled by the insecurity inherent in the globalisation of national economies and the fragmentation of social relations, and driven inexorably by the 'logic of risk'... – a world in which an all-consuming desire to eliminate threats to safety produces ever more sophisticated technologies of information-gathering, classification, surveillance, control and exclusion; in which attention shifts from the individual to the aggregate 'risk group'; and in which concepts such as individual justice, rights and accountability lose their meaning.
> (Kemshall and Maguire 2002: 170)[2]

Penal welfarism emphasised reform and rehabilitation managed exclusively by groups of professionals, each with its own expertise, culture and ethic. The new risk penology emphasises punishment and control, still largely managed by professionals but increasingly subject to informal, critical popular scrutiny.

The collective professional goal has thus become *public protection*, and the means of achieving it *risk assessment* and *risk management*. If risk is to be calculated and managed effectively, inter-agency information exchange becomes not merely desirable from the perspective of those within the system, but a necessity – 'actuarial justice' would seem to require it. The problem facing the managers, however, is how to convince an increasingly sceptical public that its protection is best left in their hands and that more widespread disclosure is undesirable.

There is an obvious tension between, on the one hand, the professional preference for information exchange to be confined to the agencies themselves – disclosure beyond the charmed circle of the agencies being very much a matter of exception and only when it will enhance offender management (disclosure conceived merely as a management tool) – and, on the other, the public's demand to be kept informed (disclosure conceived as an aspect of the 'right to know'). Certainly it is becoming increasingly difficult for the government and the agencies concerned to withstand the pressure for greater disclosure. The overwhelming public response to the campaign for 'Sarah's Law', mounted by the parents of Sarah Payne (the child victim of a sexual killing in the summer of 2000) and vigorously supported by the tabloids' 'naming and shaming' campaign aimed at forcing the government to create a public right of access to information about particular sex offenders' identities and whereabouts (*News of the World* 2000), led to the Home Office agreeing to consider ways of involving the public. It has so far resisted the central demand of the campaign for full-blown 'community notification' ('Megan's Law') along the lines adopted in some states of the USA (Matson 2001, Adams 2002),[3] whereby the names, photographs, addresses, offences and offending patterns of sex offenders released into the community are made known publicly by a variety of means, ostensibly to enchance public protection. These means include, among others, the posting of details on the internet – an increasingly common method currently employed by a majority of states[4] – the distribution of flyers and posters in and around the areas where a sex offender lives and even, in Louisiana, the placing of ads by the offender in local newspapers and mailing the notification to neighbours: for details see Adams 2002, Matson 2001, Matson and Lieb 1997.[5] The Home Office pilot study currently involving six police and probation areas, in which two members of the public are invited to apply to sit on each of the strategic management committees overseeing the work of the MAPPPs in those areas, is clearly a 'nod' towards greater public involvement. But such limited measures are unlikely to hold back the tide for long, particularly if it becomes apparent that the rationale underlying the pilot study is a bid to 'capture' public support for the notion that public protection and the management of sex offenders are better left to the professionals.[6]

The public demand for American-style community notification is not confined to the UK. In Australia and New Zealand, for instance, the publication in book form in both countries of an index of sex offenders, compiled by a journalist from media sources and court records, has provoked intense discussion (Lemin 1998; Ronken and Lincoln 2001). This would seem to suggest that the British public's demand for information in this context is not a passing phenomenon, provoked by an ephemeral moral panic which will conveniently go away; rather, like official responses to sex offending and dangerous offending, it too can be understood as a manifestation of the 'risk society' (Beck 1992, 1999; Giddens 1990). In the risk society, individuals and communities, perceiving the world to be an increasingly dangerous, insecure and risky place to live, become preoccupied with seeking ways to control risk in order to minimise their sense of insecurity. As they feel increasingly disempowered by a lack of meaningful, usable knowledge about the world around them, their desire, and thus the demand, for more knowledge becomes insistent and thus irresistible.

From the utilitarian perspective of the managers of sex offenders, such demands may be perceived as disruptive, as may the rights-based discourse within which they may be couched: they are a potential obstacle to the smooth integration and co-operation of the agencies involved in seeking to achieve public protection. A little knowledge is indeed a dangerous thing in this context, where the threat of offenders 'going underground', and thus potentially causing harm to others, in response to vigilantism and increasingly strident calls for their 'naming and shaming', is very real. It may, therefore, be tempting for managers to regard the commitment to rights represented by enactment of the Human Rights Act 1998 (HRA), which gave domestic effect to the majority of the rights contained in the European Convention on Human Rights (ECHR), as something which can only interfere with actuarial justice – rights are frankly inconvenient (indeed, '[a] relative lack of priority and importance attached to the rights of individuals' has been identified as one of the key indicators of the late, or post, modern approach to crime control: Kemshall and Maguire 2002: 178).[7] Hitherto the British judiciary has been able to engage in a relatively crude, simplistic 'balancing' of competing public interests and its inclination has been to privilege the professional discourse and its preference for a strictly 'need to know' basis for public disclosure. The HRA, of course, demands the legal privileging of those interests treated as rights by the

HRA and thus given special protection. Certainly the adoption of a rights-based approach is likely to be a complicating factor in judicial decision-making concerning disclosure of information: the judiciary cannot unproblematically be harnessed to the shared goal of the system and has to be seen to be taking the human rights agenda seriously. The judiciary's difficulty, of course, is that the rights which compete for judicial attention in this context may be claimed by all comers. Offenders' rights to life (Article 2 ECHR),[8] freedom from torture and inhuman and degrading treatment (Art 3) and respect for privacy (Art 8)[9] are potentially crucially at stake in agencies' decisions to disclose sensitive personal information about them. However, '[t]he apparently value-neutral construction of public protection and the common sense acceptability of preventing dangerous offenders from harming others masks serious implications for individual rights. The process is self-justificatory and difficult to challenge without appearing to "side with" a highly unpopular group of people' (Kemshall and Maguire 2002: 196). Consequently, '[i]f someone, or some category of persons, is categorised as a risk to public safety, there seems to remain scarcely any sense that they are nonetheless owed justice' (Hudson 2002: 100). Potential victims' rights to life, to freedom from torture, to respect for privacy and family life, and to liberty and security of the person may give the judiciary powerful reasons to strike down decisions *not* to disclose sensitive details about sex offenders living nearby, as does, perhaps most problematically of all, the public's asserted 'right to know' (not expressly protected under the ECHR but to some degree parasitic on other Convention rights). As a result, Kemshall and Maguire suggest (drawing on Scott and Ward 1999), 'the [ECHR], rather than providing a brake on any internal excesses [of panels], may inadvertently fuel the current predisposition to public protection at the expense of the individual rights of potential offenders' (2002: 196). Indeed, it may – but the future is not wholly predictable.

It has been suggested (Nash 1999) that it is political suicide for the police and the probation services not to subscribe to the public protection agenda (and indeed it would now be legal suicide, given that the pursuit of public protection is a matter of legal duty).[10] However, this is unlikely to be the case for the judiciary because of the potency of the ideology of judicial independence and the rule of law. How far the judiciary's current privileging of the professional discourse will withstand possible legal challenges to the decision-making processes of the agencies and MAPPPs mounted by offenders on the one hand, and, on the other, by victims and pressure groups representing public constituencies increasingly focused on sex offenders, it is difficult to know. Recent legal developments, both at home and in the European Court of Human

Rights, present a complicated picture. It is with that picture that the rest of this chapter is concerned.

Current law governing public authorities' powers to disclose

The relevant law is scattered across a range of statutes and the common law, and is thus not as clear as it might be. Given the sheer volume of legislation enacted in the years since 1996 relating to the management of sex offenders,[11] one might have expected that at some stage in this period parliament would have taken the many opportunities it obviously had to deal with the vexed question of disclosure of information relating to sex offenders. Indeed, an amendment to the Sex Offenders Act 1997 during its Parliamentary passage was urged on the government of the day by the then-opposition Home Office Minister Alun Michael, who thought the omission to deal with the issue created a 'black hole' in the legislation; in the event the amendment failed – the black hole remains (Power 1999). Instead, the position is largely determined by common law, a scattering of statutory provisions (principally in relation to child care proceedings under the Children Act 1989) and administrative guidelines (principally Home Office 1997). The bulk of the relevant case law is dominated by cases generated in care proceedings, an inevitable consequence of the fact that, because child care proceedings are perforce particularly sensitive, statutory provisions ensure that social workers' decisions to disclose are subject to judicial leave. Decisions by other agencies engaged in multi-agency working reach the courts only when challenges are mounted to them (this issue will be returned to in the concluding section).

Information exchange between public authorities

Where information exchange *between* public agencies involved in public protection work (including, of course, child protection) is concerned, the law is *generally* permissive. Taken together, s. 29 Data Protection Act 1998 (DPA) and s. 115 Crime and Disorder Act 1998 (CDA) largely insulate public authorities from legal liability for the exchange of sensitive information *amongst themselves*; thus, multi-agency information exchange is in most circumstances permissible, given that it is a tool used in the management of offenders in the community and is aimed at the prevention of their re-offending. Section 29 DPA exempts public authorities from the non-disclosure provisions of the Act in relation to 'sensitive personal information' (which would normally be treated as confidential), defined so as to include criminal convictions, where disclosure is necessary for the prevention or detection of crime.[12]

Section 115 CDA positively empowers 'any person [public agency or private person] who, apart from this subsection, would not have power to [do so]' to disclose information to *the police, local authorities, probation committees* and *health authorities* (or to an official working for these bodies) where it is 'necessary or expedient' to do so for any of the purposes of any provision of the Act. Section 2 of that Act creates the Sex Offender Order (SOO), breach of which is a criminal offence attracting up to five years' imprisonment. Thus, anyone – and in most cases this will be a public body or official – could pass on information to the police relating to a known or suspected sex offender if this is deemed necessary or expedient for the purpose of enabling the police to apply for a SOO. Alternatively, the police themselves could seek information from their local authority or any other agency having dealings with sex offenders if they had concerns about an individual (indeed, section 4 of the Home Office's guidance on SOOs advises that the police *should* consult with the social services and youth offending teams for their area if they are contemplating applying for a SOO against a 10- to 18-year-old), and s. 115 would clearly authorise disclosure of the requested information. Evidently, then, s. 115 provides the basis for information exchange in multi-agency settings, at least in relation to possible applications for SOOs. A difficulty with s. 115 is that it is silent as to the *source and type* of information which can be disclosed. At first glance, it might appear to enable disclosure even where this would breach confidentiality – nothing expressly qualifies the power, the nature or the source of the information to be disclosed. However, the Home Office guidance on information exchange issued after enactment of the 1998 Act suggests that the power is to be read subject to the law of confidence and existing statutory provisions (Home Office 1998: paragraphs 5.11, 5.12).

This echoes the advice contained in Home Office Circular 39/97 (concerning police handling of the notification requirements for sex offenders under the Sex Offenders Act 1997), in the Home Office's *Guidance on the Disclosure of Information about Sex Offenders who may present a risk to Children and Vulnerable Adults* (Home Office 1999)[13] and in *Working Together to Safeguard Children* (Department of Health et al. 1999).[14]

As indicated above, the case law is dominated by child-care cases, which is unsurprising given the confidential nature of such proceedings, as enshrined in statutory provisions. Nevertheless, it reveals that, generally, even such seemingly confidential information as is contained in social workers' files may usually be disclosed to other public agencies. If the information is contained in files *not filed* with a family court for care or wardship proceedings, the local authority can generally disclose it to other public agencies involved in Area Child Protection Committees (ACPCs) – indeed, the duty under s. 47, Children Act 1989 to investigate actual or suspected child abuse in effect requires such information-sharing in particular cases. As Lord Justice Butler-Sloss put it in *Re G (A Minor) (Social Worker: disclosure)* [1996] 2 All ER 65 (CA), the information obtained by social workers in the course of their duties 'cannot "be freely and widely publicised outside the proceedings [of a child protection conference]" . . . It can, however, be disclosed to fellow members of the child protection team engaged in the investigation of the possible abuse of the child concerned.' She goes on to say:

> I can see no bar to the exchange of information at any stage . . . between those engaged in the investigation of, protection from and prevention of child abuse. The exchange of information would cover those working together in inter-agency co-operation, in particular the police and social worker, including the paediatrician or other mental health involvement where appropriate and would extend to reporting to the much larger group comprising the child protection case conference.[15]

Matters are slightly more complicated when information is held by a local authority in documents *filed* with a family court. Disclosure here is governed by s. 12 of the Administration of Justice Act 1960 as amended, which provides that, while publication of information relating to proceedings in private is not of itself a contempt of court, it will be a contempt where the proceedings are, *inter alia*, brought under the Children Act 1989, unless the judge has permitted publication. Except where disclosure is to be to any of a list of persons – in which case, disclosure of court documents is automatic – the family court judge has discretion to order disclosure under rule 4.23 of the Family Proceedings Rules, 1991 on application to the court.[16] This rule is said to derive from 'a fundamental rule in legal proceedings involving children – particularly children involved in care proceedings – that documents produced to the court in the proceedings might not be disclosed to those not parties to the case' (Bedingfield 1998: 327).

It has, however, been suggested of the case law on the courts' use of their discretion under r. 4.23 that it has 'taken the whole question of confidentiality in child protection and wider proceedings under the Children Act . . . to new extremes.' (Bedingfield 1998: 534).[17] The procedural safeguards normally available to those in litigation may be dispensed with. In *Re C* [1998] 2 WLR 322 801, the Court of Appeal was for the first time faced with the question of whether the discretion to disclose extended to self-incriminating statements made by a party to family proceedings *in the course of those proceedings*. Section 98(2) of the Children Act 1989 clearly renders inadmissible in criminal proceedings self-incriminating statements made in care proceedings. Nevertheless, the Court of Appeal ruled that the family court[18] was wrong to refuse to permit the local authority to write to the police informing them of an incriminating statement made by the father of a child whose death the police had been investigating: while the *prosecution*, in any subsequent criminal proceedings against the father, would not be able to use his care proceedings statement, the *police* could use it for investigatory purposes.

It is clear that *Re C* comes very close to undermining the purpose of s. 98(2), which is to encourage candour on the part of all concerned in care proceedings. It is in danger of becoming an empty gesture and, with it, the wider principle of confidentiality which clearly under-pins the provision.

There are signs that this may be how local authorities are reading the case law, though the Court of Appeal has recently given them the red light in its decision in the consolidated appeal *Re V (Minors) (Sexual abuse: disclosure) and Re L (Sexual abuse: disclosure)* (1999) 1 FLR 267 (*Re V* is discussed below), where it was emphatically stated that local authorities do not have a discretion to disclose to other public agencies 'just in case'. In 1996, L was acquitted of the attempted rape of his step-daughter and of indecent assault on his other five children. However, two years later in care proceedings relating to one of his children, L was found to have sexually abused three of the children and to pose a significant risk to them. During the hearing, L was permitted to write down his new address for the judge. At the end of the proceedings, the local authority asked the judge to disclose L's address to them so that they could alert the local authority into whose area he had moved. Having found that L posed a considerable threat to the children of single women with whom he might cohabit, but not to children generally, the judge ordered that L's address and the findings of sexual abuse be disclosed by the applicant local authority to L's new local authority. L's appeal against the order succeeded. The Court of Appeal concluded that the public interest in the administration of justice and in the prosecution of crime did not arise to be weighed against the confidentiality of the information revealed in the course of the care proceedings: L had never been cautioned, convicted nor sentenced for any sex crime against children; there was no pending police investigation of him, nor would there be any continuing social services involvement with him, given that he was living away from the three children he had been found to have abused; and there was no perceived specific risk of his offending against other children. Consequently, if the usual presumption of confidentiality in care proceedings were to be displaced, it had to be on other grounds – and the Court of Appeal found none of those advanced by the local authorities persuasive. The local authority argued that sections 17 and 47[19] of the Children Act required them to disclose relevant information about sex abusers to other local authorities. Certainly there would be occasions where this was necessary (Lord Justice Butler-Sloss instanced children at risk moving from one area to another): in an echo of her earlier statement in *Re G* (above), Butler-Sloss stated, 'Nothing in the judgement [is] intended to inhibit the necessary exchange of relevant information between agencies'. However, the Children Act did not create any such general duty and nor could one be crafted by analogy with 'existing legislation':

> it [is] important to recognise that Parliament [has] not thought it appropriate to include such cases within the statutory and regulatory framework specifically designed for the protection of children where the man [has] neither been cautioned [for] nor convicted of any sexual abuse, and in fact where he [has] been acquitted of offences against the very children with which the family court was directly concerned. That omission [can] not be regarded as inadvertent. It reflect[s] a conscious decision that disclosure of information should be regarded as exceptional in such cases.

R v Local Authority and Police Authority in the Midlands, ex p LM [2000] 1 FLR 6122 is to similar effect. Here, a local authority and a police authority, following a multi-agency case conference, decided to disclose allegations of sexual abuse against LM to the county council to whom he had applied for a youth service teaching post and to provide school bus services. His application for judicial review of this decision succeeded: the allegations, unproven and in relation to which no proceedings were taken, were made ten years previously and in the subsequent ten-year period, during which he had been employed on school buses and in teaching youths, no further allegations had been made. The Court stressed that in these circumstances there was no pressing need to disclose and nor had the authorities considered this issue; that the rule in *ex p Thorpe* (discussed below) was not to be applied, as here, as if it sanctioned a blanket policy of disclosure; and, absent a pressing need, LM's right to privacy in relation to public authorities (Art 8, ECHR) in effect prevailed.

The generally supportive approach of the courts is, then, apparent in these cases, but so too is their desire to ensure that public agencies do not become over-zealous in their desire to share information amongst themselves 'just in case'. This position is echoed in the European Court of Human Rights' decision in *MS v Sweden* (1999) 28 EHRR 313. There, the disclosure by a hospital of MS' medical records to the Swedish state Social Insurance Office (to whom MS had applied for compensation under industrial injury legislation) was held to amount to a *prima facie* breach of her right to respect for privacy (Art 8(1)). The state was able to justify the breach by reference to Art 8(2), which basically permits interference with the right if such interference is necessary in a democratic society for the achievement of specified aims, including that relevant here – Sweden's 'economic well-being' (seeking to ensure that public funds are allocated only to deserving applicants). Nevertheless, the Court was careful to point out that had MS' records contained information irrelevant to the Social Insurance Office's determination of her claim, the disclosure by the hospital would not have been justified.[20] Clearly, then, while there is nothing in European Court jurisprudence to suggest that domestic courts – which under the HRA must have regard to that jurisprudence when determining cases involving public authorities' acts and omissions – will significantly depart from their current approach to inter-agency information exchange, they will need to pay close attention to the nature of the information to be disclosed in particular instances.

Disclosure of information by public authorities to private persons

Disclosure to private persons is governed wholly by common law, though the common law position now has to be read subject to the HRA: in arriving at their decisions on disclosure, public authorities must not act in breach of concerned parties' Convention rights.[21] At common law, the general rule is that sensitive information is not to be disclosed, unless exceptional, compelling circumstances make it necessary to do so in furtherance of some identifiable public interest – and this seems to be the rule whether or not the information is confidential as such. Those cases which have reached the courts have *generally* resulted in disclosure being permitted, albeit as a matter of exception, and to specified disclosees with a specific 'need to know'.

There appear to be only five such cases reported of direct relevance to the disclosure of information relating to sex offenders (or those found guilty of sexual abuse in care proceedings) to *private* parties, all decided within the last decade: *R v Devon CC, ex p L* [1991] 2 FLR 541; *Re V (Sexual abuse: disclosure)* (1999) 1 FLR 267; *P v West Sussex CC* [2002] EWHC 1143; *Re C* (2002) (Unreported: 15 Feb) and, finally, *R v Chief Constable of North Wales, ex p Thorpe & another* [1998] 3 All ER 310 (CA) (also reported as *ex p AB and CD*). Once again, cases involving children dominate, although not all are related to care proceedings as such. What is interesting, however, is that despite the vigilance with which the absolute integrity of child care cases is ostensibly maintained, in fact the applicable principles in such cases are becoming aligned with the principles applicable to police decisions to disclose in cases not directly concerning children.

In *ex p L* (1991), L was suspected by Devon County Council of having sexually abused C, the four-year-old daughter of his then partner, Mrs B, with whom he was living. Following examination by a paediatrician engaged by the council, C's name was placed on the child abuse register and a social worker was assigned to her. Thereafter, L lived in succession with three other women, all of whom had young children. On each occasion, social workers for the council told the woman concerned of the council's suspicions about L and told two of the women that their own children might be placed on the register and care proceedings instituted if L continued to live in the house. At no time was L charged with a crime, although he was arrested and interviewed by the police about the alleged abuse of C and was formally cautioned for an offence of indecent assault (however, the court accepted that there was uncertainty about whether the caution was legitimate in view of doubts about the genuineness of L's admission of the crime, crucial to a formal caution). L's solicitor wrote to the council, asking for an assurance that they would instruct their staff to stop disseminating their suspicions of L to others. L then applied for a judicial review of the council's refusal to give the assurance sought, said to be implicit in their letter of reply. The application was turned down primarily on the ground that the council's letter of reply was not a 'decision' and thus not capable of being reviewed at all; however, even if it was a reviewable decision, it was not unlawful as the social workers' actions were neither unfair nor in bad faith: '[S]ocial workers in the discharge of the local authority's statutory obligation to protect the welfare of children, in this case were under a duty to inform the ... mothers ... that they believed the applicant was an abuser, if they honestly believed on reasonable grounds that he was an abuser.' Disclosure here was lawful because it was limited to identified individuals for the protection of their children, reasonably felt to be at specific risk from L. Without a doubt, a similar conclusion would now be reached, L's right to respect for his privacy under Art 8(1) notwithstanding: a specific risk to specific children would provide the basis for a justifiable interference with L's right, being necessary 'for the protection of the rights and freedoms of others' (a legitimate aim specified in Art 8(2)).[22]

In similar vein is *P v West Sussex CC* [2002] EWHC 1143, in which the High Court ruled that a county council could reveal the sexual convictions of P to the daughter of his partner J, to enable the daughter to safeguard *her* children, with whom the county council feared P might have contact. Sullivan, J., stated: 'It would be difficult to conceive of someone who had a more intense interest in obtaining the information in the present case than the mother of the claimant's [J's] grandchildren.' The county council had clearly taken P's right to privacy into account in arriving at its decision and, moreover, had given J the opportunity to tell her daughter herself.

The next case, *Re V (Sexual abuse: disclosure)* (1999) 1 FLR 267, a case in which care proceedings were involved, was heard with *Re L*, discussed above. Here, the parents of four sons separated in 1987 and divorced in 1996; the four sons stayed with the mother. The father became concerned about the behaviour of his ex-wife's partner, W, towards D (at 14 the youngest of the four boys). The local authority instituted care proceedings, at the end of which the judge found relatively minor sexual impropriety in 1989 with an eight-year-old boy and overwhelming evidence of a more recent, and 'unusual and unhealthy' relationship with D. Finding that W posed a risk of significant harm to D and his 15-year-old brother, the judge made a prohibited steps order and ordered that the two youngest boys' names be retained on the child protection register. The local authority asked the judge for permission to write to the local football club for which W acted as coach to the junior teams, to other local clubs and to the league. The judge permitted the authority to write to these bodies notifying them of her decision and, in summary, of W's proven behaviour. W's appeal to the Court of Appeal was allowed. Butler-Sloss stated of the practical effects of disclosure, if it were allowed, that:

> if the dissemination is to be effective and possibly even if it is not effective, the information provided is likely to be oppressive and consequently unjust to Mr. W. These considerations illustrate the problem for the Court when faced with an application to authorise disclosure of information in a case where the risk cannot be related to a particular child or children – because it is not known whether any or which children are actually at risk from time to time.

In other words, perhaps, actuarial justice is legitimate only in so far as it is able to deal with specific risks in specific circumstances – it cannot be used as a blunt instrument.

In *Re C* (2002) 15 Feb, the most recent of the cases discussed here, the High Court ruled that the police and social services were entitled to reveal to a private housing association the findings in child care proceedings that C (a tenant, with his partner, of that association) was a serious danger to children. The purpose of disclosure was not, as in *ex p Thorpe*, to encourage C to move out of the area, but to enable the housing association to make appropriate decisions when housing other tenants in the vicinity. In short, it was not, as counsel for C argued, a 'buck-passing' exercise; rather, said Bodey J., 'it seems to me to be a good example of proposed inter-agency co-operation for the protection of vulnerable children in our complex society.' He went straight to the point in the opening passage of his judgment:

> One of the various difficulties and tensions created by serious paedophilia is the need to strike a balance between (a) taking reasonable steps to try to ensure child protection and (b) ensuring that the private lives of paedophiles and their families are respected, such that they are neither subjected to undue state interference nor hounded by the community.

C had no convictions for sex offences, though he did have two old 'cautions' for indecent assault against children (as well as convictions for non-sexual offences). The findings of serious sexual abuse in the care proceedings (which related to his and his partner's child) were, with the judge's permission, revealed to the police and social services who convened a multi-agency conference to discuss the case; the decision was made at that conference to disclose the findings to the housing association. Bodey J., having assiduously reviewed the relevant case law, weighed up the factors for and against disclosure, as required by that law. Factors telling *against* disclosure included C's and his partner's privacy rights ('the interests of the paedophile and his family; the likely impact which the disclosure might have on them in terms of vigilantism, gossip, employment difficulties and so on') and the impact on the ability of police and social services to manage C ('the risk of driving the paedophile "underground", whereby he may become a greater risk to children; [and] the difficulties in controlling sensitive information once it has been released further than to "the usual" statutory agencies . . .'). In *favour* of disclosure were the judge's findings as to the risk posed by C to children living in close proximity to him – findings made during a detailed, six-day hearing and which, 'therefore, whilst not the equivalent of criminal convictions, do carry all the weight of being [the judge's] considered conclusions in civil proceedings where the facts in issue were manifestly of a very serious nature.' Also supporting disclosure to C's housing association landlord was the fact that it 'must already have [had] some idea about Mr C's perceived proclivities' – there had been a neighbourhood petition sent to the housing association, urging it to evict C. However, Bodey J. was *not* prepared to authorise disclosure to any other housing association and landlord to whom C might apply for accommodation elsewhere in the future, principally because of 'the greater difficulties of controlling the information, if more widely released'. If, however, C and his partner were in fact to move elsewhere, a further application to disclose might have to be made and the court would have to repeat the 'balancing of factors' exercise in the light of the circumstances then prevailing.

Bodey J. was of the opinion that the grounds in Art 8(2) ECHR justifying interference with C's privacy rights 'are the same (or virtually the same) as the considerations which go into the balance [domestically] . . . The requirement of a "pressing need" and of proportionality are clearly integral to, and encompassed within, the principles laid down by the domestic authorities . . .'.

R v Chief Constable of North Wales, ex p Thorpe & another [1998] 3 All ER 310 is the only case involving disclosure outside the confines of child protection arrangements and was clearly decided by the court with a view to its being applicable to *all* public bodies in possession of sensitive information. Here, the disclosure by police of information relating to a married couple which revealed their identities and serious sex offending history to the owner of the caravan site where they were living, was held to be lawful, as it was necessary to protect children and other vulnerable people from the couple.[23] Although the decision predated implementation of the HRA, the Court nevertheless embarked on an analysis of the applicants' Convention right to respect for privacy (Art 8) and found that the disclosure by the police was justifiable within the terms of Art 8(2): it was a necessary step (meaning in Convention jurisprudence that there was a 'pressing social need' for the disclosure) required 'for the prevention of . . . crime' and 'for the protection of the rights and freedoms of others' (aims listed in 8(2)). The police were clearly acting in pursuit of their duty to prevent crime, as they had information from the probation service to the effect that the couple continued to pose a specific and significant risk to children and other vulnerable people (children were expected at the site as the Easter holidays were imminent); moreover disclosure was also a proportionate step – less intrusive measures to encourage the couple to move on had been tried and failed.

It is worth pointing out here that the Art 8 right to respect for privacy goes beyond the right to information being kept confidential (although this is, of course, included within the notion of privacy) – an important point, as doubt was cast on the confidential status of the information disclosed in this case. The police did not show the site owner the probation service report or any other confidential information from their files; rather, being uncertain as to the implications of the law on confidentiality, they chose to play safe by showing the site owner newspaper clippings about the couple in which their convictions for serious sex offences (a matter of public record in any event) were revealed. The Court's ruling thus manifests a relatively sophisticated approach to the disclosure of information: namely, that it was clearly prepared to move beyond the rather simplistic understanding of the past whereby 'facts' and 'information' could be neatly categorised as 'private' or 'in the public domain' – the latter generally being beyond the law's protection (Paton-Simpson 1998). Lord Bingham, LCJ, in the High Court's decision in the case, stated:

> When, in the course of performing its public duties, a public body (such as a police force) comes into possession of information relating to a member of the public, *being information not generally available* and damaging to that member of the public if disclosed, the body ought not to disclose such information save for the purpose of, and to the extent necessary for, performance of its public duty or enabling some other public body to perform its public duty. [emphasis added]

What is manifestly clear from this examination of the domestic law governing public authorities' powers to disclose sensitive information about sex offenders is that the courts are a long way from lending their support to American-style community notification, not least because of their increasing sensitivity to offenders' privacy rights. Indeed, in *ex p Thorpe*, the judges both in the Divisional Court and in the Court of Appeal went out of their way to eschew any approach to disclosure that might encourage 'witch hunts' and the hounding of offenders from their homes by angry residents. So far, the courts have not had to grapple with allegations that public agencies' decisions to disclose have affected, or will affect, offenders' *other* Convention rights. Arts 2 (right to protection of life) and 3 (right to freedom from torture and inhuman or *degrading* treatment) are the most likely, at any rate in the event of disclosures leading to physical attacks or to offenders' degradation by outraged mobs. The possibility of such cases coming before the courts arises because of the European Court's jurisprudence imposing certain *positive* obligations on states in relation to particular Convention rights to prevent their breach by private parties. That jurisprudence also gives rise to the possibility that public agencies may be held liable to the *victims*, actual or potential, of decisions *not* to disclose. Moreover, sooner or later, the courts will have to consider whether public agencies have the legal power to intervene in decisions by *private* persons to disclose – a possibility raised by recent developments in the case law wholly unrelated to sex offenders, but having possible implications for MAPPPs owing to their statutory managerial functions. These issues are taken up in the next section.

Future legal developments

States' positive obligations under the ECHR

An interesting and unusual feature of the European Court's jurisprudence relating to certain Convention rights is the concept of states'
positive obligations to take steps to protect those rights, even where their
actual or threatened breach emanates from private parties rather than
from the state itself. As Starmer notes of positive obligations, '[t]heir
foundation lies in the recognition that a purely negative approach to the
protection of human rights [whereby states are only required not to
interfere with rights] cannot guarantee their effective protection and that
the acts of private individuals can threaten human rights just as much
as the acts of state authorities' (2001: 139). As he suggests, while the
Court itself has never sought to define the circumstances in which
positive obligations to prevent breaches of Convention rights arise, three
sets of circumstances can be identified from the case law to date: firstly,
where fundamental rights are at stake (Arts 2, right to protection of life;
and 3, freedom from torture and inhuman or degrading treatment,
discussed below); secondly, where intimate interests such as those in Art
8 are at stake; and thirdly, where Convention rights cannot be adequately
protected by the existing domestic legal framework (Starmer 2001: 150).
The precise nature of the obligations thus imposed depends on the right
in question and the seriousness of the state's failure, but generally they
may include the need to enact laws (civil or criminal) giving the
appropriate protection from breaches, or the need to take positive,
concrete action.

Thus in *Guerra v Italy* (1998) 26 EHRR 357, the European Court ruled
that the Italian state was in breach of the applicants' Art 8 rights to
respect for their homes and family life (aspects of 'privacy' expressly
protected in the terms of 8(1)) through its *failure to disclose information* to
the applicants about a dangerous chemical factory a kilometre from their
homes in Manfredonia. Had the state disclosed such information
(including information about the risks the factory posed to health and
about necessary safety precautions in the event of a further explosion,
one having occurred in 1976 which led to the serious poisoning by
arsenic of 150 residents), the applicants could have made informed
decisions about whether to remain living in such close proximity to the
factory. While possibly somewhat strained, one reading of this case
creates interesting possibilities for those wishing to carve out a 'right to
know' – a right to American-style community notification – about sex
offenders living in their communities. Such an asserted 'right to know'
is *not* available via Art 10 of the Convention, which protects the right to

freedom of expression, including the right to receive and impart information. The Court in *Guerra* itself made this clear when, repeating the stance taken in *Leander v Sweden* (1987) 9 EHRR 433,[24] it said, 'That freedom cannot be construed as imposing on a state ... positive obligations to collect and disseminate information of its own volition' (paragraph 50). But a creative lawyer might one day argue by analogy from *Guerra* that his clients' rights under Art 8(1) to respect for their homes and family life have been breached by a MAPPP's decision to house a serious sex offender in their community *without notifying the community* of the offender's presence: had such information been given to them, they could have arrived at their own decision as to whether they were prepared to accept the risk by continuing to live in the area.

Such a reading *is* somewhat strained, it has to be conceded, as there are distinctions to be drawn. Whereas a sex offender shares with other residents of his community a right to respect for his privacy, the owners of the chemical factory had no Convention rights competing with those of the residents of Manfredonia. Moreover, the risk posed by a sex offender living in the community is, quite literally, a calculated risk which is, at least theoretically, monitored by public agencies and which may be the better managed for precisely not being disclosed to the offender's neighbours. The risk to the Manfredonians, however, was a tangible risk to their health which had previously eventuated in *actual* damage to their health long after the authorities became aware of the risk.[25] Nevertheless, it is as well to be aware of the possibility of the above line of argument: the Convention is interpreted by the Court as a 'living instrument' which therefore generates decisions lacking the force of precedents as understood in the common law world. This cuts both ways and may lead a future Court to apply the broad logic of *Guerra* as suggested above.

Still pursuing the above somewhat speculative line of argument, if an individual were to be killed, or their life seriously threatened, by the actions of a sex offender released into the community and known to pose a specific risk to persons such as that individual, it is again possible that the Convention could be invoked. Art 2(1) baldly states that '[e]veryone's right to life shall be protected by law.' This has been interpreted in two cases involving the UK as imposing on the state a positive obligation to protect individuals' lives, including, where necessary, an obligation to disclose particular information if necessary to protect lives.

In *LCB v UK* (1998) 27 EHRR 212, the Court stated that Art 2(1) requires the state 'to take appropriate steps to safeguard the lives of those within its jurisdiction ... The Court's task is ... to determine whether, given the circumstances of the case, the state did all that could have been required of it to prevent the applicant's life from being avoidably put at risk . . .' (paragraph. 36). The applicant's father was present during Britain's four Christmas Island atmospheric nuclear bomb tests in the late 1950s. The applicant was born in 1966 and, having been diagnosed with leukaemia when she was two years old, underwent chemotherapy for eight years. In 1992 she became aware of the allegedly high incidence of cancer amongst Christmas Island veterans' children and complained to the European Commission that the British government had breached her right to protection of her life through its *failure to inform her parents* that her health might be at risk because of her father's presence at the tests. Both the Commission and the Court unanimously found for the government on the facts: there was insufficient evidence to support a finding that the father's exposure and her disease were linked and, in any event, the disease was unlikely to have been diagnosed or treated earlier. However, if the government had had good reason to think that she was in danger of developing a life-threatening disease because of her father's presence, then arguably the government would have been required by Art 2(1) to disclose this fact to the applicant's parents – whether or not the government thought the information would help her (paragraph 40). As we have seen, domestic law *empowers* agencies to disclose information relating to sex offenders to private individuals with a specific need to know, and only as a matter of exception. The European Court's decision in *LCB* may impliedly be taken to *require* agencies to engage in such disclosure in life-threatening situations; furthermore, thanks to *Osman v UK* (1998) 29 EHRR 245, they may be liable for the fatal consequences of a failure to do so.

Paget-Lewis, a teacher at 15-year-old Ahmet Osman's school, developed a pathological obsession with the boy (as he had with another boy at the previous school where he taught), which ultimately led to his engaging in a series of bizarre and criminal actions culminating in his stealing a shot-gun with which he shot and killed Ahmet's father and the deputy headmaster's son, and seriously injured Ahmet and the deputy headmaster. Mrs Osman and Ahmet attempted to sue the police, essentially alleging that they were negligent in failing to prevent the killings and assaults: the Osmans had reported numerous incidents to the police prior to the final events. They failed in the Court of Appeal, owing to a House of Lords' precedent in which the police were held, on public policy grounds, to owe no duty of care to the victims of crime in relation to the way they conducted their investigations. The Osmans complained to the European Commission on a number of grounds, including that the police failed to protect the lives of Mr Osman and Ahmet as required by Article 2. They failed on this ground, both before the Commission and the Court – but on the facts, not because they had no arguable case. Having referred to its *LCB* judgement, the Court stated:

It is accepted ... that Article 2 ... may ... imply in certain well-defined circumstances a positive obligation on the authorities to take preventive operational measures to protect an individual whose life is at risk from the criminal acts of another ...

... [I]t must be established to [the Court's] satisfaction that the authorities knew or ought to have known at the time of the existence of a *real and imminent risk* to the life of *an identified individual or individuals* from the criminal acts of a third party and that they failed to take measures within the scope of their powers which, judged reasonably, might have been expected to avoid that risk. [The failure need not be] tantamount to gross negligence or wilful disregard of the duty to protect life ... [I]t is sufficient for an applicant to show that the authorities did not do all that could be reasonably expected of them to avoid a real and immediate risk to life of which they have or ought to have knowledge.

(paragraph 116)

On the facts, there was no point at which the police knew or ought to have known that the Osmans' lives were at real and immediate risk from Paget-Lewis, in relation to whom they were entitled to presume innocence. This is in contrast to the situation posited above: the operational failure by a MAPPP to disclose information about a sex offender *known* by the agencies concerned to pose a serious risk to particular individuals or types of individuals (e.g. young girls/boys, or blonde-haired women in their early twenties, and so on) might well lead to liability on the part of the police and/or probation services if the offender kills or seriously injures another and disclosure might reasonably have been expected to avoid that risk. At any rate, a domestic court might be prepared to conclude that the failure amounted to a breach of Art 2, even if it were not prepared to conclude that the failure amounted to actionable negligence as such.[27] In the case of a *sex offender* being killed by an angry mob which has been told of his presence by someone to whom it was disclosed by a public agency, there is a possibility of similar liability under Article 2, unless the agency could show that the disclosure was carried out in conformity with information-sharing protocols specifying particular precautions to obviate the risks to the offender.

Similar conclusions may be drawn in relation to Art 3. 'Degrading treatment', within the meaning of Art 3, is 'treatment which arouses in the victim feelings of fear, anguish and inferiority capable of humiliation and debasement and possibly breaking physical or moral resistance' (*Ireland v UK* (1979) 2 EHRR 25, paragraph 167). *Tyrer v UK* (1979) 2 EHRR 1 added that it is enough if the victim's treatment amounts to humiliation only in his own eyes (paragraph 23). This would seem to describe the abuse suffered by many sex offenders, actual or suspected, particularly at the hands of outraged mobs. The European Court's decision in *A v UK* (1998) 27 EHRR 611 was that the British government had to take steps to ensure that UK law be amended so as to qualify the open-ended defence of 'reasonable chastisement' (available to parents in answer to charges of violence against their children); as it stood, the defence breached Art 3, as it afforded the victims of parental abuse insufficient protection from 'inhuman and degrading treatment'[28] (which is defined as 'intense physical or mental suffering': *Ireland v UK*, paragraph 167). The Court stated that, '[Art 3] requires states to take measures designed to ensure that individuals within their jurisdiction are not subjected to torture or inhuman or degrading treatment or punishment, *including such ill-treatment administered by private individuals . . .*' (paragraph 22) [emphasis added]. The positive obligations were elaborated in *Z v UK* (2002) 34 EHRR 97 in which the Court, repeating the above passage verbatim, added that '[t]hese measures should provide effective protection, in particular, of children and other vulnerable persons and include reasonable steps to prevent ill-treatment of which the authorities had or ought to have had knowledge' (paragraph 73). In that case, five children had suffered prolonged and serious abuse at the hands of their parents; despite social services having known of the situation since 1987, they did not intervene until 1992.[29] The Court ruled that the children's suffering amounted to inhuman and degrading treatment and the state's failure to provide the children with adequate protection amounted to a breach of Art 3.

The implications of these two cases for public agencies' disclosure decisions would seem to be that liability might ensue in relation to an *offender* where disclosure carried out without proper regard to minimising the risk to the offender led to abuse.[30] In the case of an offender's *victim* suffering abuse at the offender's hands, it is conceivable that, again as with Art 2, the *failure* to disclose to that victim or to those who might fall within the offender's preferred victim typology might lead to liability – at any rate, if the agency concerned knew or ought to have known that there was a high risk of the offender's engaging in such conduct.

Intervening to prevent general disclosure

Two recent decisions by British courts create the intriguing possibility that a form of 'prior restraint' may be available both to sex offenders and to the public agencies responsible for their management, to prevent disclosure by private parties which threaten to interfere with the agencies' statutory managerial functions or with an offender's rights. The cases are *Broadmoor Hospital v Robinson* [2000] 1 WLR 1590 and *Venables & Thompson v NG Newspapers Ltd* [2001] 1 WLR 1038.

At issue in the *Robinson* case was 'whether a statutory body is entitled to be granted an injunction in civil proceedings to support its performance of its statutory duties.' Broadmoor Hospital had been granted two court orders, restraining Robinson, detained in Broadmoor following conviction for manslaughter, from delivering the manuscript of a book he had written in hospital to his publishers; the second ordered him to deliver up to the hospital all documents relating to the book. The hospital's concern was that if published, the book would expose Robinson to the risk of assault, undermine his mental state and distress other patients and his victim's family. The orders were discharged on appeal by Robinson, and the hospital appealed to the Court of Appeal. The Court ruled that a public body *could* gain an injunction to prevent interference with the performance of its statutory functions; however, no injunction was available to protect patients' rights as such and so the appeal was turned down. The case is significant, because it extends the jurisdiction of the courts to grant civil injunctions relating to the exercise of public powers and duties. Essentially, the position hitherto was that such injunctions were available only to the Attorney-General (and, rarely, to Chief Constables in relation to the enforcement of the criminal law).[31] Lord Woolf MR summarised the position arrived at as follows:

> if a public body is given a statutory responsibility which it is required to perform in the public interest, then, in the absence of an implication to the contrary in the statute, it has standing to apply to the court for an injunction to prevent interference with its performance of its public responsibilities and the courts should grant such an application when 'it appears to the court to be just and convenient to do so.'

The implications for the police and probation services and their MAPPPs are clear. Section 67(2) CJCSA 2000 establishes the services' statutory duty to set up MAPPPs: 'The responsible authority[32] for each area must establish arrangements for the purpose of assessing and *managing the risks* posed in that area by' sex or violent offenders. There is nothing in that Act implying that the two services lack standing to apply for an injunction. It would therefore seem to follow from the ruling in *Robinson* that if a MAPPP's ability to manage a particular offender is being undermined by the 'naming and shaming' activities of the press, then the chief officer of police and the local probation board could *in principle* jointly apply for an injunction to restrain the press' activities. Two caveats must be entered. The first is that it is not altogether clear from the Court's decision whether the third party's activity must be *intended* to interfere with performance of the statutory function, or whether it is enough that the activity *as a matter of fact* so interferes. Lord Woolf suggests that injunctive relief would be available to Broadmoor to restrain a third party's activity 'if it is an activity which can be shown to be having a sufficiently significant impact on the security of the hospital or the treatment of a patient.' Lord Waller LJ, however, having expressly endorsed Woolf's *general* statement of the rule, then gave examples which seemed to suggest that the third party's interference may be restrained only if it is intended to frustrate the performance of the statutory function:

[F]or example, if a third party were *to set out* to frustrate the authority in its treatment of a patient, I can see no reason why the court should not grant an injunction to prevent that conduct. If a third party *attempted to interfere* with the discipline at Broadmoor, I would see no reason why the court should not assist the authority by injunction if necessary. [emphasis added]

If an intention to interfere is required, the press would doubtless argue (as indeed did the *News of the World* in response to criticism of its 'naming and shaming' campaign of summer 2000) that its purpose was to *enhance* public agencies' public protection functions by promoting public vigilance. The second caveat is far more significant – namely, that the press' Art 10 freedom to publish would be centrally at stake. *Robinson* was decided before the HRA came into effect. Would a court, particularly in view of s. 12 HRA, which requires courts to pay particular attention to the press' Art 10 rights, be convinced that an injunction was, as required by Art 10(2), necessary for the protection of the rights and freedoms of others, or for the prevention of disorder or crime? Possibly: the former would embrace the rights of the offender himself and those of potential victims who might be at greater risk if the press' activities drive the offender underground and thus beyond the control of the MAPPP. The latter – prevention of crime or disorder – might be a strong justification for the injunction, given the serious disorder in some British cities that followed in the wake of the Sarah Payne case.

What of an *offender's* ability to apply for injunctive relief in such circumstances if the police or probation services decline, or simply fail, to do so? The offender cannot make a free-standing application under the Convention, directly alleging that the press is interfering with his right to privacy: he is a private party suing another private party and thus has to base his application on an existing common law cause of action[33] – which would be breach of confidence. But if the press is simply publishing his name and photograph, it is highly unlikely that he has a cause of action (his address might well be a different matter).[34] But could a sex offender, co-operating with his probation officer and with any surveillance measures put in place by the MAPPP, and perhaps co-operating with a Sex Offender Order taken out against him by the police, apply for an injunction to restrain the press from further publicising his whereabouts, or to restrain his neighbours from laying siege to his home, on the basis that these activities were undermining his management and thus undermining the police and probation services' statutory duty to manage him? There is a tantalising hint of this possibility in the *Venables & Thompson* case, although Butler-Sloss was there clearly not enamoured of the idea. Counsel, basing himself on the *Robinson* principle,

> advanced the argument that, in circumstances where the public responsibilities of a public authority were, or were likely to be, interfered with and that public authority refused or failed to take proceedings to obtain an injunction, the beneficiary of those responsibilities has standing to make the application himself ... I recognise that, if a public authority were unable to carry out its public functions, which were and were intended to be in the interests of the recipients, such interference might be very unjust to the recipients. *It does, however, seem to me to be a considerable extension of the, so far, untested remedy approved [in Robinson]. I have considerable reservations about the basis for the granting of such an injunction, one problem being its potential ambit width which would be likely ... to be extended far too widely.* [emphasis added]

It remains to be seen whether applications for injunctions based on the *Robinson* principle will be applied for at all, whether by the police and probation services, or by offenders – and whether the courts will be willing to grant them. The courts might, however, be persuaded to do so if it could convincingly be argued that such legal remedy is required, in appropriate cases, to fulfil the state's positive obligations, discussed above, under Arts 2 and 3 (protection of life and freedom from torture, *inhuman* or *degrading* treatment).

A final word is required as to the basis on which Venables and Thompson succeeded in getting the life-long injunctions for which they applied. Venables and Thompson, the killers of two-year-old James Bulger (killed when the defendants were 10 years old) were now adults and were about to be released from prison. They sought permanent injunctions to restrain the press from revealing, *inter alia*, their new identities, their addresses and their photographs, on the grounds that any such publicity would breach their right to confidentiality, and would pose a very real threat to their lives and to their freedom from inhuman and degrading treatment (Arts 2 and 3, ECHR). The response of the press was that the granting of such injunctions would breach the press' right under Art 10 to impart important information to the public. The Court of Appeal granted the requested injunctions, after conducting a careful balancing exercise in relation to all the parties' Convention rights. The Court had to be particularly mindful of the press' Art 10 right, thanks to s. 12 HRA, which enjoins the courts to pay particular regard to this right in cases where it is at stake. Indeed, Butler-Sloss, LJ, noted that the old approach in breach of confidence cases, whereby competing public interests were crudely balanced, 'cannot . . . now stand in the light of s. 12 . . . and Article 10 . . ., which together give an enhanced importance to freedom of expression and consequently the right of the press to publish.' She went on to state, however, that this did not mean that the Art 10 right has a presumptive priority over other Convention rights; rather, it meant that any exception to freedom of expression has to fall within Art 10(2) – which permits such exceptions where necessary in a democratic society for the achievement of certain stated purposes (protection of national security, protection of the rights and freedoms of others, and so on).

This case is significant for a number of reasons. It confirms that Convention rights have indirect horizontal effect[35] domestically – that is, they are relevant to the determination of private proceedings in so far as the courts, as 'public bodies' under the HRA, are impliedly required by s. 6 of that Act to develop the common law in accordance with Convention rights, even in cases involving no state party. It is also significant in so far as it is the first case in which a permanent, life-long injunction has been issued to safeguard an individual's rights. For our purposes, however, it has a yet wider significance: it *may* provide the basis for the obtaining of an injunction by a sex offender against private persons, including the press, who might be contemplating a 'naming and shaming' campaign, to include the complainant. It must be conceded – again – that this may be an over-ambitious reading of the case, as there are distinctions which can be drawn. Venables and Thompson were given, in effect, mandatory life sentences; their release suggests that they were no longer regarded as posing a significant risk to anyone. Sex offenders, on the other hand, unless given life sentences, are released despite the strong possibility in many instances that they continue to pose a significant risk of re-offending, and the press could claim to be alerting the public to this risk. Nevertheless, Butler-Sloss chose to avoid the point made by counsel for the newspapers that if injunctions were granted in this case, they would have to be granted to protect paedophiles. Instead, she went out of her way to stress the exceptional nature of the case: 'the claimants are uniquely notorious . . . their case is exceptional.' Moreover,

I do not see this extension of the law of confidence, by the grant of relief in the exceptional circumstances of this case, as opening a door to the granting of general restrictions on the media *in cases where anonymity would be desirable* [emphasis added]. In my judgment, that is where the strict application of Article 10(2) bites. It will only be appropriate to grant injunctions to restrain the media where it can be convincingly demonstrated, within those exceptions, that it is strictly necessary.

Conclusions

In conclusion, then, the following general statements can be made, some tentatively, about the law governing the disclosure of information relating to sex offenders:

- Inter-agency exchange is generally permitted for the fulfilment of the relevant agencies' duties; what is not permitted, however, is such exchange for 'just in case' purposes.

- Disclosure to private parties is, as a general rule, not allowed: a blanket policy of disclosure to anyone who might usefully be told is unlawful. It will be justified as a matter of exception only, on the basis of a strict 'need to know' and, in the wake of enactment of the HRA, where Convention rights may be at stake, justification must be brought within the terms of the relevant Convention article.

- Disclosures that might have an impact on offenders' rights under Arts 2, 3 and 8 in particular should be accompanied by positive measures aimed at ensuring that private third parties do not breach those rights (the state's 'positive obligations').

- The state's 'positive obligations' under Convention jurisprudence may *require* (not merely permit) disclosure to private parties (including, perhaps – and speculatively – by way of community notification).

- Recent developments in the British courts suggest the *possibility* of the police and probation services being able to make proactive use of injunctions to restrain widespread public disclosure if this interferes, or is likely to interfere, with the ability of MAPPPs to carry out their statutory function of managing sex offenders in the community. The further – though currently unlikely – possibility is that offenders might have standing to gain such injunctions.

The picture which emerges from this survey of the law is that rumours of the death of offenders' individual rights may be somewhat premature and overly pessimistic. This is not to suggest that we should be complacent about the courts' ability to resist the logic of risk – but to acknowledge that case outcomes are not wholly predictable. The Convention rights guarantee a 'due process' approach to justice and entail that the 'as yet unresolved struggles over the relative roles of "experts" and the general public in determining crime control strategy' (Kemshall and Maguire 2002: 191) will not be resolved solely by reference to the balance of convenience.

Given the obvious minefield created for agencies by the human rights agenda, and given that demands for community notification are unlikely to recede, it is interesting that there appears to have been no suggestion from any quarter that ultimate responsibility for disclosure decisions could be taken out of the hands of the agencies concerned in managing sex offenders and made subject to *ex ante* judicial control – that MAPPPs and individual members thereof should have to apply for court orders permitting (or indeed restraining) the disclosure of information. Such a system has a precedent in the context of child care proceedings (as seen above) and, in the context of sex offender management, would not be wholly without precedent: some states in the USA require the courts to determine which offenders are to be subject to community notification, based on the court's risk assessment either at the sentencing or release stages (Matson and Lieb 1997: 12). What is (very tentatively) envisaged here is, admittedly, different in that judicial control would be available at any point throughout the period of the offender's presence in a community, in so far as a MAPPP (or its members) would have to obtain judicial review of their decision to disclose. If we are imaginative, it may be possible to devise ways of ensuring the presence at such hearings of members of the affected community (a limited form of 'restorative justice'), though of course this would have to be subject to carefully conceived safeguards for the offender. Such a procedure might go some way towards enhancing the currently woefully inadequate, uncertain and diffuse public accountability of MAPPPs (Maguire et al. 2001).

Notes

1 See Home Office (2002b), Maguire et al. (2001), Kemshall (2001). For an account of the development of multi-agency working in England and Wales, largely driven by the probation service, see Nash (1999); for a brief historical account, see Kemshall and Maguire (2002: 171–5). Multi-agency working, originally based on informal arrangements, in relation to sex and violent offenders is now a legal requirement imposed specifically on the police and

probation services: sections 67 and 68, Criminal Justice and Court Services Act 2000 (CJCSA).

2 For further discussion, see, for instance, Garland (2001 passim).

3 Matson's account is a valuable, largely descriptive account; for an evaluative account of notification arrangements, see Hebenton and Thomas (1997).

4 See Adams (2002) for details of methods of community notification as of February 2001.

5 Three broad types of notification are evident in the North American arrangements, characterised by the degree of notification required: broad community notification; notification to specific individuals and organisations; access to registration information. See generally Matson and Lieb (1997). American public support for notification appears to be high: see Philips (1998).

6 The Home Office's guidance to MAPPPs on the preparation of their annual reports makes fascinating reading in terms of its desire to encourage a degree of appeasement by the MAPPPs of their local publics: see Home Office (2002a, 2003).

7 Kemshall and Maguire's research for the Home Office seems to confirm the low priority afforded to rights in the work of MAPPPs: 'concern was rarely expressed about possible violations of rights to privacy or of the fundamental distinction between those who are under statutory supervision or control . . . and those who are not . . .' (2002: 190). It should be pointed out, however, that they are far from uncritical of the theorists of the 'new penality'; their research confirms their view that the picture on the ground is far more complicated than these supposedly key indicators would suggest.

8 Hereafter, 'Article' will be referred to as 'Art'.

9 The rights to liberty and security of the person (Art 5) and to a fair trial (Art 6) are also potentially at stake; the discussion here will focus on those rights referred to in the text.

10 See Part 1, CJCSA.

11 The power to extract DNA samples without consent, created by s. 63, Police and Criminal Evidence Act 1984 (PACE), has been extended by the Criminal Evidence (Amendment) Act 1997 to those convicted of sexual offences prior to the coming into force of PACE. In a bid to eliminate the pornographic use of certain types of criminal evidence, the Sexual Offences (Prohibited Material) Act 1997 restricts access by defendants accused of certain sexual offences to photographs and victims' statements. Section 2 of the Crime (Sentences) Act 1997 provides for the imposition of a mandatory life sentence on anyone of 18 years or older receiving a second conviction for rape, attempted rape or unlawful sexual intercourse with a girl under 13. The Crime and Disorder Act 1998 introduces extended sentences (and abolishes ss. 10–27 of the Crime (Sentences) Act 1997, never implemented) for sex offenders. The Sex Offenders Act 1997 has already been amended: CJCSA and Police Reform Act 2002.

12 Section 29, DPA. See for details chapter 5, 'Exemptions and Modifications', in guidance issued by the Information Commissioner (who oversees enforcement of the DPA).

13 This document also stresses the desirability of information-sharing protocols and their integration into a risk assessment and management system.

14 See generally Bedingfield (1998: 323–32).

15 See also *Re W* [1998] 2 All ER 801.

16 SI 1991/1247 as amended by Family Proceedings (Amendment) Rules 2001, SI 2001/821.

17 See, for instance, *Oxfordshire County Council v M* [1994] 2 All ER 269.

18 [1996] 2 FLR 123.

19 Section 17 places a general duty on local authorities to safeguard and promote the welfare of children in need in their area. Section 47 requires a local authority to investigate when, *inter alia*, it reasonably suspects that a child in its area is suffering, or is likely to suffer, significant harm.

20 See also *Z v Finland* (1998) 26 EHRR 357.

21 While the HRA expressly relates only to *legislative* powers, it appears to be widely accepted that the courts are obliged by s. 6 of the Act to interpret the common law in conformity with Convention rights; thus public authorities exercising common law powers must do so with reference to those rights.

22 This case was in any event cited without critical comment in *Re C* (2002), discussed below.

23 For discussion of this case, see Barber (1998a, 1998b), Mullender (1998) and Power (1999).

24 'Article 10 guarantees the freedom to receive as well as impart information, but it does not confer a right of access to information.' (*Leander*, paragraph 116)

25 'We can presume that the long history of pollution from this particular factory was a decisive factor in the Court's willingness to find the authorities liable for failing to provide advice to the local population.' (Mowbray 2001: 386).

26 *Hill v Chief Constable of West Yorks* [1989] AC 53.

27 The precise contours of the duty of care owed by the police to the victims of crime in domestic tort law is currently somewhat uncertain, owing to a degree of confusion generated by the *Osman* ruling on the Article 6 aspects of the Osmans' complaint.

28 The British government has since indicated that it will not be amending the law in England and Wales on this point, in response to a consultation exercise (Department of Health 2000 and Department of Health Press Release 2001) which showed that 70 per cent of respondents favoured retention of the 'right' to 'smack' a child; see also *The Times*, 9 November 2001. However, the Court of Appeal's ruling in *R v H* (2002) 1 Cr App R 7 in effect implements the European Court's decision, by stipulating the conditions which must be fulfilled before the defence can succeed.

29 The children's bid to win damages domestically for social services' alleged negligence had failed: *X v Bedfordshire CC and Others* [1995] 2 AC 633.

30 Furthermore, even if the initial disclosure is carried out sensitively, it is possible that the police might be liable for a subsequent failure to intervene if they have been made aware that an offender is being seriously harassed.

31 Local authorities, by s. 222 Local Government Act 1972, have power to apply for an injunction to support the criminal law.

32 'Responsible authority' is defined in s. 67(1) as meaning 'the chief officer of police and the local probation board for that area acting jointly.'
33 Convention rights have only *indirect* horizontal effect in proceedings between private parties: *Douglas v Hello! Ltd* [2001] 2 WLR 992 and *Venables & Thompson v News Group Newspapers Ltd* [2001] 2 WLR 1038.
34 See, however, text below.
35 For excellent summary accounts of the concept of horizontal effect and of the significant body of legal literature it has generated, see Feldman (2002: 99–102) and Fenwick (2002: 161–4).

References

Adams, D. (2002) 'Summary of State Sex Offender Registries, 2001', *Bureau of Justice Statistics Fact Sheet* (March). US Department of Justice.

Barber, I. (1998a) 'Privacy and the police: private right, public right or human right?', *Public Law* 15, pp. 19–24.

Barber, I. (1998b) 'Disclosure of information by police', *Journal of Criminal Law*, pp. 115–17.

Beck, U. (1992) *Risk Society: towards a new modernity.* London: Sage.

Beck, U. (1999) *World Risk Society.* London: Sage.

Bedingfield, M. (1998) *The Child in Need: children, the State and the law.* Bristol: Family Law 1998.

Department of Health (2000) *Protecting Children, Supporting Parents: a consultation document on the physical punishment of children.* London: Department of Health.

Department of Health, Home Office and Department of Education and Employment (1999) *Working Together to Safeguard Children.* London: Department of Health.

Department of Health Press Release 2001/0524. London: Department of Health.

Feldman, D. (2002) *Civil Liberties and Human Rights in England and Wales.* Oxford: Oxford University Press.

Fenwick, H. (2002) *Civil Liberties and Human Rights.* London: Cavendish Publishing.

Garland, D. (2001) *The Culture of Control: crime and social order in contemporary society.* Oxford: Oxford University Press.

Giddens, A. (1990) *The Consequences of Modernity.* Cambridge: Polity Press.

Hebenton, B. and Thomas, T. (1997) *Keeping Track? Observations on sex offender registration in the US*, Police Research Series Paper 83. London: Home Office.

Home Office (1997) *HOC 39/97: Sex Offenders Act.* London: Home Office.

Home Office (1998) *Guidance on the Crime & Disorder Act 1998: crime & disorder partnerships*, Chapter 5. London: Home Office.

Home Office (1999) *Guidance on the Disclosure of Information about Sex Offenders who may present a risk to Children and Vulnerable Adults.* London: Home Office.

Home Office (2002a) *Guidance to Police and Probation Services on the Criminal Justice & Court Services Act 2000, Sections 67 & 68 (Multi-Agency Public Protection Arrangements – MAPPA).* London: Home Office.

Home Office (2002b) *Protection Through Partnership: Multi-Agency Public Protection Arrangements Annual Report 2001–2002*. London: Home Office.

Home Office (2003) *Further Guidance to Police and Probation Services on the Criminal Justice & Court Services Act 2000, Sections 67 & 68 (Multi-Agency Public Protection Arrangements – MAPPA)*. London: Home Office.

Hudson, B. (2002) 'Balancing Rights and Risk: dilemmas of justice and difference', in N. Gray, J. Laing and L. Noaks (eds) *Criminal Justice, Mental Health and the Politics of Risk*. London: Cavendish Publishing, pp. 99–122.

Kemshall, H. (2001) *Risk Assessment and Management of Known Sexual and Violent Offenders: a review of current issues*, Police Research Series Paper 140. London: Home Office.

Kemshall, H. and Maguire, M. (2002) 'Public Protection, Partnership and Risk Penality: the multi-agency risk management of sexual and violent offenders', in N. Gray, J. Laing and L. Noaks (eds) *Criminal Justice, Mental Health and the Politics of Risk*. London: Cavendish Publishing, pp. 169–98.

Lemin, J. (1998) 'To Know or Not to Know? The privacy law implications of the 1996 Paedophile and Sex Offender Index', *Victoria University of Wellington Law Review* 28:2, pp. 415–40.

Maguire, M., Kemshall, H., Noaks, L., Sharpe, K. and Wincup, E. (2001) *Risk Management of Sexual and Violent Offenders: the work of public protection panels*, Police Research Series Paper 139. London: Home Office.

Matson, S. (2001) *Community Notification and Education*. Center for Sex Offender Management (available on the Center's website: www.csom.org).

Matson, S. and Lieb, R. (1997) *Megan's Law: a review of state and federal legislation*. (Washington State Institute for Public Policy: Document No. 97/10/1101).

Mowbray, A. (2001) *Cases and Materials on the European Convention on Human Rights*. London: Butterworths.

Mullender, R. (1998) 'Privacy, paedophilia and the European Convention on Human Rights: a deontological approach', *Public Law* (Autumn), pp. 384–8.

Nash, M. (1999) *Police, Probation and Protecting the Public*. London: Blackstone Press.

News of the World 'Named Shamed' (23 July 2000).

Paton-Simpson, E. (1998) 'Private circles and public squares: invasion of privacy by the publication of "private facts" ', *Modern Law Review* 61:3, pp. 318–40.

Philips, D. (1998) *Community Notification as Viewed by Washington's Citizens*. (Washington State Institute for Public Policy: Document No. 98/03/1101).

Power, H. (1999) 'Sex Offenders, Privacy and the Police', *Criminal Law Review*, pp. 3–16.

Ronken, C. and Lincoln, R. (2001) 'Deborah's Law: the effects of naming and shaming on sex offenders in Australia', *Australian and New Zealand Journal of Criminology* 34:3, pp. 235–55.

Scott, J. and Ward, D. (1999) 'Human rights and the probation service', *Vista*, 5:2, pp. 106–18.

Starmer, K. (2001) 'Positive obligations under the Convention', in J. Jowell and J. Cooper (eds) *Understanding Human Rights Law*. Oxford: Hart Publishing, pp. 139–59.

Chapter 5

Sex offenders, risk penality and the problem of disclosure to the community

Hazel Kemshall and Mike Maguire

Introduction

Recent legislation and administrative arrangements for the 'management' of sexual and dangerous offenders (described in detail elsewhere in this volume) raise major normative questions relating to human rights and civil liberties, such as the extent to which it is justifiable to imprison or control the movements of people on the basis of assessments of their risk of future offending. They also raise important evaluative questions about the relative 'effectiveness' of the various policies and their implementation. Our aims here, however, are geared mainly towards *explanation* rather than discussion of principles or policy.

Our first aim is simply to help 'set the scene' by raising questions about the broad social context and the key influences shaping contemporary debates and policy-making in the 'public protection' area: not least, how do we start to explain the unprecedented rise in public and media concern about sex offenders that has been apparent over the last decade, and the equally unprecedented 'ratcheting up' of punishment and control measures against them? A second aim is to look at specific questions about relationships and communications between 'professionals' and local communities, especially regarding the frequent demands for greater public involvement in decision-making processes, including a right to 'community notification' of the whereabouts of convicted offenders. For example, it will be asked why – especially at a time when public protection work by relevant agencies is better co-ordinated and probably more effective than it has ever been – local communities have become so reluctant to trust professionals to 'risk manage' people who have convictions for sex offences, demanding instead their public exposure and exclusion from the neighbourhood. It will also be asked to what extent it may be possible to develop a more productive 'dialogue' about risk, in which the professionals assist the community towards a different kind of response.

In tackling the above questions, we shall draw on some important theoretical literature that has emerged in recent years under the general label of the sociology of punishment. This explores the effect of major social and economic changes in the late 20th century – often referred to as the conditions of 'late capitalism' or 'late modernity' – on public perceptions of crime and on penal thought and practice, with a particular focus on the move to centre stage of the concept of *risk*. As will be outlined, many social theorists have identified the decline of the 'disciplinary', 'transformative' or 'penal-welfare' approaches to crime control associated with the 'modern' period, and the emergence since the 1970s of a new form of 'penality' in which crime is accepted to a large extent as a 'given' and fewer efforts are made to change or 'rehabilitate' offenders, the focus being instead on assessing the risks posed by particular categories of people (or by particular situations or locations) and 'managing' these risks through a variety of measures ranging from routine surveillance to long-term preventive detention. Social theorists have also identified a growing sense of insecurity and fear of crime among the public, and rising demands for greater punishment of offenders and the exclusion of anyone considered to pose a risk.

Another key plank in our argument is generated by related literature which suggests that there are two very different understandings of 'risk' at work in the arena of contemporary crime control: one, driving the policy of governments and criminal justice agencies, is an understanding based on 'economic rationality' and the statistical calculation of risk; the other is the 'cultural' understanding of risk held by many ordinary members of the public (and reflected in and magnified by the media), in which factors such as the vividness of the danger and the perceived extent of control over events tend to play a greater part than the cold calculation of the odds of an event occurring. It will also be argued that, under 'late modern' conditions, not only has this difference in perceptions grown wider, but, ironically, the very efforts of government and professionals to improve 'risk management' procedures and to convince the public that these are sound, may have themselves inadvertently increased the general fear of crime and the feelings of dissatisfaction and distrust.

Such issues are not merely of academic interest. They raise important questions about the nature of communication between professionals and the general public, including practical questions about how best to counteract the problems of differing perceptions of risk and of unintended effects. Understanding of such issues is clearly of great importance to policy-makers at a time of frequent calls for greater public involvement in decision-making.

We begin with an outline of some of the key ideas and theoretical arguments around the concept of 'risk penality', and then illustrate them through a brief reminder of some of the key developments around 'public protection' over the past decade. The remainder of the chapter focuses on issues surrounding the involvement of the public, either through the release of information ('community notification') or through efforts to incorporate non-professionals into risk management processes.

The rise of a 'risk penality'

The growing prominence of the concept of risk in contemporary criminal justice and in penal policy and practice is well documented. Indeed, the prevalence of risk concerns and the impact of actuarialism on the organisation and delivery of crime prevention, policing, criminal justice and penal sanctions have been offered as evidence of a major shift in the philosophy and practice of crime control, and the emergence of what has been variously described as a 'new penology' (Feeley and Simon 1992, 1994), 'risk penality' (Garland 2001) or 'late modern' or 'postmodern' penality (Pratt 1995, 2000; Ericson and Haggerty 1997). This in turn is regarded by many sociologists as part of a much broader trend in contemporary ('late modern') Western democracies identified by Giddens (1990, 1998), Beck (1992) and others as the emergence of the 'risk society' – a world in which the identification and management of risk become structuring principles of the work of almost every agency or organisation, and a pervasive preoccupation in ordinary social life.

In the criminological literature, the growing dominance of risk-focused thinking and 'risk management' approaches and techniques has been identified in a variety of developments which, although initially distinct, have become increasingly blurred or in some cases consciously 'joined up'. These include:

1. The continuing growth of 'situational' approaches to crime prevention (especially CCTV) aimed at surveillance and opportunity reduction in locations identified as particularly vulnerable to crime (both whole categories of location, such as post offices or underground trains and stations, or specific 'hot spots').

2. The massive expansion of private policing and security firms, which have traditionally had rather different aims and approaches to the

public police, being concerned primarily with the prediction, control and management of risks to people or property in particular locations or institutions, rather than with bringing individual offenders to justice (Shearing and Stenning 1981; Johnston 2000).

3. An increasing focus on risk issues by the public police. This has been expressed most forcefully by Ericson and Haggerty (1997), who argue that policing globally is now driven primarily by the 'logic of risk', its core work being the collection and distribution of risk information. In the UK, one can point to the rapid development of 'intelligence led policing' (Maguire 2000) and, more recently, of the national intelligence model, which includes provision for a regular 'strategic risk (or 'threat') assessment' by every police force.

4. The expansion of crime management by means of increasingly formalised and co-ordinated multi-agency work and information sharing. The most prominent examples in England and Wales are probably the local community safety partnerships created under the Crime and Disorder Act 1998 (Hughes 1998, Pease 2002) and the Multi-Agency Public Protection Arrangements (MAPPAs) discussed below.

5. Legislation enabling courts to pass civil orders restricting the movements or behaviour of people thought to pose a risk or nuisance to others, breach of which constitutes a criminal act punishable by imprisonment. This applies to both Sex Offender Orders (see Power 1998) and Anti-Social Behaviour Orders (the latter highlight a further trend towards a blurring of the dividing line between criminal offences and non-criminal actions which cause annoyance: see Maguire 1998, 2000).

6. The growth of risk-focused policy and practice in the penal realm, particularly in prisons and probation (Kemshall 1998; Kemshall and Maguire 2001, 2002; Robinson 2002). This includes the now standard use of instruments such as the Level of Service Inventory Revised (LSI-R) and the Offender Assessment System (OASys) to assist the classification of offenders into risk groups (and hence to inform advice to sentencers and allocate decisions within penal agencies) and, again, the elaborate risk assessment and management systems concerning sexual and dangerous offenders which are the subject of this volume.

There is no space here to go into detail about the arguments and evidence in all these complex areas, but as a general background to the discussion it may be helpful to outline very briefly some of the main features, explanations and interpretations of this shift in 'penality' that have been put forward by criminologists.

The failure of the 'disciplinary agenda'

One of the core factors said by most of the above writers to underlie the changes they identify is the collapse of the 'modernist' disciplinary agenda in the wake of the failure of the penal-welfare system to deliver its promise of crime control (Garland 1995, 1996, 2001). We are living, Garland argues, in an era in which high crime rates have come to be seen as normal and there is little prospect of 'reforming' large numbers of offenders. Consequently, we are witnessing the rapid replacement of disciplinary mechanisms of crime control (including efforts to 'change', 'train' or 'rehabilitate' offenders) by mechanisms concerned with the management of risk distribution, or an actuarial, insurance-based concept of crime control (Reichman 1986: 153).

Simon (1988: 773–4) has characterised this as a strategy of 'accommodation' rather than of 'normalisation': 'because changing people is difficult and expensive ... In our present social circumstances, it is cheaper to know and plan around people's failings than to normalise them.' Feeley and Simon (1994: 173) likewise state that the 'new penology' they identify is predicated upon the acceptance of 'deviance as normal'. They argue, in a highly pessimistic account of contemporary crime control, that the role of penology is being transformed from a mechanism of guilt attribution and reformation, to a merely administrative function of risk categorisation and the regulation and management of 'dangerous people'. Key features they identify as evidence of this include the replacement of 'clinical diagnosis and retributive judgement' by risk calculations and risk probability assessments (hence the term 'actuarialism'); an increased emphasis upon 'managing' offenders as aggregate risk groups, rather than pursuing strategies to 'change' individuals; and the special targeting, increased surveillance and control of groups and individuals categorised as 'high risk' or 'dangerous'.

While the importance of the concept of risk in penal policy is now widely acknowledged, it should be emphasised that there is by no means full agreement on the precise nature and extent of its role. Furthermore, the notion of the framing of justice or its delivery as entirely 'actuarial' is quite strongly contested, both in broad theoretical terms (O'Malley 2000; Garland 1995, 2001; Loader and Sparks 2002; Hudson 2002) and on empirical grounds. Some recent studies of probation practice, for example, suggest that the case may have been overstated and that contemporary penal policy and practice are in reality more ambivalent: in short, actuarial justice is (so far, at least) largely rhetorical, with actual frontline practice little transformed by risk calculations (Lynch 1998, 2000; Kemshall and Maguire 2001; Robinson 2002). Similar findings have emerged from policing studies (Maguire and John 1996; Maguire 2000; Innes and Fielding, unpublished 2002).

The dispersal of social control and 'responsibilisation'

The specifically risk-focused developments outlined above are often linked to a number of other significant changes in the field of crime control, driven less by concerns about high crime rates than by other social, economic and political changes associated with 'late capitalism' (or 'late modernity') and centring around issues of governance and responsibility. Many sociologists argue that a combination of the impact of globalisation, economic uncertainty and the ascendancy of neo-liberal economic thinking (including low taxation) have made it impossible for national governments in Western democracies to maintain previous levels of provision for their citizens' welfare. This has led to a tacit recognition that there are serious limits to the capacity of the police or criminal justice agencies to protect people from crime, and an increasing use of 'economic rationality' in deciding the priorities into which police or other public resources will be put. Consequently, there has been a general shift towards new, dispersed forms of governance and social control (see, for example, Giddens 1990; Stenson and Sullivan 2001). This includes a process of 'responsibilisation', whereby individuals – theoretically in return for greater individual freedom and reduced regulation – are expected to a large extent to 'manage their own risks' by both refraining from criminal behaviour and protecting themselves against crime (Giddens 1990, 1991; Rose 1995, 2000; Garland 1996, 2001).

However, this process tends to produce greater inequalities in the distribution of risk, in that those with the means to protect themselves effectively or to buy houses in low-crime areas carry a much lower burden of the risk than others. The repeat victimisation of 'disadvantaged communities' is well established (Velez 2001), and it is often these sites where re-housing of sex offenders post-custody is sought. The 'gated communities' of the middle class are rarely the site of public housing or the 'forced' relocation of sex-offending risks by professionals. The inequitable distribution of risks can only add to lack of trust and exacerbate low thresholds of acceptability ('acceptable' risks have been defined as those which are perceived as carrying some benefit as well as cost, are well managed, are equitable, and are regulated by systems that have trust and public accountability: see Hood and Jones 1996 and below).

Further negative effects that have been noted include a general reduction in commitment to the 'public good' in terms of willingly playing a part in the collective management of risks – for example in the acceptance of a hostel for ex-offenders in one's neighbourhood – and a corresponding perception among those in poorer communities that protection from crime risks is in reality a 'club good' rather than a 'public good', accessible only to some and withheld from those most in need of it (Crawford 1998; Johnston 2000).

Finally, and perhaps most importantly, the 'responsibilisation' process can encourage a tendency to adjudge certain groups of people (particularly offenders or potential offenders) as undeserving of the extra freedoms accorded to the majority, and hence a greater preference for exclusionary actions rather than attempts to rehabilitate or reintegrate.

Fear of crime and 'populist punitiveness'

The other major factors in the equation appear to be the linked phenomena of a growth in 'fear of crime' and the emergence of what Bottoms (1995) has called 'populist punitiveness'. While it can be argued that enhanced concerns about crime – reflected both in public surveys and in constant media attention to the topic – are partly a reaction to rising crime rates, they can also be linked to the same global economic forces referred to above, which have fragmented and dislocated many communities, producing a loss of old certainties (such as the relative 'permanence' of job, family and residence) and contributing to a generalised sense of insecurity, of which fear of crime is simply one manifestation.

This sense of insecurity, it is widely argued, has been one of the driving forces behind a sustained increase, particularly since the early 1990s, in demands for 'tougher' punishments, not just of 'dangerous' offenders (though the demands are particularly insistent where 'paedophiles' are concerned), but of offenders of many kinds. Such calls have also frequently been combined, particularly in the popular press, with expressions of distrust of professionals, who – despite a clear toughening of attitudes among the latter, including probation officers – are presented as 'do-gooders' out of touch with the feelings of the public.

Criminal justice policy and practice have been influenced to a considerable degree by this rise in populism, and have been characterised by sudden punitive reactions, often involving major transfers of resources, to a series of media-inflamed 'panics' about a wide variety of offences of varying seriousness and risk to public safety (recent examples in the UK being 'street robbery' and 'anti-social behaviour', as well as sex offences of all kinds). This pattern (which applies to the United States and many other countries as well as to the UK) appears significantly out of step with the picture presented by Feeley and Simon of the emergence of 'coldly rational' penal systems based on scientific assessment of risk and carefully considered distribution of resources to allow the effective management of those categories of offender posing the highest risk. However, the subject of crime has always given rise to high emotions and, especially in an era of uncertainty and rapid change, public feelings about crime and its risks may be given vent through an 'expressive' and 'symbolic' rationality of punishment that can challenge or even supersede 'economic' rationality. In a sense, indeed, this can be seen as the other side of the coin to actuarialism and equally part of the new 'late modern penality'. This view is supported by O'Malley (1999), who challenges Feeley and Simon's distinction between risk management and retribution, seeing the relationship between, on the one hand, 'healing the past' and symbolic punishment, and on the other, future-orientated risk reduction strategies, as a symbiotic one. Garland (1997) has argued that the relationship between economic and expressive rationalities of crime control should be similarly understood. Recent media and legislative responses to sex offenders and paedophiles in the UK are a case in point, with policy and practice driven by a mix of penal populism, expressive punishment and actuarialism.

Sexual and dangerous offenders: the rise of 'public protection'

Two of the main features of 'risk penality' identified above – the importance of risk classification in determining what is done with offenders, and the continual salience of public concern about crime risks – can readily be illustrated by a brief look at the recent history of responses to sexual (and, to a lesser extent, serious violent) offending in England and Wales. These include both criminal justice responses and those of vocal sections of the public (aided and abetted by the media): as noted above, these two kinds of response have become increasingly intertwined, the government introducing new (and ever harsher) legislation at short notice in response to individual cases or to pressure from the media or victims' families.

The 1980s saw the acceleration of an emerging trend towards 'bifurcation' (Bottoms 1977) or a twin-track approach to sentencing, in which the perpetrators of more serious offences and those considered to pose a danger to the public received much longer prison sentences (or were denied parole) while sentences for less serious offenders were generally reduced. This trend, which was encouraged by legislation such as the 1982 Criminal Justice Act and government policies such as the 1983 'Brittan rules' on parole (Maguire 1992), reflected the New Right's preoccupation with both spiralling crime rates and spiralling costs (Bottoms 1977; Flynn 1978; Hudson 1993). The Criminal Justice Act 1991 cemented this process in that, despite an overt 'just deserts' approach intended to reduce the use of imprisonment overall, sentences longer than the accepted 'tariff' were encouraged on the grounds of 'public protection' from those convicted of sexual, violent or drugs offences – a system later dubbed 'punitive bifurcation' by Cavadino and Dignan (1997; see also Wasik and Taylor 1991). It has been further argued that, in terms of political realities, the Criminal Justice Act 1991 was concerned with two contradictory objectives: reducing the use of (costly) custody, and being seen to be 'tough on crime' (Nash 1999). The former aim was in effect obscured by the overtly tougher measures taken against particular types of offenders for whom there was little public sympathy: an 'early sign that certain offenders were to be isolated within the criminal justice system for special attention' (Nash 1999: 45).

Sex offenders in particular were targeted for special attention, including both longer prison sentences and extended parole supervision (section 44). These offenders, and particularly 'paedophiles', had already emerged in the late 1980s as a primary focus of concern (Worrall 1997), highlighted by a series of high-profile cases and the spectre of organised and pervasive paedophilia in society at large (for example the stories about 'satanic abuse' and the Butler-Schloss inquiry in Cleveland in 1988). During the 1990s this process continued apace. Although accounting for less than one per cent of recorded offences (Home Office 2000), sex offenders came to dominate the political and penal policy agenda for much of the decade, resulting in what has been called a 'criminal apartheid' towards them (Soothill et al. 1998). As Cobley (2000: 2) also noted, ' "Paedophile" has become a household word', illustrated by her computer search of newspaper articles that revealed its use in '712 articles in six leading British newspapers' in the first four months of 1998, 'whereas the word only appeared 1,312 times in total in the four year period between 1992–1995'.

One of the main factors in this continuing attention has been the construction of the 'predatory paedophile' as a constant major threat to children. Playing on fears of 'stranger-danger' and building on the strong feelings aroused by particularly horrific – though very rare – cases of child abduction and homicide, the media have continually reinforced the spectre of an invisible stranger in our midst, preying on the vulnerable young (Kitzinger 1999a, b; Thompson 1998; Wilczynski and Sinclair 1999). In just a few years, it has been pointed out, the 'spectre of the mobile and anonymous sexual offender' has become a terrifying and ever-present concern for many people (Hebenton and Thomas 1996: 249) and the paedophile has been constructed as a 'demon' to be 'put under surveillance, punished, contained and constrained' (Young 1996: 9). In Britain, Kitzinger (1999b) identifies the roots of this 'moral panic' in the mid-1980s and the key impetus given by the BBC 'Childwatch' programme and the inception of 'Childline'. More recently, public attention has been caught at frequent intervals by sex offender releases from prison, relocation in the community (often against the wishes of local residents) and central government initiatives around sex offender registers (Thomas 2001).

Ironically, it can be argued that initiatives aimed at reducing risk in this area inadvertently unleashed an even greater feeling of risk and danger, accelerating a spiral of action and reaction that has become difficult to control. From 1996 onwards there have been several major outbreaks of vigilante action,[1] exacerbated by a feeling of siege in some communities, especially council house tenants on 'sink estates' who have come to feel that they are being asked to accept a disproportionate level of risk (Walters 2001).

The government and criminal justice agencies in turn have felt constrained to promote a series of ever harsher penal policies against sex offenders – the effect of which has been described by Sanders and Lyon (1995) as 'repetitive retribution'. By the end of the century, a battery of punitive and preventive legislation had been passed, primarily against sex offenders (although clearly often the main target, 'paedophiles' are not normally specified in statutes as a distinct group), but also against 'dangerous' offenders more generally. In addition to a series of extensions to the permitted length of post-release licence periods (now up to ten years), this included the introduction of a mandatory life sentence on a second conviction for a serious violent or sexual offence; a requirement for convicted sex offenders to register with the police for at least five years; a civil Sex Offender Order, breach of which is punishable by imprisonment up to five years; and statutory duties on probation and police to jointly risk assess and manage sexual and serious violent offenders in the community (for details of all the above legislation, see the introduction to this volume). The latest proposals, set out in the White Paper *Justice for All* (Home Office 2002), go much further, including discretionary life sentences (and lifelong supervision) for sexual or violent offenders who are assessed as 'dangerous'.

Community notification and public involvement

As illustrated above, populist calls for more draconian sentences for sex offenders have been heeded in large measure by the government, although these tend to be justified by the latter in terms of preventive goals or 'public protection', rather than as a combination of retribution and protection, which is more common in media comment. By contrast, a somewhat different media-led campaign – for 'community notification' of the whereabouts of sex offenders – has been strongly resisted by the government. Although most professionals consider that this would be a disastrous policy, likely to result in offenders being hounded from their homes and driven 'underground' (and hence more difficult to 'risk manage'), it is nevertheless worth asking whether it might be feasible as part of a more comprehensive and carefully implemented strategy to involve local communities directly in the risk management of offenders. We begin, however, with a brief reminder of the background.

The murder of Sarah Payne in the summer of 2000 stimulated intense media debate about the appropriate monitoring of paedophiles and led to calls for 'Sarah's Law' (a UK version of the American 'Megan's Law'), whereby the local community would have a right to be informed of the names and addresses of people with convictions for sexual offences.[2] It also led to a campaign by the *News of the World* to 'name and shame paedophiles'. The campaign, which resulted in public disorder and vigilante action (some against wrongly identified people) in several towns, was eventually suspended after protests from police, probation and other agencies that it was counter-productive to public protection. The National Association for the Care and Resettlement of Offenders, for example, described the *News of the World* reporting as 'grossly irresponsible'; and the Association of Chief Police Officers stated that it would 'put children's lives at risk by driving sexual offenders underground' (Thomas 2001: 103; *Guardian* 24 July 2000). This campaign also highlighted the growing divide between professionals and public in penal matters and the strength of the belief that parents have 'the right to know'. It resulted in some apparent compromises from the government, although not in the direction of community notification. Rather, ministers proposed further controls over sex offenders, including tightening the operation and extending the remit of the Sex Offender Register, and discussed the possibility of law reform and yet heavier sentences.

The subsequent trial and conviction of Roy Whiting in December 2001, a man on the Sex Offender Register and known to the local MAPPP, rekindled calls for a Sarah's Law and challenges to the expertise and professionalism of those agencies tasked with the community risk management of sex offenders. This time, however, the media coverage was less inflammatory, and more people with relevant knowledge and experience joined the debate on both sides.[3] Home Office ministers continued to argue that a 'Sarah's Law' would be 'unworkable': it would be very difficult in practice to provide all parents with useful information on all registered offenders (110,000 at the time), and any attempt to do so would create more mobility among offenders, making the situation worse.[4]

At the same time, however, an interesting debate was opened up about the detail of how a community notification system might work in practice if such a law *were* to be passed in England and Wales. This included questions such as what information might be given out, to whom, in what form, about which kinds of offenders, and of what level of risk; and perhaps most importantly, how parents and communities might be encouraged to respond 'appropriately' to the information they were given.

It is questions relating to this last issue that we wish to explore in more depth in the final part of the paper. In particular, are the preoccupation with risk and danger, and the intolerant and exclusionary attitudes which are prevalent in contemporary ('late modern') Britain, so strong that any disclosure of information about a sex offender is doomed to produce vigilante action? Or is it possible to counteract these forces with a creative approach to 'dialogue with the community'?

Communicating and debating risk with the public: challenges and contrasting approaches

Perhaps the greatest challenge in communicating with the public on this topic arises from some major differences, alluded to earlier, between 'expert' and 'lay' perceptions of risk. The complexity of risk perception has been well researched, with the following significant features of everyday perceptions well established:

- Risks that are vivid and easily imaginable are inflated.

- Risks that are involuntary are resented.

- Risks that are perceived as inequitable are resisted.

- Negative risks without any perceived benefit are seen as unacceptable.

(See, for example, Freudenberg 1988; Slovic 1992).

These would all appear to be common characteristics of sex offender risks: many ex-prisoners with convictions for sexual offences are settled in deprived housing areas, where residents are likely to feel that they are bearing a grossly unequal share of the risk in comparison with wealthier areas (inequitable risk); that they have no say in these decisions (involuntary risk); that the consequences of an offence against their children would be dire (vivid risk); and that there is no conceivable benefit to themselves in accepting this burden of risk (wholly negative risk). This is the backdrop against which experts and professionals must engage with the public about the risk management of sex offenders. In this climate, which communication strategies are likely to be useful and which are not?

In England and Wales, the basic position in most areas has been to disclose as little as possible, under the assumption that unless a particular person or group of people is thought to be in clear danger of victimisation and would clearly benefit from a warning, the best strategy is to maintain secrecy and 'leave it to the experts'. Certainly, the notion of general community access to the Sex Offender Register or to specific information about individuals living in one's area, which is common in the United States, is quite alien to current thinking among both practitioners and policy-makers. Nevertheless, in attempting to offset public calls for a full-blown 'Sarah's Law', the government has made some concessions to engagement with the general public, particularly through a requirement on local MAPPPs to produce an annual report on their activities, and the appointment of 'lay members'.

The first annual reports were published in summer 2002, but there is little evidence to suggest that they have succeeded in stimulating a broader debate or any serious engagement with local communities about the problem of the community management of high-risk offenders. The main result was a predictable, though fairly short-lived, furore in the local and national media. The reports thus seem to represent something of a missed opportunity for wider debate and dialogue. Lay members are currently in the process of appointment,[5] but are to be appointed only to strategic management boards. As such they will not have direct access to individual cases or MAPPP decision-making. It remains to be seen how effectively the role functions as a mechanism of public accountability and communication.

However, a somewhat more open attitude has been evident in Scotland, where the Cosgrove (2001) report on work with sex offenders emphasised the importance of communication and wider debate with the public about the problem of sex offending and the effective management of offenders in the community. The report advocated:

- Active work in schools on child safety and protective strategies against potential abuse.

- 'Improved understanding within communities about sex offending and the positive involvement of communities in the development of local strategies for the management of sex offenders.' (p. 5)

- 'Better protection through the development of education based programmes and the provision of public information which deals with the dangers of sex offending.' (p. 19)

- Workshops to bring agencies and communities together to discuss sex offending.

- A national education campaign, for example via television and leaflets for parents, on the extent and nature of sex offender risks to children.

The report went on to say:

> We have noted the concerns expressed by local communities about sex offenders living in their area. Emotive responses may be understandable but they are counter-productive. It is important for lead agencies to engage local communities by helping them to understand the risks posed when a sex offender goes underground, making it more difficult for the police to keep track of him. It is far better for communities to be involved in finding solutions as part of a strategic plan than feeling that they themselves must take on what is likely to be a less effective response in a way that does not reduce the risk posed by the offender. Our recommendations will help to involve communities, although the statutory responsibility for community protection must remain with the appropriate agencies ... The public information strategy which we advocate will help to inform communities. Closer links between communities and those agencies involved in child safety/crime prevention issues will also help to build confidence and increase the credibility of the information provided, helping to reduce tensions at times of difficulty. The aim should be to harness the concerns of local communities through open dialogue.
>
> (Cosgrove 2001: 20)

These comments are very much in tune with the six main recommendations made by Donnelly (1997) to improve the prevention of (violent) child abuse, which appear to translate fairly readily into the arena of reducing sex offender risks to children. In brief, the recommendations were:

- Develop public awareness and education.
- Public education needs to be long-term and repetitive.
- Education needs to be mainstream.
- Communities need to be engaged in risk management.
- Professionals should be key players in engaging the public.
- The focus should be on prevention.
  (Adapted from Freeman-Longo and Blanchard 1998: 179)

The Scottish Cosgrove Report emphasises a broader approach to sex offenders and there is some evidence from public health campaigns to suggest that such approaches can be helpful (Mercy et al. 1993). A key principle seems to be that if a significant item of 'risk knowledge' is passed to the public (and with it the burden of anxiety, fear and resentment), then this should be supported with practical advice on risk management techniques and responsible use of the information – in other words, potentially vulnerable people need guidance on what to do once they have been notified (www.parentsformeganslaw/communityapproach, 14/10/02).

The better-managed community notification schemes in the USA (for example New York) accept and apply this principle, combining 'active' dissemination of information on high-risk sex offenders with the provision of advice and written material on child sex abuse prevention. At neighbourhood level, this means that a law enforcement officer will call at every home within a certain distance of the offender's location and inform residents about him (or her): the minimum suggested is 10 houses in each direction. Active dissemination at a broader community level involves the controlled release of information to 'vulnerable entities' – for example, nurseries, schools, day care centres, local youth groups and places of worship. In both cases, educational inputs form a major element in the disclosure process.

The key ingredients, then, appear to be controlled disclosure; adequate information and support to those who receive information; and assistance to parents, children and communities to 'self-risk manage'. This position acknowledges that the agencies involved have some responsibility for managing community responses to risk as well as for managing individual sex offender risks. There is recognition that information dissemination and school education must be handled with care to avoid creating fearful children, and that further crime through vigilante action must be avoided. As a police officer responsible for the register and notification in Seattle has expressed it: 'Doing community notification without doing community education is like smoking a cigarette while you're standing in a pool of gasoline. You are setting yourself up for a disaster.' (Freeman-Longo and Blanchard 1998: 110).

Finally, it is emphasised that such schemes are highly local, and dependent upon face-to-face contact between professionals (particularly the police) and community at public meetings, parents meetings and in schools (as advocated by Cosgrove) – all of which are intended to enable and encourage communities to protect themselves on an informed and considered basis, rather than blindly resorting to vigilante action.

Other possibilities

One might speculate further whether local and personal contact helps to build trust in professionals and their risk management systems, and

helps to reduce community anxiety and resentment. The
Support' initiative may offer some insight here (Petrunik 20(
the initiative recognises that many sex offenders are social i
literally provides a 'circle of support' in the community for the offender
once released from either prison or treatment centre. Such circles are
comprised of volunteers with whom the offender will have significant
contact (for example, local church leaders, mentors, etc.). In addition to
social support the volunteers are trained to identify 'warning signals' for
risky behaviours and to assist offenders with relapse prevention, as well
as informing the statutory authorities if the risky behaviour warrants it.
At present there are two pilots in the UK, and long-term evaluation of
the programme here is awaited. In addition to testing its effectiveness in
reducing re-offending, it will be important to establish whether community resentment and fear are reduced by such circles, and whether this
is a technique that may assist in establishing greater acceptability of sex
offender risk management in the community.

A further initiative is 'Stop it Now', originating in the USA and
supported by an alliance of key voluntary and statutory agencies
working with child sexual abuse. This initiative recognises that most
child sexual abuse is not perpetrated by 'monsters' or strangers, but by
people children know. It combines education, awareness raising and a
strong preventive element, provided by a helpline offering 'advice and
support to people who suspect abuse and to those seeking help to stop
their own abusive thoughts and behavior' (Stop it Now leaflet). Stop It
Now claims that pilot projects in the USA have shown that abusers do
come forward and benefit from treatment programmes,[6] and that the
awareness raising does result in more people able to recognise child
sexual abuse (www.stopitnow.com). Within the UK and Ireland there are
pilot programmes running (e.g. Surrey and Derbyshire), although as yet
there is no long-term evaluation of such programmes in the UK
(www.stopitnow.org.uk). These projects are based on partnerships
between local agencies such as police, probation and social services, and
emphasise treatment through accredited programmes as well as
monitoring and family support. As in the USA, public education and
awareness are emphasised, publications and resource packs to train
members of the public in the early identification of 'warning signs' are
provided, and sex offenders are urged to come forward for treatment
and advice.

Both these initiatives recognise that sex offenders are present in
communities (and always will be) and aim to broaden the responsibility
for 'policing' them beyond the traditional boundaries of statutory
agencies such as police and probation. Circles of Support, for example,
combines reintegration and support with community surveillance. Stop

It Now places responsibility for dealing with sex offenders within the wider community, as well as offering treatment for those prepared to self-disclose. Importantly, both seek to redress the demonisation of sex offenders and to offer constructive, community-based techniques for their long-term management. In addition, they may offer better mechanisms for disseminating information about sex offender risk levels to the public, and demonstrate practical techniques for their acceptable reintegration. It remains to be seen whether MAPPPs could have a key co-ordinating role in such public information and education campaigns.

Finally, restorative justice has also been advocated as one possible approach to the more effective reintegration and management of sex offenders in the community; and mediation and restitution (for example through apologies and community service) have been used quite widely for familial sexual abuse in Canada and the USA (Freeman-Longo and Blanchard 1998). In essence, the approach aims to reduce the shaming and punishment components of traditional responses to sex offenders on the grounds of their ineffectiveness (Gilligan 1996; Freeman-Longo and Blanchard 1998). However, the effectiveness of such approaches has yet to be fully evaluated, as has the role of restorative justice in promoting a more effective communication with the public about sex offenders.

Concluding comments

The difficulties in developing a more productive dialogue with communities about sex offenders in a climate of distrust are acute. The current distance between professionals and public, and the growing sense of public insecurity, serve only to exacerbate these difficulties. The result is an ever-increasing spiral of exclusion and 'tougher punishment' – a process which itself is likely to produce heightened anxiety and the demonisation of sex offenders. In the long term, this is an unproductive and ineffective approach to the risk management of sex offenders, resulting in vigilante action and sex offenders retreating 'underground'. It will also create an ever-increasing core of sex offenders beyond the bounds of natural community surveillance who will require ever-increasing resources merely to manage them in place. In this scenario, risks are bound to outstrip continually the professional resources available to manage them.

An alternative approach is to aim at developing a partnership between professionals and public, in which communities have an active and appropriately regulated part in the management of sex offenders alongside professionals. This needs to be placed within a broader strategy of public education and communication that emphasises:

- A national educative campaign on the extent and nature of sex offending against children.

- Joint work in local communities to develop locally sensitive strategies for the management of sex offenders.

- Educative campaigns for communities, parents and children, with an emphasis upon prevention.

- Positive community engagement in risk management in order to avoid vigilante action.

- Inclusionary strategies such as 'Circles of Support' to enhance risk management, community surveillance and reintegration.

- Proactive communication with the public and avoidance of reactive, crisis driven strategies.

This, of course, is a highly ambitious aim, and to have any chance of success it will require carefully co-ordinated policy at both national and local levels. It will also need further evaluative work to identify the most effective communication strategies.

Finally, a broader question of major relevance to the chances of success is whether there is something intrinsically different about work with sex offenders that places it beyond the usual processes of public accountability and engagement, or whether it is merely a question of establishing how to use these processes without generating unmanageable and unintended consequences. Given that risks with similar characteristics, both environmental and social, are not treated as intrinsically different, it is perhaps time to consider *how* not *if*. Effective risk management requires trust, and trust comes out of transparency, accountability and good governance. Public trust in the professional management of sex offenders in the community can be enhanced only by increased attention to these key features of any effective risk management system (cf. Hood and Jones 1996).

Notes

1 For example, the cases of Robert Oliver and Sydney Cooke, released to public outcry and vigilante action after serving approximately eight years for the abduction and manslaughter of a 14-year-old boy.

2 Under the federal Megan's Law, passed in 1996, community notification is mandatory in cases where it is adjudged 'necessary and relevant for public protection' – a judgement normally dependent upon assessed risk level (Hebenton and Thomas 1997: 7, 24–32). Low-risk offenders are generally

subject to a principle of 'passive release of information' (i.e. the information is available to the public, but must be individually requested).

3   See, for example, www.bbc.co.uk/news 'Do we need a "Sarah's Law?"' (13 December 2001), with Michelle Elliott, the director of Kidscape, arguing that it would work for the most dangerous paedophiles, and others such as Harry Fletcher of the National Association of Probation Officers arguing that it would fuel vigilante action and lead some offenders to avoid registration.

4   See, for example, the remarks of Beverley Hughes at www.bbc.co.uk/news ('Sarah's Law Unworkable', 13 December 2001). However, little reference was made in these debates to American research evidence, which has raised broader questions about the effectiveness of systems built around the combination of sex offender registration and community notification. Zevitz and Farkas (2000a, b), for example, claim that there are often negative effects in terms of community anxiety. Prentky (1996) describes a marginalizing impact which can be detrimental to offenders' reintegration and avoidance of re-offending. A study by Schram and Milloy (1995) found no statistically significant difference between sex offenders subject to registration and community notification and those who were not. Equally, an evaluation in Washington found no reduction in sex abuse reports (Association for the Treatment of Sexual Abusers 1996). Three main reasons have been offered for such findings: inaccuracies in American registers, the mobility of sex offenders, and the high level of sex offending within families that community notification is unable to reduce (Freeman-Longo 1996, Rudin 1996, Freeman-Longo and Blanchard 1998, Tewksbury 2002). It should, however, be noted that compliance with registration requirements is generally much lower in the US than in England and Wales (where it is generally over 90 per cent: see Plotnikoff and Woolfson 2000).

5   Their role will be subject to evaluation by the Home Office.

6   For example, the Vermont 'Stop It Now' programme (Freeman-Longo and Blanchard 1998). Further information can be obtained from: STOP IT NOW!, PO Box 495, Haydenville, Massachusetts 01039, USA.

References

Association for the Treatment of Sexual Abusers (ATSA) (1996) 'Public notification of sexual offender release' (ATSA statement, 6 November 1996).

Beck, U. (1992) *The Risk Society: Towards a New Modernity*. London: Sage.

Bottoms, A. (1977) 'Reflections on the Renaissance of Dangerousness', *Howard Journal of Criminal Justice*, 16, pp. 70–96.

Bottoms, A. (1995) 'The Politics and Philosophy of Sentencing', in C. Clarkson and R. Morgan (eds) *The Politics of Sentencing*. Oxford: Clarendon Press.

Cavadino, M. and Dignan, J. (1997) *The Penal System: an introduction*, 2nd edition. London: Sage.

Cobley, C. (2000) *Sex Offenders: law, policy and practice*. Bristol: Jordans.

Cosgrove (2001) 'The Report of the Expert Panel on Sex Offending'. Edinburgh: The Scottish Executive.

Crawford, A. (1998) *Crime Prevention and Community Safety: politics, policies and practices*. London: Longman.

Donnelly, A. C. (1997) 'Public Education about Child Abuse and Neglect from 1971–1997: educating ourselves and the future', The 25th Annual Child Abuse and Neglect Symposium, Keystone, Colorado (Sponsored by the Kempe Center, Denver, Colorado).

Ericson, R. V. and Haggerty, K. D. (1997) *Policing and the Risk Society*, Clarendon Studies in Criminology. Oxford: Oxford University Press.

Feeley, M. and Simon, J. (1992) 'The New Penology: notes on the emerging strategy for corrections', *Criminology* 30:4, pp. 449–75.

Feeley, M. and Simon, J. (1994) 'Actuarial Justice: the emerging new criminal law', in D. Nelken (ed.) *The Futures of Criminology*. London: Sage.

Flynn, E. E. (1978) 'Classification for Risk and Supervision – A Preliminary Conceptualization', in J. C. Freeman (ed.) *Prisons Past and Future*. London: Heinemann, pp: 131–49.

Freeman-Longo, R. E. (1996) 'Feel Good Legislation: prevention or calamity?', *Child Abuse and Neglect* 20:2, pp. 95–101.

Freeman-Longo, R. E. and Blanchard, G. T. (1998) *Sexual Abuse in America: epidemic of the 21st century*. Vermont: The Safer Society Press.

Freudenberg, W. R. (1988) 'Perceived Risk, Real Risk: social science and the art of probabilistic risk assessment', *Science* 242, pp. 44–9.

Garland, D. (1995) 'Penal Modernism and Postmodernism', in T. G. Blomberg and S. Cohen (eds) *Punishment and Social Control: essays in honor of Sheldon L. Messinger*. New York: Aldine de Gruyter, pp. 181–209.

Garland, D. (1996) 'The Limits of the Sovereign State: strategies of crime control in contemporary society', *British Journal of Criminology* 36:4, pp. 445–71.

Garland, D. (1997a) 'The Social and Political Context', in R. Burnett (ed.), *The Probation Service: responding to change*, Proceedings of the Probation Studies Unit First Annual Colloquium, December 1996. Probation Studies Unit, Oxford.

Garland, D. (2001) *The culture of crime control: Crime and social order in contemporary society*. Oxford: Oxford University Press.

Giddens, A. (1990) *The Consequences of Modernity*. Cambridge: Polity Press.

Giddens, A. (1998) 'Risk Society: the context of British politics', in J. Franklin (ed.) *The Politics of Risk Society*. Cambridge: Polity Press, pp. 23–4.

Giddens, A. (1991) *Modernity and Self-Identity*. Cambridge: Polity Press.

Gilligan, J. (1996) *Violence: Reflections on a National Epidemic*. New York: Vintage Books.

Guardian (2000) 'Tabloids Naming of Paedophiles is Condemned by Police Chief' (24 July 2000), p. 1.

Hebenton, B. and Thomas, T. (1996) 'Tracking sex offenders', *The Howard Journal* 35:2, pp. 97–112.

Home Office (2001a) 'Initial Guidance to the Police and Probation Services on Sections 67 and 68 of the Criminal Justice and Court Services Act 2000'. London: Home Office.

Home Office (2001b) 'Criminal Justice and Police Act 2001'. London: Home Office.

Home Office (2002) *Justice for All*, Cm 5563, White Paper. London: Home Office.

Hood, C. and Jones, D. K. C. (1996) *Accident and Design: contemporary debates in risk management*. London: University College London.

Hudson, B. (1993) *Penal Policy and Social Justice*. Basingstoke: Macmillan.

Hudson, B. (2002) 'Punishment and Control', in M. Maguire, R. Morgan and R. Reiner (eds) *The Oxford Handbook of Criminology*. Oxford: Oxford University Press, pp. 233–63.

Hughes, G. (1998) *Understanding Crime Prevention: social control, risk and late modernity*. Milton Keynes: Open University Press.

Innes, M. and Fielding, N. (unpublished, 2002) 'The Intelligence Process: information work and the theory and practice of intelligence-led policing', Paper to British Criminology Conference (Keele University, July 2002).

Johnston, L. (2000) *Policing Britain: Risk, Security and Governance*. Harlow: Longman.

Kemshall, H. (1998) *Risk in Probation Practice*. Aldershot: Ashgate.

Kemshall, H. and Maguire, M. (2001) 'Public Protection, Partnership and Risk Penality: the multi-agency risk management of sexual and violent offenders', *Punishment and Society* 3:2, pp. 237–64.

Kemshall, H. and Maguire, M. (2002) 'Community Justice, Risk Management and Multi-Agency Public Protection Panels', *Community Justice* 1:1, pp. 11–27.

Kitzinger, J. (1999a) 'Researching Risk and the Media', *Health, Risk and Society* 1:1, pp. 55–70.

Kitzinger, J. (1999b) 'The Ultimate Neighbour from Hell: media framing of paedophiles', in B. Franklin (ed.), *Social Policy, Media and Misrepresentation*. London: Routledge, pp. 207–21.

Loader, I. and Sparks, R. (2002) 'Contemporary Landscapes of Crime, Order and Control: governance, risk and globalisation', in M. Maguire, R. Morgan, and R. Reiner (eds) *The Oxford Handbook of Criminology*. Oxford: Oxford University Press, pp. 83–111.

Lupton, D. (1999) *Risk*. London: Routledge.

Lynch, M. (1998) 'Waste Managers? The New Penology, Crime Fighting and the Parole Agent Identity', *Law and Society Review* 32:4, pp. 839–69.

Lynch, M. (2000) 'Rehabilitation and Rhetoric: the ideal of reformation in contemporary parole discourse and practices', *Punishment and Society* 2:1, pp. 40–65.

Maguire, M. (1992) 'Parole', in E. Stockdale and S. Casale (eds) *Criminal Justice Under Stress*. London: Blackstone Press.

Maguire, M. (1998) 'POP, ILP and Partnership', *Criminal Justice Matters* 32, pp. 21–2.

Maguire, M. (2000) 'Policing by Risks and Targets: some dimensions and implications of intelligence-led crime control', *Policing and Society* 9, pp. 315–36.

Maguire, M. (2002) 'Crime Statistics: the "data explosion" and its implications', in M. Maguire, R. Morgan and R. Reiner (eds) *The Oxford Handbook of Criminology*. Oxford: Oxford University Press, pp. 322–75.

Maguire, M., Kemshall, H., Noaks, L. and Wincup, E. (2001) 'Risk Management of Sexual and Violent Offenders: the work of public protection panels', Police Research Series Paper 139. London: Home Office.

Mercy, J. A., Rosenberg, M. L., Powell, K. E., Broome, C. V. and Roper, W. L. (1993) 'Public Health Policy for Preventing Violence', *Health Affairs* 12, pp. 7–29.

Muncie, J. (1999) 'Exorcising Demons: media, politics and criminal justice', in B. Franklin (ed.) *Social Policy, The Media and Misrepresentation*. London: Routledge, pp. 174–89.

Nash, M. (1999) *Police, Probation and Protecting the Public*. London: Blackstone.

O'Malley, P. (1992) 'Risk, Power and Crime Prevention', *Economy and Society* 21:3, pp. 252–75.

O' Malley, P. (1999) 'Volatile and Contradictory Punishment', *Theoretical Criminology* 3:2, pp. 175–96.

O'Malley, P. (2000) 'Risk Societies and the Government of Crime', in M. Brown and J. Pratt (eds) *Dangerous Offenders: punishment and social order*. London: Routledge, pp. 17–33.

Pease, K. (2002) 'Crime Reduction' in M. Maguire, R. Morgan and R. Reiner (eds), *The Oxford Handbook of Criminology*. Oxford: Oxford University Press, pp. 947–79.

Petrunik, M. G. (2002) 'Managing Unacceptable Risk: sex offenders, community response, and social policy in the United States and Canada', *International Journal of Offender Therapy and Comparative Criminology*, 46:4, pp. 483–511.

Plotnikoff, J. and Woolfson, R. (2000) 'Where Are They Now? An evaluation of sex offender registration in England and Wales'. London: Home Office.

Pratt, J. (1995) 'Dangerousness, Risk and Technologies of Power', *Australian and New Zealand Journal of Criminology* 29, pp. 236–54.

Pratt, J. (2000) 'The Return of the Wheelbarrow Men: or, the arrival of postmodern penality?', *British Journal of Criminology* 40, pp. 127–45.

Prentky, A. (1996) 'Community Notification and Constructive Risk Reduction', *Journal of Interpersonal Violence* 11:2, pp. 295–8.

Reichman, N. (1986) 'Managing Crime Risks: towards an insurance based model of social control', *Research in Law and Social Control* 8, pp. 151–72.

Robinson, G. (2002) 'Exploring Risk Management in Probation: Contemporary Developments in England and Wales', *Punishment and Society*, 4:1, pp. 5–26.

Rose, N. (1995) 'Governing "Advanced" Liberal Democracies' in A. Barry, T. Osbourne and N. Rose (eds) *Foucault and Political Reason*. London: UCL Press, pp. 37–64.

Rose, N. (2000) 'Government and Control', *British Journal of Criminology* 40, pp. 321–39.

Rudin, J. (1996) 'Megan's Law: can it stop sexual predators – and at what cost to constitutional rights?', *Criminal Justice* 11:3, pp. 2–10.

Sanders, C. R. and Lyon, E. (1995) 'Repetitive Retribution: media images and the cultural construction of criminal justice', in J. Ferrell and C. Sanders (eds) *Cultural Criminology*. Boston, Mass: Northeastern University Press, pp. 25–44.

Schram, D. and Milloy, C. (1995) *Community Notification: a study of offender characteristics and recidivism*. Seattle: Urban Policy Research.

Shearing, C. and Stenning, P. (1981) 'Modern Private Security: its growth and implications' in M. Tonry and N. Morris (eds) *Crime and Justice: An Annual Review of Research* 3. Chicago: University of Chicago Press, pp. 193–245.

Simon , J. (1988) 'The Ideological Affects of Actuarial Practices', *Law and Society Review* 22:4, pp. 772–800.

Slovic, P. (1992) 'Perceptions of Risk: reflections on the psychometric paradigm' in S. Krimsky and D. Golding (eds) *Social Theories of Risk*. Westport, USA: Praeger, pp. 117–52.

Soothill, K., Francis, B. and Ackerley, E. (1998) 'Paedophilia and Paedophiles', *New Law Journal* 148, pp. 882–3.

Stenson, K. and Sullivan, R. (eds) (2001) *Crime, Risk and Justice: the politics of crime control in liberal democracies*. Devon: Willan Publishing.

Tewksbury, R. (2002) 'Validity and Utility of the Kentucky Sex Offender Registry', *Federal Probation* June, pp. 21–6.

Thomas, T. (2001) 'Sex Offenders, the Home Office and the Sunday Papers', *Journal of Social Welfare and Family Law* 23:1, pp. 103–4.

Thompson, K. (1998) *Moral Panics*. London: Routledge.

Velez, M. B. (2001) 'The Role of Public Social Control in Urban Neighbourhoods: a multi-level analysis of victimization risk', *Criminology* 39:4, pp. 837–64.

Walters, A. (2001) *Acid Row*. London: MacMillan.

Wasik, M. and Taylor, R. D. (1991) *Blackstone's Guide to the Criminal Justice Act 1991*. Oxford: Blackstone Press.

Wilczynski, A. and Sinclair, K. (1999) 'Moral Tales: representations of child abuse in the quality and tabloid media', *The Australian and New Zealand Journal of Criminology* 32:3, pp. 262–83.

Worrall, A. (1997) *Punishment in the Community: The Future of Criminal Justice*. London: Longman.

www.bbc.co.uk (2001), 'Do We Need a "Sarah's Law"', 13 December 2001.

www.parentsformeganslaw/communityapproach 'Understanding Your Local School's Role and the Role of Parents for Megan's Law in Helping to Manage Sex Offender Notifications in Your Community'.

Young, A. (1996) *Imagining Crime: textual outlaws and criminal conversations*. London: Sage.

Zevitz, R. and Farkas, M. (2000a) 'Sex Offender Community Notification: managing high risk criminals or exacting further vengeance?', *Behavioural Sciences and the Law* 18:2/3, pp. 375–91.

Zevitz, R. and Farkas, M. (2000b) 'Sex Offender Community Notification: examining the importance of neighbourhood meetings', *Behavioural Sciences and the Law* 18:2/3, pp. 393–408.

Chapter 6

Interpreting the treatment performance of sex offenders

Michael C. Seto

Introduction

Treatment is a common component of the criminal justice response to sexual offending in many jurisdictions. For example, in Canada, incarcerated sex offenders who are applying for conditional release into the community are expected to participate in institutional treatment, and many will receive community-based treatment while under parole supervision. In addition, information about sex offenders' performance in treatment influences decisions made about them with regard to sentencing, institutional placement, conditional release and level of community supervision. It is, therefore, important to determine the best way to interpret the treatment performance of sex offenders.

I will comment briefly on a number of methodological issues to consider before reviewing the relevant literature on treatment performance. These issues include the definition of treatment performance, how it is measured and how it is typically analysed.

Methodological issues

Definition of treatment performance

Treatment performance is defined broadly as an offender's involvement in treatment (reflected in his attendance, motivation for treatment and level of participation in therapy sessions), compliance with treatment rules and expectations, and attainment of treatment goals (learning the principles underlying the treatment approach, understanding treatment concepts and developing new skills). These variables can be distinguished conceptually between those having to do with non-specific aspects of treatment performance (such as motivation for treatment and compliance with programme rules and expectations), and those having to do with specific aspects of treatment performance (such as skills acquisition). Researchers who have examined treatment performance have rarely distinguished between these two domains.

Measurement

Most measures of treatment performance are based on clinician ratings (e.g. Anderson, Gibeau and D'Amora 1995; Stirpe, Wilson and Long 2001). Although therapists can obviously shed a great deal of light on how participants in treatment programmes have done, they may also be vulnerable to biases in making their ratings because of their close involvement with the participants. Measures of treatment performance might be less influenced by these biases if the measuring process were undertaken (at least in part) by raters who were not involved in providing treatment and who used specific, objective criteria (e.g. demonstrating new skills in a role-playing situation).

Static or dynamic risk factor

Another conceptual and methodological issue to consider in this research literature is when treatment performance is measured. Treatment performance can be analysed as a potential static risk factor or as a potential dynamic risk factor. Static risk factors are defined here as those predictors of recidivism that are historical or very unlikely to change. Examples of static risk factors include prior offence history and psychopathy (Rice and Harris 1997). Actuarial risk scales for use with sex offenders – such as the Static-99 (Hanson and Thornton 2000) and Sex Offender Risk Appraisal Guide (Quinsey et al. 1998) – are comprised of static risk factors and are good predictors of recidivism over the long term (see Hanson, Morton and Harris, 2003, for a review). In contrast, dynamic risk factors are defined here as those predictors of recidivism that can change over time. To be truly dynamic, changes in a putative dynamic risk factor must be shown to be associated with changes in the likelihood of recidivism. Examples of potential dynamic risk factors include peer relationships, attitudes tolerant of sexual offending, and noncompliance with supervision or treatment requirements (Quinsey et al. 1997; Hanson and Harris 2000; Hudson et al. 2002; Quinsey 2002).

Treatment performance is commonly assessed at the end of a treatment programme, to determine whether an individual has successfully completed the treatment and to make decisions about conditional release, among other considerations. In these situations, treatment performance is measured once and is therefore a potential static risk factor. Changes in treatment performance can also be considered among those who are already at risk to re-offend, such as participants in community-based treatment programmes. In these situations, treatment performance can be measured repeatedly, and can therefore be a potential dynamic risk factor.

Interpreting treatment performance

Outcome studies have typically examined treatment performance as a potential static risk factor. In non-forensic clinical practice, there is some evidence that better treatment performance is related to better outcomes (e.g., Chamberlain et al. 1984; Startup and Edmonds 1994; Murran et al. 1995). However, this relationship may not be true for offenders seen in forensic practice. Unlike voluntary treatment participants in many areas of clinical practice, a substantial proportion of offenders, including sex offenders, deny that they have a problem requiring treatment. Sex offenders claim they have not committed the offences for which they were convicted (Barbaree 1991, Kennedy and Grubin 1992), and many say they do not want to participate in treatment focusing on sexual offending, although they are often willing to participate in other kinds of treatment (Langevin, Wright and Handy 1988). Nonetheless, these people often enter sex offender treatment because it is ordered by the courts, it is a condition of their probation or parole, or they are pressured by their spouse or romantic partner, family members or social service workers.

No published studies have compared the outcomes of sex offenders who enter treatment voluntarily with those who entered treatment as a result of external pressure. Looking to related areas of practice, there is some evidence from substance abuse research that legally pressured clients do not differ from voluntary clients in terms of treatment retention and other outcomes. For example, Brecht, Anglin, and Wang (1993) reported that differences in the amount of legal pressure experienced by methadone maintenance clients were not related to subsequent drug use and criminal involvement. Prendergast et al. (2002) found that legally pressured and voluntary inmates who participated in substance abuse treatment did not differ in terms of self-reported within-treatment change on psychological variables such as self-esteem, depression and anxiety, discharge on parole, or agreeing to participate in treatment once in the community. Ryan, Plant, and O'Malley (1995) studied 98 alcoholic outpatients and found that treatment participation as a condition of probation was unrelated to treatment attendance and retention. However, the best treatment attendance and retention were found for participants who were required to participate as a condition of probation and who at the same time reported high levels of interest in their involvement in treatment.

There is even some evidence that legally pressured clients do better. Knight et al. (2000) found that both readiness for change assessed at the beginning of treatment and legal pressure independently predicted programme retention among offenders in substance abuse treatment. Young and Belenko (2001) found that substance abuse treatment clients recognised the degree of legal pressure applied to them, and that greater legal pressure was associated with lower dropout rates.

Sex offender treatment performance

A number of studies have examined the relationship between aspects of treatment performance and outcomes among sex offenders. All of these studies examined treatment performance as a potential static risk factor. Two studies found no relationship, one found a positive relationship, and three found a negative relationship.

Jenkins-Hall (1994) assessed acceptance of responsibility, attendance and level of participation in therapy sessions to predict mastery of programme content in a sample of sex offenders. These aspects of treatment performance predicted proficiency with the principles and concepts of rational-emotive therapy, but did not predict proficiency with the principles and concepts of relapse prevention, which is currently among the most popular approaches in the treatment of sex offenders (see Marshall et al. 1998). Quinsey, Khanna, and Malcolm (1998) reported on a follow-up study of sex offenders treated at the Regional Treatment Centre, a treatment programme based in a Canadian maximum-security penitentiary, and found that a clinician rating of treatment gain was unrelated to either serious recidivism in general or sexual recidivism in particular among 193 treated sex offenders, even though treated sex offenders showed significant improvements on within-treatment measures.

In terms of a positive relationship, Marques and her colleagues recently reported on sex offenders who participated in an institutional treatment programme in California (the well-known Sex Offender Treatment and Evaluation Project, or SOTEP). Participants who obtained positive post-treatment scores on phallometrically-measured sexual arousal, attitudes and beliefs about sexual offending, and ratings of their relapse prevention assignments, were less likely to re-offend than those who did not obtain positive post-treatment scores, even after statistically controlling for actuarially-estimated risk to reoffend (Marques et al. 2002). These results were consistent with those previously reported for a smaller sample of child sexual abusers who participated in the SOTEP programme (Marques et al. 1994).

In terms of a negative relationship, Sadoff, Roether, and Peters (1971) found that sex offenders who, when asked at the end of treatment, reported that group psychotherapy was helpful were more, rather than less, likely to be re-arrested than sex offenders who complained about their involvement in group therapy.

We recently reported the results of a follow-up study of 224 sex offenders who were treated at the Warkworth Sexual Behaviour Clinic, a Canadian prison-based treatment programme (Seto and Barbaree 1999). This programme followed a relapse prevention model and provided treatment in daily three-hour group sessions, five days a week, over a five-month period. Some participants also attended individual physiological conditioning sessions to reduce deviant sexual arousal, if this was identified as a treatment target in initial phallometric testing for sexual interests in prepubescent children or non-consenting sex. The main treatment targets at the Warkworth Sexual Behaviour Clinic were acceptance of responsibility for offences, victim empathy, understanding of one's offence cycle (the typical sequence of thoughts, feelings and behaviours preceding sexual offences and related problematic behaviour such as masturbating to deviant sexual fantasies), and development of an individually tailored relapse prevention plan.

As shown in Table 6.1, our measure of treatment performance included items tapping non-specific aspects such as the offender's attendance, level of participation in therapy, and interactions with others during group sessions, as well as items tapping specific aspects of skills and knowledge acquisition, including quality of homework assignments in victim empathy exercises, understanding of offence cycle, and development of a relapse prevention plan. The measure also included therapist ratings of motivation for treatment and overall behaviour change. Except for the two therapist ratings, the items on our measure were coded by research assistants based on clinical notes kept by the therapists and the original written homework assignments completed by the offenders.

Contrary to our expectations, good treatment performance was not associated with lower rates of recidivism during the average follow-up period of 32 months. In fact, good treatment performance was associated with higher rates of recidivism. This was especially true among individuals scoring higher in psychopathy. Men who scored higher on psychopathy on the Psychopathy Checklist-Revised (PCL-R: Hare 1991) and who performed well in treatment were almost four times as likely to commit a new serious offence, defined as a new non-sexually violent or new sexual offence, during the follow-up (see Figure 6.1). This was a very interesting finding because other studies have found

Table 6.1 Treatment performance measure used in Seto and Barbaree (1999, 2003)

Item	Rating
Behaviour in group	
Attendance (tardiness or absence)	1 = very poor
	2 = poor
	3 = good
Level of participation	1 = very poor
	2 = poor
	3 = good
Helpfulness to others in group	1 = unhelpful
	2 = helpful
Appropriateness of interactions with other clients and staff	1 = very inappropriate
	2 = inappropriate
	3 = appropriate
Disruptiveness of conduct in group sessions	1 = very disruptive
	2 = disruptive
	3 = not disruptive
Treatment progress	
Change in victim empathy	1 = less empathic
	2 = unchanged
	3 = more empathic
Understanding of offense cycle	1 = very poor
	2 = poor
	3 = good
	4 = very good
Quality of relapse prevention plan	1 = poor
	2 = satisfactory
	3 = good
Clinician ratings	
Motivation for treatment	Rated 1 (low) to 5 (high)
Overall behaviour change	Rated 1 (low) to 5 (high)

that psychopathic offenders are adversely affected by treatment, while non-psychopathic offenders appear to benefit (Hare et al. 2000; Rice, Harris and Cormier 1992).

Looman et al. (2002) recently reported results similar to those described above in a different sample of convicted sex offenders treated at a correctional psychiatric centre (Regional Treatment Centre) using a diagnostic Psychopathy Checklist-Revised (PCL-R) cutoff score of 25 for identifying psychopaths. They also found that men who performed well

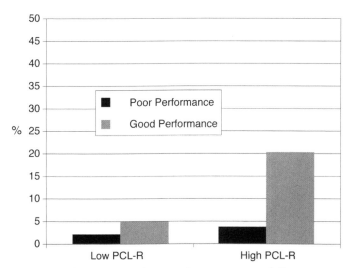

Figure 6.1 Rates of serious recidivism after an average follow-up period of 32 months
Followed to November 1996, using federal agency recidivism data (Seto and Barbaree 1999). PCL-R = Psychopathy Checklist-Revised Score. Offenders divided into groups according to median splits on PCL-R and treatment performance scores.

in treatment, in terms of ratings of change in victim empathy, under-standing of offence cycle, quality of relapse prevention plan, and global performance, and who scored higher in psychopathy were more likely than other offenders in the sample to seriously re-offend during the follow-up period of four to five years.

We have since extended the follow-up of the sex offender sample studied by Seto and Barbaree (1999), almost doubling the average time at risk in the community from 32 to 62 months, to determine whether the relationship between treatment performance and recidivism held up over time (Seto and Barbaree 2003). In the latest follow-up, treatment performance was not related to either general or serious recidivism (see Figure 6.2). As in Seto and Barbaree (1999), sex offenders who scored higher in psychopathy were approximately twice as likely to seriously re-offend as sex offenders who scored lower in psychopathy. A recent follow-up study of a larger sample of sex offenders assessed at the same clinic also found that treatment performance was unrelated to serious recidivism (Langton et al. 2002).

One explanation for the difference between Seto and Barbaree (1999) and Seto and Barbaree (2003) was the source of recidivism data that was used. The original follow-up study was conducted using correctional

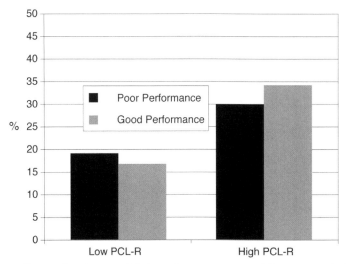

Figure 6.2 Rates of serious recidivism after an average follow-up period of 62 months
Followed to April 2000, using national police recidivism data. PCL-R = Psychopathy Checklist-Revised Score. Offenders divided into groups according to median splits on PCL-R and treatment performance scores.

and parole board records, and could have missed re-offences that resulted in provincial sentences (in Canada, sentences of two years or more are served in federal penitentiaries while shorter sentences are served in provincial institutions). In contrast, the new follow-up study used a national police database that captures all new convictions in Canada, regardless of sentence length. Although this change in data source did make a noticeable difference in the magnitude of the effect, men who were better in treatment performance and higher in psychopathy still tended to be more likely to seriously re-offend when we analysed recidivism up to November 1996 (the end-date of the Seto and Barbaree (1999) follow-up study), using the more comprehensive source of outcome data (see Figure 6.3).

Conclusion

Overall, there is little evidence to support the claim that sex offender treatment performance is a static risk factor, such that good treatment performance is related to lower long-term risk to seriously re-offend among sex offenders. This is an important finding because it suggests that adjusting estimates of long-term risk to re-offend based on treatment

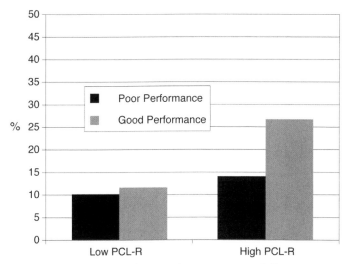

Figure 6.3 Rates of serious recidivism after an average follow-up period of 32 months
Followed to November 1996, using national police recidivism data. PCL-R = Psychopathy Checklist-Revised Score. Offenders divided into groups according to median splits on PCL-R and treatment performance scores.

performance or reporting that a sex offender is lower in risk because of good treatment performance exhibited while participating in a treatment programme is not empirically supported (cf. Looman et al. 2002; Quinsey et al. 1998, but see also Marques et al. 2002).

It is still possible, however, that treatment performance is a dynamic risk factor that predicts the imminence of any serious recidivism that might occur among individuals at a given level of long-term risk to re-offend. In this view, treatment performance is an assay of offender motivation, attitudes and compliance; there is some evidence that these variables are dynamic risk factors (Quinsey et al. 1997; Hanson and Harris 2000; Quinsey 2002).

No studies have yet examined whether changes in treatment performance, requiring at least two measurements over time, predict recidivism over and above the established static risk factors that comprise validated actuarial risk scales. Such studies will probably need to be conducted in community-based treatment programmes for sex offenders, because opportunity to sexually re-offend is limited in institutional settings (although problematic behaviour such as masturbating to deviant sexual fantasies or sexually harassing staff can occur anywhere). Multiple measurements are required because demonstrating that information about treatment performance, assessed once, predicts recidivism does not tell us whether treatment performance is a dynamic risk factor. As some have noted, any variable (changeable or not) assessed at only one point in time is just like a static variable (Rice, Harris and Quinsey 2002; Harris and Rice 2003). Such an empirical demonstration tells us only that treatment performance is a potential actuarial risk scale item, if it adds to the predictive accuracy provided by existing actuarial risk scales (Beech et al. 2002; Thornton 2002).

To establish treatment performance as a dynamic risk factor, we need research to determine whether changes in treatment performance are related to problematic behaviour and recidivism among sex offenders who are at risk in the community. This research is methodologically difficult, but it can be done. The Ontario Forensic Risk Study, a study of dynamic risk factors among mentally disordered offenders, is an excellent example of how to conduct this kind of research (Quinsey 2002; see http://pavlov.psyc.queensu.ca/~ofrs/).

Future directions

The development of valid actuarial risk scales has allowed professionals working with sex offenders to determine accurately *who* is more likely to seriously re-offend (e.g. Barbaree et al. 2001). In fact, high levels of predictive accuracy can be obtained when actuarial risk scales are scored under optimal conditions, including no missing items, high rater reliability and constant follow-up periods (Harris and Rice 2003). Even if future research does demonstrate that treatment performance, assessed once, is related to recidivism among sex offenders, it will remain to be determined whether information about treatment performance adds to the predictive accuracy that can already be obtained by existing actuarial risk scales.

At the same time, we know much less about *when* offences are more likely to occur. Determining the imminence of any re-offence that might occur among individuals at a particular level of long-term risk to re-offend would be of obvious importance to clinicians and criminal justice officials who must make decisions about treatment and supervision. Putative dynamic risk factors such as changes in treatment performance, assessed on at least two occasions, could be a valuable aid to sex offender management efforts in the community. However, we need research on this question before we can interpret treatment performance in this manner.

Distinguishing genuine treatment performance

An important issue for this line of research is to distinguish genuine from simulated treatment performance. Sex offender treatment is predicated on the assumption that offenders who want to refrain from re-offending will be more successful if they understand the principles and concepts of the treatment approach, learn the skills that are being taught, and use those skills when they are in risky situations. However, some offenders can develop their understanding and learn the skills without intending to apply what they have gained from treatment to avoid re-offending once they are released (cf. those sex offenders who are on the approach path described by Hudson and Ward 2000, and who are excited rather than worried by the prospects of committing a sexual offence). We need methods to assess genuine treatment performance.

Reliable behavioural competency measures could be very useful in this regard (see Miner 2000). Another approach is to focus on initial treatment performance scores. Marques et al. (1989) found that only about a third of sex offenders who participated in the SOTEP programme had a satisfactory understanding of their offence cycles and relapse prevention plans after completing six months of treatment, whereas all of them had developed a satisfactory understanding by the third time they were assessed in these areas, presumably because they had received sufficient feedback and coaching from therapists and other treatment participants. The possibility that treatment performance scores are less likely to be predictive of future outcomes, to the extent that they represent help by others, is an intriguing one, especially in light of data recently reported by Beech and Fisher (2000). These investigators found that sex offenders with child victims who were treated in English or Welsh prisons and who showed improvement in their understanding of offence cycles and relapse prevention, but who did not show positive changes in their empathy for victims and attitudes about sex with children, did not maintain their improvement nine months after the programme ended. They also reported a qualitative observation that these men relied more on staff and others for help in developing their relapse prevention plans than men who showed improvement in all of the areas described above.

Yet another approach is to focus on sex offenders who had no obvious external incentives for participating in treatment. One explanation for the difference in findings reported by Marques et al. (2002) for the SOTEP programme and those reported for the other treatment programmes – Warkworth Sexual Behaviour Clinic and Regional Treatment Centre – is the absence of an obvious external incentive for participating in the SOTEP programme. Offenders were eligible for the two-year SOTEP programme only if they had 18–30 months remaining of their prison term, and they were released on parole independent of any clinical assessment of their treatment progress or risk to re-offend. In contrast, many sex offenders are legally pressured to participate in treatment, and clinical assessments of treatment response are highly related to decisions made about offenders, such as receiving parole (e.g. Barbaree and Seto 1998; Quinsey, Khanna and Malcolm 1998). Treatment performance in a sex offender programme without external incentives may be a more genuine measure than treatment performance in a programme in which sex offenders have obvious incentives to participate. Of course, the large majority of sex offenders are legally pressured to participate in treatment, so the theoretical value of Marques et al.'s (2002) findings is high, but the clinical utility is unclear without more work in this area. We need measures of motivation to change that are not vulnerable to socially desirable response if we are to address the question of whether offenders who are truly motivated to refrain from re-offending differ in outcomes from those who are not so motivated.

Treatment refusal and drop-out

If future studies confirm that treatment performance is unrelated to recidivism among sex offenders, we will need to reconcile such findings with evidence that poor treatment performance is related to higher rates of treatment drop-out, and treatment drop-out is a significant predictor of recidivism among sex offenders (Hanson and Bussière 1998) and non-sex offenders (Wormith and Olver 2002). Moreover, a recent re-examination of the sex offender treatment outcome studies reviewed in a meta-analysis by Hanson et al. (2002) suggests that refusing to participate in treatment is also associated with greater rates of recidivism (Rice and Harris 2003). How can refusal to participate in treatment and dropping out of treatment be significantly and positively related to sex offender recidivism when poor treatment performance is not?

One possibility is that refusing to participate or dropping out of treatment is a purer indicator of motivation for treatment and compliance than typical indicators of treatment performance such as attendance and level of participation in group therapy sessions. A related possibility is that treatment refusal or drop-out is a purer indicator of antisociality than treatment performance. However, in the sample described by Seto and Barbaree (2003), scores on a very good indicator of antisociality (the PCL-R) had the same correlation (.12) with both treatment drop-out and treatment performance. A third possibility is that the amount of variance in motivation to change and other aspects of treatment performance is reduced among offenders who participate in treatment after those who refuse treatment or drop out of treatment early on are eliminated from the study sample. This lowers the potential for treatment performance to be significantly associated with recidivism.

More research on the predictors of treatment drop-out among sex offenders is needed. A meta-analysis of the general psychotherapy literature found that individual characteristics such as participant age, education and socio-economic status predicted drop-out (Wierzbicki and Pekarik 1993). Research on substance abuse treatment can also shed light on the relevant predictors of drop-out among sex offenders. For example, Sung, Belenko and Feng (2001) found that offenders participating in substance abuse treatment varied in their compliance with programme rules and expectations. A small group of severe non-compliers accounted for the majority of incidents recorded, but many offenders engaged in some non-compliance during treatment. Not surprisingly, treatment non-compliance was a significant predictor of treatment drop-out, and was in turn predicted by offender age, poor education and employment history, and early involvement in the criminal justice system. Sung et al. noted that these factors are also predictors of substance abuse and crime, and suggest that substance abuse, crime and treatment non-compliance may originate from the same causes. A number of studies have similarly found that empirically established risk factors among sex offenders – offender age, offence history, marital status and antisocial personality disorder – are associated with drop-out among sex offenders (Abel et al. 1988; Browne, Foreman and Middleton 1998; Moore, Bergman and Knox 1999; Dillinger and Strassberg 2002; but see Shaw, Herkov and Greer 1995).

It would be interesting to see if sex offenders who voluntarily drop out of treatment differ from those who are expelled from treatment programmes because of their non-compliance and disruptive behaviour. Abel et al. (1988) found that a majority of sex offenders who dropped out of treatment did so voluntarily, while only a small minority were terminated because of their disruptive behaviour. Of note, Wormith and Olver (2002) found that non-sex offenders who were expelled from treatment did not differ in their rates of recidivism from those who chose to withdraw from the programme. The two groups also did not differ from each other in ratings of their attendance, motivation, attitude toward treatment, acceptance of responsibility, global improvement and homework completion. However, they did differ in their disruptiveness on the treatment unit, with expelled offenders rated as more disruptive than those who withdrew.

Finally, it would be informative to determine whether therapeutic engagement techniques such as motivational interviewing and orientation sessions are effective in reducing treatment refusal and drop-out among offenders. It would also be useful to determine whether these therapeutic engagement interventions have an impact on recidivism.

Effectiveness of treatment

More research on the relationship between treatment performance and recidivism among sex offenders will shed a great deal of light on the crucial question of sex offender treatment efficacy. Hanson et al.'s (2002) meta-analysis of 43 treatment outcome studies found that sex offenders who participated in cognitive-behavioural treatments had lower rates of sexual (10 per cent) and general (32 per cent) recidivism than those who did not (17 per cent and 51 per cent, respectively).[1] If it is true that contemporary sex offender treatment methods such as cognitive-behaviour therapy and relapse prevention can reduce recidivism, one would expect good treatment performance in a cognitive-behavioural relapse prevention programme to be related to treatment outcome. In other words, we would expect those who learn more in an appropriate treatment to be less likely to re-offend than those who learn less.

This kind of research could advance both our knowledge of the causes of sexual offending and the likely components of effective sex offender treatment. For example, finding that treatment performance in social skills training – level of participation, compliance with training requirements and actual change in social skills – predicts sex offender recidivism would suggest that social skills deficits are one of the causes of sexual re-offending, and would suggest that social skills training is an important part of sex offender treatment. Of course, demonstrating such a relationship is a necessary but not sufficient condition. Failing to find this relationship, on the other hand, would indicate that social skills deficits are not causally related to sexual re-offending, and would indicate that other targets should be the focus of treatment planning.[2]

Careful consideration of theoretically-derived types of sex offender could also guide the matching of treatments to sex offenders. Different sex offender types may have different causal factors, and therefore different treatment targets. For example, future research may find that improvement in social skills is actually associated with greater recidivism among psychopathic sex offenders, who hypothetically use the skills they learn to manipulate others more effectively and gain access to victims; at the same time it is associated with lower recidivism among non-psychopathic sex offenders, who hypothetically use the skills to develop more stable relationships with consenting adult partners. Failure to distinguish between these two theoretically and empirically different types of sex offender would obscure the interpretation of treatment performance results. It is clear that systematic investigation of the relationship between performance on different components of treatment and recidivism should be a top priority in future sex offender treatment research, because the results of this research could guide the evolution of more effective treatments.

Contact details and acknowledgements

Correspondence should be addressed to Michael Seto, Law and Mental Health Program, Centre for Addiction and Mental Health, Unit 3 – 1001 Queen Street West, Toronto, Ontario, Canada, M6J 1H4. Email: Michael_ Seto@camh.net.

I would like to thank Lucy Berliner, Grant Harris, Martin Lalumière, Calvin Langton, Janice Marques, Vern Quinsey, Marnie Rice, and David Thornton for their very helpful comments on an earlier version of this chapter.

Notes

1 Whether this is evidence of treatment efficacy has been debated, however, given the fact that the methodologically best studies, those involving random assignment to treatment versus comparison conditions, did not find a positive effect for treatment (see Rice and Harris, 2003).

2 This approach assumes that changes observed within treatment persist during the course of the follow-up period.

References

Abel, G. G., Mittelman, M., Becker, J. V., Rathner, J. and Rouleau, J.-L. (1988) 'Predicting child molesters' response to treatment', *Annals of the New York Academy of Sciences* 528, pp. 223–34.

Anderson, R. D., Gibeau, D. and D'Amora, B. A. (1995) 'The Sex Offender Treatment Rating Scale: initial reliability data', *Sexual Abuse* 7, pp. 221–7.

Barbaree, H. E. (1991) 'Denial and Minimization Among Sex Offenders: assessment and treatment outcome', *Forum on Corrections Research* 3, pp. 30–3.

Barbaree, H. E. and Seto, M. C. (1998) 'The Ongoing Follow-up of Sex Offenders Treated at the Warkworth Sexual Behaviour Clinic' (Research report prepared for the Correctional Service of Canada).

Barbaree, H. E., Seto, M. C., Langton, C. M. and Peacock, E. J. (2001) 'Evaluating the Predictive Accuracy of Six Risk Assessment Instruments for Adult Sex Offenders', *Criminal Justice and Behavior* 28, p. 490–521.

Beech, A. and Fisher, D. (2000) 'Maintaining relapse prevention skills and strategies in treated child abusers', in D. R. Laws, S. M. Hudson and T. Ward (eds), *Remaking Relapse Prevention with Sex Offenders: a sourcebook*. Thousand Oaks, California: Sage, pp. 455–65.

Beech, A., Friendship, C., Erikson, M. and Hanson, R.K. (2002) 'The Relationship between Static and Dynamic Risk Factors and Reconviction in a Sample of U.K. Child Abusers', *Sexual Abuse* 14, pp. 155–67.

Brecht, M. L., Anglin, M. D. and Wang, J. (1993) 'Treatment Effectiveness for Legally Coerced versus Voluntary Methadone Maintenance Clients', *American Journal of Drug and Alcohol Abuse* 19, pp. 89–106.

Browne, K. D., Foreman, L. and Middleton, D. (1998) 'Predicting Treatment Drop-out in Sex Offenders', *Child Abuse Review* 7, 402–19.

Chamberlain, P., Patterson, G., Reid, J., Kavanagh, K. and Forgatch, M. (1984) 'Observation of Client Resistance', *Behavior Therapy* 15, pp. 144–55.

Dillinger, R. J. and Strassberg, D. S. (2002, October) 'Factors in Assessing Likelihood of Treatment Completion of Sex Offenders', Paper presented at the 21st Annual Conference of the Association for the Treatment of Sexual Abusers (Montréal, Québec).

Hanson, R. K. and Bussière, M .T. (1998) 'Predicting Relapse: a meta-analysis of sexual offender recidivism studies', *Journal of Consulting and Clinical Psychology* 66, pp. 348–62.

Hanson, R. K., Gordon, A., Harris, A. J. R., Marques, J. K., Murphy, W., Quinsey, V. L. and Seto, M. C. (2002) 'First Report of the Collaborative Outcome Data Project on the Effectiveness of Treatment for Sex Offenders', *Sexual Abuse* 14, pp. 169–94.

Hanson, R. K. and Harris, A. J. R. (2000) 'Where should we intervene? Dynamic predictors of sex offence recidivism', *Criminal Justice and Behavior* 27, pp. 6–35.

Hanson, R. K., Morton, K. E. and Harris, A. J. R. (2003) 'Sexual Offender Recidivism Risk: what we know and what we need to know', *Annals of the New York Academy of Sciences*, 989, 154–66.

Hanson, R. K. and Thornton, D. (2000) 'Improving Risk Assessments for Sex Offenders: a comparison of three actuarial scales', *Law and Human Behavior* 24, pp. 119–36.

Hare, R. D. (1991) *Manual for the Revised Psychopathy Checklist*. Toronto: Multi-Health Systems.

Hare, R. D., Clark, D., Grann, M. and Thornton, D. (2000) 'Psychopathy and the Predictive Validity of the PCL-R: an international perspective', *Behavioral Sciences and the Law* 18, pp. 623–45.

Harris, G. T. and Rice, M. E. (2003) 'Actuarial Assessment of Risk among Sex Offenders', *Annals of the New York Academy of Sciences*, 989, 198–210.

Hudson, S. M., Wales, D. S., Bakker, L. and Ward, T. (2002) 'Dynamic risk factors: the Kia Marama evaluation', *Sexual Abuse* 14, pp. 103–19.

Hudson, S. M. and Ward, T. (2000) 'Relapse Prevention: assessment and treatment implications', in D. R. Laws, S. M. Hudson and T. Ward (eds), *Remaking Relapse Prevention with Sex Offenders: a sourcebook*. Thousand Oaks, California: Sage, pp. 102–122.

Jenkins-Hall, K. (1994) 'Outpatient Treatment of Child Molesters: motivational factors and outcome', *Journal of Offender Rehabilitation* 21, pp. 139–50.

Kennedy, H. and Grubin, D. (1992) 'Patterns of Denial in Sex Offenders', *Psychological Medicine* 22, 191–96.

Knight, K., Hiller, M. L., Broome, K. M. and Simpson, D. D. (2000) 'Legal Pressure, Treatment Readiness, and Engagement in Long-term Residential Programmes', *Journal of Offender Rehabilitation* 31, pp. 101–15.

Langevin, R., Wright, P. and Handy, L. C. (1988) 'What Treatment Do Sex Offenders Want?' *Annals of Sex Research* 1, pp. 363–85.

Langton, C. M., Barbaree, H. E., Seto, M. C., Harkins, L. and Peacock, E. (2002) 'How Should We Interpret Behavior in Treatment?' Paper presented at the 21st Annual Conference of the Association for the Treatment of Sexual Abusers (Montréal, Québec).

Looman, J., Abracen, J., Serin, R. and Marquis, P. (2002) *Psychopathy, Treatment Change and Recidivism in High Risk High Need Sexual Offenders.* (manuscript submitted for publication). [See also Marquis, P., Abracen, J. and Looman, J. (2001) 'Psychopathy, Treatment Change and Recidivism with Sexual Offenders', Paper presented at the 20th Annual Conference of the Association for the Treatment of Sexual Abusers (San Antonio, Texas).]

Marques, J., Day, D. M., Nelson, C. and Miner, M. H. (1989) 'The Sex Offender Treatment and Evaluation Project: California's relapse prevention programme', in D. R. Laws (ed.), *Relapse Prevention with Sex Offenders.* New York: Guilford, pp. 247–67.

Marques, J., Day, D. M., Wiederanders, M. and Nelson, C. (2002) 'Main Effects and Beyond: new findings from California's Sex Offender Treatment and Evaluation Project (SOTEP)', Paper presented at the 21st Annual Conference of the Association for the Treatment of Sexual Abusers (Montréal, Québec).

Marques, J., Nelson, C., West, M. A. and Day, D. M. (1994) 'The Relationship between Treatment Goals and Recidivism among Child Molesters', *Behaviour Research and Therapy* 32, pp. 577–88.

Marshall, W. L., Fernandez, Y. M., Hudson, S. M. and Ward, T. (eds) (1998) *Sourcebook of Treatment Programmes for Sexual Offenders.* New York: Plenum.

Miner, M. H. (2000) 'Competency-based Assessment', in D. R. Laws, S. M. Hudson and T. Ward (eds), *Remaking Relapse Prevention with Sex Offenders: a sourcebook.* Thousand Oaks, California: Sage, pp. 213–24.

Moore, D. L., Bergman, B. A. and Knox, P. L. (1999) 'Predictors of Sex Offender Treatment Completion', *Journal of Child Sexual Abuse* 7, pp. 73–88.

Murran, J. C., Gorman, B. S., Safran, J. D., Twining, L., Samstag, L. W. and Winston, A. (1995) 'Linking In-session Change to Overall Outcome in Short-term Cognitive Therapy', *Journal of Consulting and Clinical Psychology* 63, pp. 651–7.

Prendergast, M. L., Farabee, D., Cartier, J. and Henkin, S. (2002) 'Involuntary Treatment within a Prison Setting: impact on psychosocial change during treatment', *Criminal Justice and Behavior* 29, pp. 5–26.

Quinsey, V. L. (2002, September) 'Static and Dynamic Risk Factors in the Prediction of Violent and Sexual Recidivism', Paper presented at the 7th Conference of the International Association for the Treatment of Sexual Abusers (Vienna, Austria).

Quinsey, V. L., Coleman, G., Jones, B., Altrows, I. F. (1997) 'Proximal Antecedents of Eloping and Reoffending among Supervised Mentally Disordered Offenders', *Journal of Interpersonal Violence* 12, pp. 794–813.

Quinsey, V. L., Harris, G. T., Rice, M. E. and Cormier, C. A. (1998) *Violent Offenders: appraising and managing risk*. Washington, DC: American Psychological Association.

Quinsey, V. L., Khanna, A. and Malcolm, P. B. (1998) 'A Retrospective Evaluation of the Regional Treatment Centre Sex Offender Treatment Program', *Journal of Interpersonal Violence* 13, pp. 621–44.

Rice, M. E. and Harris, G. T. (1997) 'Cross-validation and Extension of the Violence Risk Appraisal Guide for Child Molesters and Rapists', *Law and Human Behavior* 21, pp. 231–41.

Rice, M. E. and Harris, G. T. (2003) 'The Size and Sign of Treatment Effects in Sex Offender Therapy', *Annals of the New York Academy of Sciences*, 989, 428–40.

Rice, M. E., Harris, G. T. and Cormier, C. (1992) 'Evaluation of a Maximum Security Therapeutic Community for Psychopaths and Other Mentally Disordered Offenders', *Law and Human Behavior* 16, pp. 399–412.

Rice, M. E., Harris, G. T. and Quinsey, V. L. (2002) 'The Appraisal of Violence Risk', *Current Opinion in Psychiatry* 15, pp. 589–93.

Ryan, R. M., Plant, R. W. and O'Malley, S. (1995) 'Initial Motivations for Alcohol Treatment: Relations with patient characteristics, treatment involvement, and dropout', *Addictive Behaviors* 20, pp. 279–97.

Sadoff, R. L., Roether, H. A. and Peters, J. J. (1971) 'Clinical Measure of Enforced Group Psychotherapy', *American Journal of Psychiatry* 128, pp. 116–19.

Seto, M. C. and Barbaree, H. E. (1999) 'Psychopathy, Treatment Behavior, and Sex Offender Recidivism', *Journal of Interpersonal Violence* 14, pp. 1235–48.

Seto, M. C. and Barbaree, H. E. (2003) *Psychopathy, Treatment Behavior, and Recidivism: an extended follow-up of Seto and Barbaree (1999)*. Manuscript accepted pending revisions.

Shaw, T. A., Herkov, M. J. and Greer, R. A. (1995) 'Examination of Treatment Completion and Predicted Outcome among Incarcerated Sex Offenders', *Bulletin of the American Academy of Psychiatry and the Law* 23, pp. 35–41.

Startup, M. and Edmonds, J. (1994) 'Compliance with Homework Assignments in Cognitive-behavioral Psychotherapy for Depression: relation to outcome and methods of enhancement', *Cognitive Therapy and Research* 18, pp. 567–79.

Stirpe, T. S., Wilson, R. J. and Long, C. (2001) 'Goal Attainment Scaling with Sexual Offenders: a measure of clinical impact at posttreatment and at community follow-up', *Sexual Abuse* 13, pp. 65–77.

Sung, H.-E., Belenko, S. and Feng, L. (2001) 'Treatment Compliance in the Trajectory of Treatment Progress among Offenders', *Journal of Substance Abuse Treatment* 20, pp. 153–62.

Thornton, D. (2002) 'Constructing and Testing a Framework for Dynamic Risk Assessment', *Sexual Abuse* 14, pp. 139–54.

Wierzbicki, M. and Pekarik, G. (1993) 'A Meta-analysis of Psychotherapy Drop-out', *Professional Psychology: Research and Practice* 24, pp. 190–5.

Wormith, J. S. and Olver, M. E. (2002) 'Offender Treatment Attrition and its Relationship with Risk, Responsivity and Recidivism', *Criminal Justice and Behavior* 29, pp. 447–71.

Young, D. and Belenko, S. (2002) 'Program Retention and Perceived Coercion in Three Models of Mandatory Drug Treatment', *Journal of Drug Issues* 32, pp. 297–328.

Chapter 7

The Machiavellian sex offender

David Thornton

Introduction

Men who sexually abuse children are commonly seen as using cognitive distortions to give themselves permission to offend. In line with this characterisation of the process of offending, child-molesters tend to score higher on psychometric instruments that assess degree of belief in various general attitudes that would make it easier to 'give yourself permission to abuse' (e.g. Segal and Stermac 1990; Hanson, Gizzarelli and Scott 1994). The content of the beliefs commonly identified as distortions generally relates to representations of children (e.g. as sexually interested and seductive little adults), to norms about sex (e.g. ideas about consent or sexual entitlement), or more specifically to representations of the sexually abusive act itself (e.g. as harmless so long as the adult is gentle or kind). Notably missing from the range of distortions are beliefs that might serve to justify the grooming process used to set up opportunities to abuse or to silence victims.

Grooming is a ubiquitous feature of the sexual abuse of children. Common techniques include selecting vulnerable families or vulnerable children within families, gaining the family's trust, sharing pornography with the child, using alcohol or drugs to incapacitate, rewarding the child for increasing compliance through displays of 'affection' and gifts, desensitising the child through gradually increasing the intimacy of physical contact, or frightening the child into compliance through threats of harm to the child him/herself or to those the child cares about such as siblings, their mother or family pets.

Based on these observations, men who sexually abuse children are often characterised as 'manipulative'. Manipulating other people is something that in itself is often thought of as reprehensible. Many people will therefore be, to some extent, inhibited from too consciously engaging in manipulation of others. Some people, however, have general beliefs that condone or justify manipulation and they would therefore find it easier to engage in the manipulative tactics that are commonly required to create the opportunity to offend. Of course, an individual might accidentally find themselves with an opportunity to offend, perhaps having particular access to one or two potential victims (say, their own children) but the more repetitive their offending the more they will have to depend on deliberate manipulation to create the opportunity and so, it is hypothesised, the more likely it is that their offending will be facilitated by a general belief system that justifies manipulation.

What kind of belief system would justify manipulation? One such belief system is the construct of Machiavellianism as developed by Christie and Geis (1970).

The construct of Machiavellianism

The construct of Machiavellianism was developed by Christie and Geis (1970) on the basis of their analysis of the writings of classic power theorists, including notably Machiavelli's *The Prince* and *The Discourses* (1940). They see it as a system of beliefs combining a somewhat cynical view of human nature that represents people as weak, cowardly, selfish and easily misled, with a willingness to use manipulative tactics that take advantage of this weakness, and with disrespect for conventional morality. Through an elaborate series of social psychological experiments they delineate the behavioural patterns typical of people who endorse these beliefs to an above average extent (high Machs) as compared to those who reject them (low Machs). High Machs emerge as characterised by a cool, cognitive analysis of interpersonal situations that enables them to resist social influences and to initiate and create structure. In contrast, low Machs emerge as empathically enmeshed in the feelings and desires of other people so that they are susceptible to social influence, and inclined to accept and follow the structures projected by others.

According to this research, high Machs and low Machs sometimes behave in similar ways but differences emerge in situations that involve face-to-face interaction, where there is opportunity for improvisation, and where irrelevant affect is aroused. In such circumstances high Machs consistently dominate low Machs. More specifically, in such situations high Machs successfully manipulate, persuade but are not persuaded by, or just outperform low Machs.

Machiavellianism and sexual offending

Given this more detailed characterisation of the construct of Machiavellianism, how well fitted is it to play the suggested role of facilitating repetitive offending?

Part of the construct consists of beliefs that directly justify the use of interpersonal manipulation, thus high Machs should be more willing to use the tactics.

Additionally, however, it would seem likely that the cognitive style characteristic of high Machs (the cool cognitive analysis of interpersonal situations) would make them more skilled at dominating and manipulating, as would the fact that they presumably have more practice at this kind of behavioural tactic. This seems particularly likely to be so since the situations in which high Machs successfully dominate and manipulate low Machs (face-to-face interaction, where there is opportunity for improvisation, and where irrelevant affect is aroused) commonly arise in the grooming process used to set up the opportunity to offend.

Being more skilled at dominating and manipulating will mean both that more opportunities to offend are created, and that attempts to offend are more often successful, so that the behaviour of attempting to offend is more often reinforced.

Taking these considerations together there seem strong grounds for hypothesising that men who sexually abuse children repetitively will tend to be rated higher on Machiavellianism.

Machiavellianism in repeated and once-sentenced child-molesters

An opportunity to investigate this hypothesis arose during the early years of the operation of the national sex offender treatment programme run by Her Majesty's Prison Service (Thornton and Hogue 1993). A battery of questionnaires was administered to imprisoned sex offenders prior to their beginning treatment. Included in this battery was a shortened form of the Mach-IV questionnaire (shortened because space was at a premium in the battery). Items were selected on the basis of the published item-total correlations and factor loadings (Christie and Geis 1970). The resulting scale had a retest reliability (from before treatment to after it) of 0.55 in a mixed sample of 82 sex offenders. Internal consistency as measured by Cronbach's alpha was in the mid 0.7s. Data from the questionnaires along with conviction data were returned, by higher security prisons that ran the programme, to a central database.

A sample of 157 adult male child-molesters was extracted from this database; child-molester being defined as someone currently serving a sentence for a sexual offence against a child under the age of 14. This group was then split into two categories. The first category consisted of those whose index conviction was for a sexual offence against a child but who had not been previously convicted for such an offence. The second category consisted of those whose index conviction was for a sexual offence against a child but who, in addition, had been previously convicted and sentenced for a similar offence. The analysis then compared the Machiavellianism scores of those child-molesters who had been sentenced on a single occasion for this kind of offence (N = 104) to those who had been sentenced on two or more occasions (labelled as 'repetitive'). The 'repetitive' group is, in effect, composed of men who have been convicted once for sexual offences against children and then gone on to be reconvicted for this offence. Table 7.1 shows means and standard deviations on the short Machiavellianism scale for these two groups.

Table 7.1 Mean Machiavellianism scores for single sentence and repeatedly sentenced child-molesters

	N	Mean	SD
Sentenced once for child-molesting	104	8.580	2.372
Sentenced repeatedly for child-molesting	53	9.585	3.461

The difference between the two groups amounts to about a third of a standard deviation, a moderate sized effect. It is statistically significant (t-test = 2.138; d.f. = 155; p = 0.034; Mann-Whitney U = 2087, p = 0.013).[1] Thus, more repetitive child-molesters do seem to be more inclined to endorse general Machiavellian beliefs.

Machiavellianism and sexual reconviction

The effect reported in Table 7.1 can be interpreted in a number of ways. One possibility is that pre-existing Machiavellian beliefs make it easier for someone to repeatedly commit sexual offences against children. An alternative view is that engaging in the manipulative grooming needed to repeatedly sexually abuse children leads the offender to look more favourably on manipulative behaviour in general. This second possibility suggests that holding more Machiavellian beliefs may relate to having repeatedly molested children in the past but would not be useful in predicting whether an offender would do so again.

It was possible to investigate this issue when reconviction data later became available for this data set. Using a follow-up limited to four years, five of these child-molesters were identified as being sexually reconvicted. The average time at risk for this group was a little over three years. These offenders can be contrasted to child-molesters who were not sexually reconvicted during the follow-up period. Only those who had been at risk for at least 18 months were considered in the analysis so that their not being reconvicted was not solely due to lack of opportunity. This produced a group of 94 not-sexually reconvicted child-molesters whose average at risk period was similarly a little over three years.

Table 7.2 shows the mean scores of these two groups on the short Machiavellianism scale.

Table 7.2 Mean Machiavellianism scores and sexual reconviction

	N	Mean	SD
Not reconvicted in four years	94	8.737	2.748
Reconvicted in four years	5	12.600	2.793

It is striking that the mean Machiavellianism score of those child-molesters who went on to be sexually reconvicted is much higher than those who were not reconvicted. The difference is over one standard deviation in magnitude. And despite the small number who were reconvicted, the difference is statistically significant (Mann-Whitney $U = 74$, $p = 0.01$; t-test $= 3.061$; d.f. $= 97$; $p = 0.003$).

Machiavellianism and sexual reconviction controlling for prior sexual convictions

The results in Table 7.2 indicate that Machiavellianism is related to future sexual offending by child-molesters as well as to how often they have offended in the past. This, however, still leaves the question of whether knowing an offender's Machiavellianism tells us more about his likelihood of being reconvicted than we could know simply from his past record. This issue was examined by applying logistic regression to these data. Here, sexual reconviction was taken as the dependent variable. An equation was fitted predicting sexual reconviction from whether the offender had been previously convicted for child-molesting. Then the

Machiavellianism score was added to the equation and the degree of improvement in the Log-Likelihood Ratio was examined to see whether a significant improvement in predictive accuracy resulted. Table 7.3 shows the resulting regression equation.

Table 7.3 Logistic regression equation predicting sexual reconviction by child-molesters

	B	SE	p
Repeatedly sentenced for child-molesting?	1.621	1.209	NS
Machiavellianism	0.518	0.233	0.026

The table shows the p derived from the Wald χ^2 approximation. The more exact improvement in Log-Likelihood Ratio gave $\chi^2 = 7.045$ (1) $p = 0.008$. Thus adding Machiavellianism to the equation led to a significant improvement in predictive accuracy over that provided by knowing whether the offender had been repeatedly sentenced for child-molesting. The equation shows that the direction of this relationship is, as expected, that the more an offender endorses general Machiavellian beliefs, the more likely they are to re-offend.

Implications of these findings

The theoretical proposition that Machiavellian beliefs make it easier to repeatedly commit sexual offences against children led to two related predictions: that those men with a history of having been sentenced more than once for child-molesting will score higher on Machiavellianism than those who have only been sentenced once; and that independent of their past record, those who go on to be reconvicted for a sexual offence will score higher than those who are not reconvicted. Both these predictions were supported. This gives some credibility to the proposed link between Machiavellian beliefs and repeated sexual offending.

If Machiavellian beliefs do make it easier to commit sexual offences, then three potential practical implications need to be considered. First, treatment programmes for sexual offenders ought to assess for generalised Machiavellian beliefs and should target them for change. Existing cognitive therapy techniques would seem as applicable here as they are to other pro-offending beliefs. Second, Machiavellian beliefs should be included in the range of psychological factors assessed in comprehensive systems designed to assess the risk presented by sexual offenders. Both the Structured Risk Assessment framework (Thornton 2002) and SONAR (Hanson and Harris 2001) might benefit from incorporating this new factor. Third, processes for managing and supervising sexual offenders in the community need to take account of the likely vulnerability of low Mach supervisors to high Mach offenders. Several suggestions might be made here. Supervisors should probably be selected for moderate degrees of Machiavellianism – thus reducing their vulnerability. Supervision processes should be structured so that they avoid the situations in which high Machs consistently win (situations where there is direct interpersonal contact, opportunity for improvisation, and where irrelevant affect is aroused). Since interpersonal contact is a required part of supervision, it is necessary to focus on the other two dimensions, so supervision for high Mach sexual offenders should be structured, with limited opportunity for 'flexible individualisation', and conducted in a calm unemotional way. Additionally, having key supervision decisions (such as about revocation) being made by people who are not in direct contact with the offender might be helpful.

This prescription might seem overly rule-bound and rigid. Some support for it comes from an unpublished study carried out by the author. Here the degree to which young offenders (mainly aged 18 to 20 years old) behaved delinquently (fighting, stealing, etc.) within a correctional facility was examined as a function of Machiavellianism and type of regime. One facility ran a highly structured, organised regime in which offenders were assigned to regime activities based on categorisations and no attempt was made to individualise their treatment. The other regime prided itself on the flexible way in which it individualised the regime activities made available to inmates based on their needs. In the flexible regime high Machs tended to be more delinquent than their peers. Furthermore, their delinquency was successful; they were both more delinquent and behaving delinquently was associated with lower stress. In contrast, in the structured regime, high Machs were no more inclined to behave delinquently than their peers and those who behaved pro-socially experienced lower stress.

'Flexible individualisation' too easily creates vulnerabilities that Machiavellian offenders exploit.

The present findings could do with being replicated in an independent sample. Additionally, however, future research could usefully examine the relationship between generalised Machiavellian beliefs and the use of specific grooming tactics in offending. Do high Mach sex offenders commit specific kinds of crime, ones that draw on their ease and skill in interpersonal domination and manipulation?

Finally, two theoretical issues need addressing. Does the present model suggest that high Machs in general are liable to sexually abuse children? And how does the construct of Machiavellianism relate to that of psychopathy?

The present model suggests that Machiavellianism will be relevant to risk for sexually abusing children only when the individual concerned has a sexual interest in children. Additionally, the individual would have to overcome the other internal inhibitors against such activity. Thus Machiavellianism is best regarded as relevant to the sexual abuse of children among those who have already begun to engage in this kind of offending rather than among the general public.

There are some conceptual similarities between Machiavellianism and psychopathy. Both involve a certain emotional coolness (shallow emotionality in psychopathy, a cool cognitive approach in Machiavellianism), a lack of empathic emotional engagement with others (callousness in psychopathy, low Machs being empathically enmeshed in the feelings and desires of other people), and both involve a willingness to engage in interpersonal manipulation. However, there are important differences. High Machs are not more inclined to lie than low Machs, nor are they more impulsive (Christie and Geis 1970), whereas pathological lying, a lack of long term goals, and impulsiveness are core features of psychopathy (Hare 1991). Thus despite some similarities, high Machs are importantly different from psychopaths.

Note

1 Parametric t-tests and non-parametric Mann-Whitney U tests are reported as there is a marked difference between the SDs in some analyses.

References

Christie, R. and Geis, F. L. (1970) *Studies in Machiavellianism*. New York: Academic Press.

Hanson, R. K., Gizzarelli, R. and Scott, H. (1994) 'The Attitudes of Incest Offenders: sexual entitlement and acceptance of sex with children', *Criminal Justice and Behavior* 21, pp. 187–202.

Hanson, R. K. and Harris, A. (2001) 'A Structured Approach to Evaluating Change Among Sexual Offenders', *Sexual Abuse* 13, pp. 105–122.

Machiavelli, N. (1940) *The Prince. The Discourses*. New York: Modern Library.

Hare, R. D. (1991) *The Hare Psychopathy Checklist-Revised*. Toronto, Ontario: Multi-Health Systems.

Segal, Z. V. and Stermac, L. E. (1990) 'The Role of Cognition in Sexual Assault', in W. L. Marshall, D. R. Laws and H. E. Barbaree (eds) *Handbook of Sexual Assault: issues, theories and treatment of the offender*. New York: Plenum.

Thornton, D. and Hogue, T. (1993) 'The Large Scale Provision of Programmes for Imprisoned Sex Offenders: issues, dilemmas and progress', *Criminal Behaviour and Mental Health* 3, pp. 371–80.

Thornton, D. (2002) 'Constructing and Testing a Framework for Dynamic Risk Assessment', *Sexual Abuse* 14, pp. 137–51.

Chapter 8

The role of the polygraph

Don Grubin

The use of actuarial techniques to assess the risk of reconviction by sex offenders has become increasingly popular over the last decade. Studies have demonstrated their efficacy in predicting long-term risk, which appears to be greater than more clinically based approaches; retrospective research employing ROC statistics suggests that when comparing sex offenders who are reconvicted for sexual crimes with sex offenders who are not, actuarial techniques will, at their best, correctly classify the recidivists as higher risk 75 per cent of the time.

Actuarial approaches, however, provide an estimate of the *likelihood* of reconviction only. Because they are based on historical, present or absent, and either unchanging or slow to change variables (for example, age, number of convictions, history of cohabitation), they provide no guidance on other key aspects of risk evaluation that form the basis of day-to-day risk management, such as the degree of harm that might be caused by a re-offence or the imminence of offending behaviour. In order to make accurate predictions regarding these issues, it is now well recognised that consideration must be given to so-called dynamic risk factors that relate more specifically to the individual offender. Hanson and Harris (2000) have further pointed out that dynamic risk factors themselves are best divided into two types: those that are relatively stable such as an offender's attitudes, his ability to form relationships, or his capacity to 'regulate' himself in respect of sexual and more general behaviour, and 'acute' factors that can change relatively rapidly, such as his co-operation with supervision, his level of hostility and his access to victims.

Thus, while actuarial risk assessment provides a baseline that can anchor judgement regarding an individual, it is the beginning rather than the end of the risk assessment/risk management process. It should also be remembered that actuarial variables are empirically driven, and do not come with theoretical explanations of why they are important: for example, we know that a history of sex offence convictions is predictive of further convictions over time, but not why. Dynamic variables can help determine the relevance of static factors in specific cases, allowing a more sophisticated assessment of risk to be carried out.

Researchers, therefore, have been attempting to develop instruments that can identify and measure dynamic factors that, while being responsive to change, will be capable of quantifying risk in a manner similar to actuarial tools. Amongst the most advanced of these efforts are the psychometric approach taken by the SOTEP team in the UK (Beech et al. 2002), the Structured Risk Assessment being developed by Thornton (2002) which has been partly influenced by the SOTEP psychometric findings, and SONAR, which was designed and is currently being tested at a number of sites in North America (Hanson and Harris 2000).

As yet, the search for dynamic risk factor assessment tools has not produced an instrument capable of quantifying risk that can be confidently used to adjust the results of actuarial risk assessment. However, what the work referred to above has done is highlight the components that need to be included in any systematic and well targeted formulation of risk, emphasising in particular those characteristics of an individual that need to be addressed in treatment (for example, cognitive distortions, emotional regulation, and life management skills), and those that must be monitored with a view to intervention if necessary (such as increases in sexual preoccupation, breakdown in the supervisory relationship between offender and probation officer, or the emergence of behaviours that bring the offender into contact with potential victims).

An analogy with the formulation of risk relating to the possibility of an individual suffering a myocardial infarction can help illustrate this approach to risk assessment and management. A person with a strong family history of heart disease – for example having close relatives who died at young ages from myocardial infarctions – would be said to have a high *long-term* risk of suffering a myocardial infarction himself because of genetic factors. There is not much he can do about this apart from recognising that he is at risk. However, other factors will increase his risk generally, such as having raised blood pressure or a high blood cholesterol level (and which may turn out to be the mediators of the genetic risk). These are things that can be influenced by treatment, and could be called stable dynamic risk factors. Similarly, there is another set of factors that markedly increase his short-term to immediate risk of myocardial infarction, such as smoking and stress. These last items are the sorts of thing that can be observed to fluctuate over short periods of time, and which can be influenced immediately by intervention. These are the equivalent to acute dynamic risk factors. This comparison with the assessment and management of risk of myocardial infarction is represented in Figure 8.1.

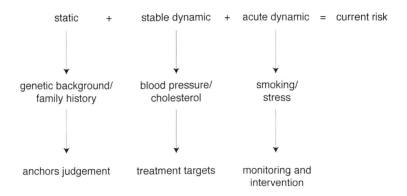

Figure 8.1 Risk assessment and management in respect to myocardial infarction

Combining estimates of long-term risk with treatment intervention, monitoring and appropriate intervention can result in what might be called an integrated risk management strategy, regardless of whether this is applied to patients at risk of a heart attack or sex offenders at risk of re-offending.

An important difference between patients and sex offenders, however, is that sex offenders are generally less likely to disclose fully (or sometimes at all) the types of information needed for this type of approach to be successful. Although this is not usually an issue in respect of static risk factors like previous convictions, given that these are part of the public record, offenders may not report reliably, or even recognise, relevant aspects of their sexual behaviour histories, their patterns of sexual arousal, or what took place in an offence, and they may try to conceal current behaviours and activities about which a supervisor would want to know. It is as if a doctor has to rely on the patient's self report of diet in order to estimate blood cholesterol levels, or the patient receiving treatment for angina neglects to tell the doctor that he smokes. But whereas a patient who hides important information from his doctor in the end harms only himself, the sex offender who does so also puts others at risk from his re-offending.

Unfortunately, we know from experience that sex offenders often do fail to disclose important pieces of both historical and current information about themselves. Because of this, assessors and treatment providers make use of a variety of techniques and more objective measures to form an understanding of an offender's risk, including group processes in sex offender treatment, behavioural observation, psychometric testing, PPG and other measures of sexual interest and arousal, tagging, and police surveillance.

In the United States, the polygraph has become an important addition to this armoury in many places, beginning in the 1970s but becoming more common from the early 1990s. Surveys carried out by English and her colleagues suggest that polygraphy is used in the management of sex offenders by between a quarter and a third of probation services in the United States (English et al. 2000). It is also used widely within treatment programmes (Abrams and Simmons 2000). The use of the polygraph in this way is probably most developed in the state of Colorado where mandatory testing of sex offenders is seen as an essential component of a containment model also comprising treatment and supervision.

Practitioners who make use of polygraphy tend to be enthusiastic about its benefits, and reports often describe substantial increases in numbers and types of victim, previously unknown offences, and deviant fantasies, together with a decrease in the age of onset of deviant behaviour and offending, and interestingly, a reduction in self-reported histories of their own abuse claimed by offenders. For instance, when comparing what was known about offenders before and after polygraph examinations, English et al. (2000) reported an 80 per cent increase in offenders who disclosed having had male victims, and over a 200 per cent increase in those admitting to offences against both child and adult victims, while Hindman and Peters (2001) noted increases in numbers of known victims from an average of 2.5 to 13.6, and a reduction from 65 per cent to 32 per cent of those claiming to have been themselves sexually abused as children. In a small UK study involving 14 sex offenders, Wilcox and associates reported a decrease in age of first known sex offence from 28 to 13.5 (personal communication). Similar findings are reported by Emerick and Dutton (1993).

Although clinically persuasive, from a research perspective studies such as these suffer from a lack of genuine comparison or control groups, at best comparing samples from before and after the introduction of polygraphy into a programme. Similarly, there is only limited, largely anecdotal evidence to show that the use of polygraphy reduces re-offending, although data from Colorado suggests that when polygraphy is introduced into a programme there is an initial increase in high-risk behaviours and detected offences, followed by a reduction in both (English, personal communication).

To examine polygraph efficacy, we carried out a study in England comparing two groups of offenders who were on probation in three different areas (this study is described more fully in Grubin et al., in press). After a research interview to clarify high-risk behaviours, one group was informed that they would be polygraphed in three months to assess whether knowledge of this would help them avoid engaging in risky behaviours, while the members of the other group were told that they would act as a comparison group. At three months (time 1), however, both groups were in fact polygraphed, the hypothesis being that those who were expecting a polygraph examination would have engaged in fewer high-risk behaviours over the three month period than those in the comparison group. After the polygraph examination at time 1, those who passed were to be told that they would simply be reviewed in a further three months time (time 2), while those who failed the exam were to be warned about their behaviour and told that in three months they would be polygraphed again. As at time 1, both groups would be polygraphed at time 2. Because this was a research study, the participation of offenders was voluntary, and they were free to drop out of the study at any time.

Of the 116 men who were approached for the study, just 50 (43 per cent) agreed to take part and were interviewed by a researcher to establish their individual 'high-risk behaviours'. At three months, two men had been recalled to prison and one had significant mental health problems, but a further 14 defaulted from the polygraph assessment; in addition, one offender from the comparison group dropped out of the study when asked to undergo a polygraph. This left 32 men who agreed to be polygraphed – 28 per cent of those initially approached and 64 per cent of those who had agreed to take part in the study (Figure 8.2). Drop-outs were evenly distributed between both groups.

All of the 32 offenders who agreed to be polygraphed were thought to be doing well in treatment, and apart from one man who was known to be masturbating to deviant fantasies, there were no particular concerns about any of them. When they were polygraphed at time 1, however, 30 of the 32 men disclosed behaviours of concern, and the one who did not (apart from the offender who was known to be masturbating to deviant fantasies) failed his polygraph examination (Figure 8.3). Furthermore, as can be seen from Figure 8.3, many of the offenders made more than one disclosure, giving some information to the interviewer, more to the

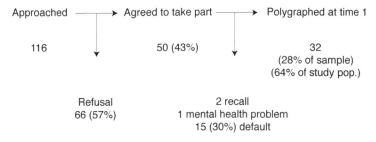

Figure 8.2 Subjects taking part in Newcastle polygraph study

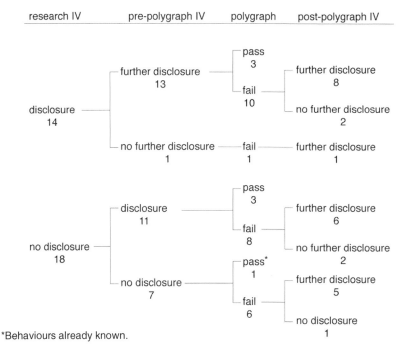

*Behaviours already known.

Figure 8.3 Disclosure at time 1 (3 months) in Newcastle polygraph study. All interviews were carried out at the same session (n = 32).

polygrapher prior to being polygraphed, and then disclosing still more after failing the polygraph. Only seven (22 per cent) offenders passed the polygraph exam itself.

A wide variety of behaviours of concern were disclosed. Twenty-seven offenders (84 per cent) admitted to masturbating to deviant fantasies, nine (28 per cent) to obtaining pictures of children for the purposes of sexual arousal, nine (28 per cent) to going to places where they knew children would be, and 11 (34 per cent) to having unsupervised contact with children. One man reported approximately 50 separate incidents of frottage involving young girls, another to having unsupervised contact with the 12-year-old girl who had been the victim of his original offence, and a third to prowling public toilets in search of potential young male victims.

Because all but one of these men disclosed behaviours of immediate relevance to their treatment and supervision, the initial hypothesis that the expectation of a polygraph examination would inhibit men from engaging in high-risk behaviours appeared to be invalidated, and rather than allocating the seven men who managed to pass the polygraph to the 'comparison' group for time 2, all were told that they would be polygraphed again three months later.

At time 2, a further 11 men defaulted from the study, leaving just 21 (42 per cent) of the original research sample. Interestingly, of those 11 who did not return at time 2, four were from the group of seven men who had passed their polygraphs at time 1.

The findings at time 2 were encouragingly different from what they were at time 1. As can be seen from Figure 8.4, on this occasion 15 (71 per cent) passed the polygraph, and disclosures tended to occur initially and fully, rather than in a piecemeal manner.

All but one of the offenders at time 2 said that the polygraph had helped them not to re-offend, and 12 (57 per cent) said knowledge of the impending exam inhibited them from engaging in high-risk behaviours. Over half the offenders said they were now reporting more information about their behaviour to their probation officers. Given that these 21 men represented just 18 per cent of the 116 men who were originally approached for the study, one can only wonder about the other 82 per cent of offenders on these three programmes.

Although a small study, this trial suggests that the polygraph can act as an important 'truth facilitator' for sex offenders in treatment, and it is this function rather than its more commonly thought of role as a 'lie detector' that may be most relevant for its contribution to the management of risk in sex offenders. It brought dynamic acute risk factors, in other words, behaviours that increase the risk of re-offending in the short term, to the attention of supervising probation officers so that preventative steps could be taken, and it also made clear to those providing treatment where further work needed to be done (for example, regarding continued masturbation to deviant fantasies). It appeared to assist those who were motivated not to offend to stick to their relapse prevention plans. The original hypothesis – that knowledge of an impending polygraph examination inhibits behaviours of concern, thereby having an impact on dynamic acute risk factors – appeared to be supported after all, although experience of the polygraph examination rather than just an expectation of having one seems to be necessary.

Based on results such as this, it would appear that the polygraph can be of potentially great value, not only in respect of sex offenders on treatment programmes, but also for the management of sex offenders generally. For example, using the actuarial tool Risk Matrix 2000, about 55 per cent of sex offenders are allocated to a 'medium risk' group, of whom about 20 per cent are expected to be reconvicted of a sexual offence over a 20-year period, and 15 per cent to a 'low risk' group with a reconviction rate of ten per cent. Most police and probation strategies focus resources on the smaller number of 'very high risk' offenders

research IV   pre-polygraph IV   polygraph   post-polygraph IV

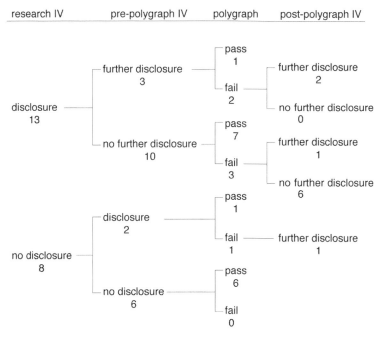

Figure 8.4 Disclosure at time 2 (6 months) in Newcastle polygraph study (n = 21)

(about 10 per cent), who have a 60 per cent reconviction rate. In absolute terms, however, the 70 per cent of offenders in the 'low' and 'medium' risk groups will be responsible for nearly as many reconvictions as those in the very high risk group. A technique that could identify the minority of 'low' and 'medium' risk offenders whose behaviour (i.e. acute dynamic risk factors) indicates that they are currently a higher risk and should be treated as such would contribute greatly to public protection, while being able to identify those 'very high risk' offenders whose immediate risk is in fact lower would result in great savings in time and money. This is illustrated in Figure 8.5 below.

One can only speculate about the motives of those who avoided the polygraph, but clearly if the polygraph is to have its intended impact, then testing will need to be mandatory. Polygraphy, however, is not used at all in the UK, and its use in North America is not without controversy. What, then, is the problem? Why is the polygraph not used universally in the management of sex offenders in the community?

The absence of polygraphy in the UK can be linked directly to a strongly worded negative review carried out by the British Psychological Society (BPS) in the 1980s, commissioned in the wake of the Geoffrey

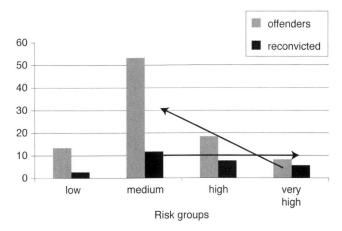

Figure 8.5 Illustrative figures from Risk Matrix 2000 to indicate the way in which 'higher risk' medium risk offenders (determined by polygraph recognition of dynamic acute risk factors) could be managed as if they were very high risk, while some very high risk offenders whose dynamic risk was low could be treated as if they were medium risk

Prime spy scandal (British Psychological Society, 1986). In effect, the BPS argued that polygraphy is unscientific. This also has been the theme of subsequent, equally withering critiques, for example by Cross and Saxe (2001) and most recently by an expert panel convened by the National Academies of Sciences (NAS) in the United States (2002). For example, the NAS review concluded that, 'polygraph testing now rests on weak scientific underpinnings despite nearly a century of study', criticising polygraph research as lacking in 'scientific rigor' (interestingly, they refer to the 'available evidence', perhaps taking a swipe at the large amount of research carried out by the American Department of Defense and other security agencies that is not in the public domain), and also noting the 'unverified' nature of the link between physiological response and deception. The BPS in 1986 also raised concerns about the monitoring of polygraphers, and the ethical issues associated with 'inducing anxiety' in polygraph subjects.

Specific scientific issues raised by the various critical reviews can be summarised as follows:

- Inter-rater and test–retest reliability is uncertain.

- The validity (i.e. accuracy) of the polygraph remains to be demonstrated – estimates range from under 70 per cent (Iaccono and Lykken 1997) to over 90 per cent (Forensic Research 1997).

- There is a lack of standardisation in the way testing is carried out.

- Subject differences have not been taken into account.

- The theoretical basis of the various examination techniques is weak.

These concerns are all almost certainly valid. However, it is worth noting that they reflect a lack of evidence and 'scientific rigor', rather than negative evidence regarding polygraphy *per se*. One can either dismiss what appears on the face of it to represent a useful and valuable clinical tool because of the inadequacies of its research pedigree, or one can set out to examine the technique properly, producing evidence that will either support or condemn it once and for all. If the latter course is to be taken, a number of issues will need to be addressed.

Distinguishing between uses of polygraphy

First, researchers and those interpreting the research findings need to distinguish between the various uses of polygraphy. The BPS review, for example, and much of that of the NAS, focused on security vetting, pre-employment screening and criminal investigation. Similarly, almost all of the 'validity studies' involve investigative type protocols – having subjects view mock crimes, for example, or comparing the results of police polygraphs with the outcome of criminal cases. The issues associated with these types of use, however, and the types of outcomes they seek, are very different from the post-conviction polygraph testing of sex offenders who are taking part in treatment programmes or are being supervised on probation. The implications of failing a polygraph, and the risk of 'false positives' are very different in the post-conviction setting.

Realistic settings

Second, in order to determine the validity of the polygraph, tests need to be carried out in realistic settings, with an objective means of establishing underlying truth that will allow both false negatives and false positives to be identified: laboratory experiments are by their nature unrealistic and hence of questionable generalisability, while retrospective field studies have difficulty in establishing representative samples and deciding upon 'ground truth'. As one solution to this, we are organising an American-based study in which sex offenders whose supervision involves abstinence from drugs are polygraphed immediately before they receive an unexpected drug test, allowing us to compare polygraph chart interpretation with actual recent drug consumption.

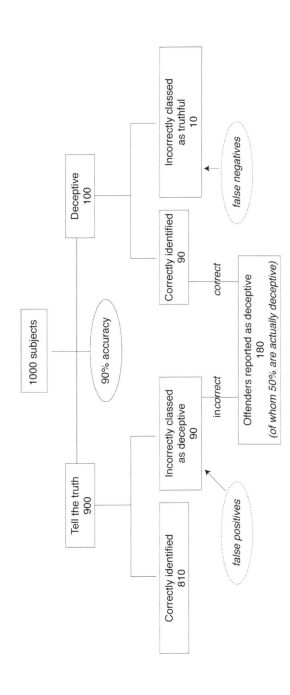

Figure 8.6 Proportion of offenders correctly identified as 'telling the truth' and 'being deceptive' if the polygraph has an accuracy of 90 per cent, and 90 per cent of offenders 'tell the truth'

Interpreting the results

The third issue is the way in which 'deception indicated' charts are to be interpreted. As Kokish (unpublished) and others have observed, even if polygraph testing is highly accurate, in cases where most offenders tell the truth most of the time the reliability of 'deception indicated' findings is problematic. As can be seen in Figure 8.6, if the polygraph has an accuracy of 90 per cent, and 90 per cent of 1,000 offenders 'tell the truth', then while the deception of only ten subjects will be missed (i.e. they 'beat the polygraph') and 810 of 820 individuals reported as telling the truth actually have done so, 50 per cent of the 180 offenders who are identified as being deceptive are in fact telling the truth, in spite of an overall false positive rate of just 9 per cent.

Of course, in post-conviction sex offender testing one does not rely solely on the results of a failed polygraph: corroboration will be sought, either through an admission by the offender, or from other sources. In this setting the polygraph is only one of a number of tools that contribute to treatment and management, and its results need to be interpreted just as with any other type of assessment procedure. Unlike in security vetting, the issue here is less about the 'accuracy' of the polygraph and more about facilitating disclosure.

There is, however, also the allied problem of 'false confessions', that is, offenders who make something up in order to explain a failed polygraph. There is little data about how common this is. Kokish and Blasingame gave anonymous questionnaires to participants in a California treatment programme in which polygraphy is used routinely and found that five of 95 men reported that on at least one occasion they admitted to things they had not done when confronted with a polygraph finding indicative of deception (unpublished data).

Using other indicators of deception

The final issue is that given the arguments about the link between deception and what the polygraph measures physiologically, ways need to be sought to correlate the autonomic responses recorded by the polygraph when the subject is deceptive with other neurophysiological indicators of deception, making use, for example, of techniques such as functional brain imaging.

Conclusion

Where, then, does this leave clinicians and policy-makers? If the results of our study and the reports of others using the polygraph in clinical and supervisory settings are to be believed, then the individual risk assessments we carry out and our evaluation of how offenders are responding to treatment are often flawed. Offenders themselves appear to recognise the potential worth of the polygraph, even if they do not want to co-operate with it. One could argue that the time has come to move from theoretical arguments about the scientific status of the polygraph, and to initiate a properly designed research programme aimed at determining whether or not it has a role in the treatment and management of sex offenders. If such a foundation can be established, then it should be possible to standardise and regulate practice to ensure that the integrity of its delivery is maintained.

References

Abrams, S. and Simmons, G. (2000) 'Post-conviction Polygraph Testing: then and now', *Polygraph* 29, pp. 63–7.

Beech, A., Friendship, C., Erikson, M. and Hanson, R.K. (2002) 'The Relationship between Static and Dynamic Risk Factors and Reconviction in a Sample of U.K. Child Abusers', *Sexual Abuse* 14, pp. 155–67.

British Psychological Society (1986) 'Report of the Working Group on the Use of the Polygraph in Criminal Investigation and Personnel Screening', *Bulletin of the British Psychological Society* 39, pp. 81–94.

Cross, T. P. and Saxe, L. (2001) 'Polygraph Testing and Sexual Abuse: the lure of the magic lasso', *Child Maltreatment* 6, pp. 195–206.

Emerick, R. L. and Dutton, W. A. (1993) 'The Effect of Polygraphy on the Self Report of Adolescent Sex Offenders: implications for risk assessment', *Annals of Sex Research* 6, pp. 83–103.

English, K., Jones, L., Pasini-Hill, D., Patrick, D. and Cooley-Towell, S. (2000) *The Value of Polygraph Testing in Sex Offender Management*. Research report submitted to the National Institute of Justice (Denver, Colorado: Department of Public Safety, Division of Criminal Justice, Office of Research and Statistics).

Forensic Research (1997) 'Validity and Reliability of Polygraph Testing', *Polygraph* 26, pp. 215–39.

Grubin, D., Madsen, L., Parsons, S., Sosnowski, D. and Warberg, B. (in press) 'A Prospective Study of the use of polygraphy on high risk behaviours in adult sex offenders', *Sexual Abuse: A Journal of Research and Treatment*.

Hanson, R. K. and Harris, A. J. R. (2000) 'Where Should We Intervene? Dynamic predictors of sexual offense recidivism', *Criminal Justice and Behavior* 27, pp. 6–35.

Hindman, J. and Peters, J. M. (2001) 'Polygraph Testing Leads to Better Understanding Adult and Juvenile Sex Offenders', *Federal Probation* 65, pp. 8–15.

Iaccono, W. and Lykken, D. T. (1997) 'The Scientific Status of Research on Polygraph Techniques: the case against polygraph tests', in D. L. Faigman,

D.H. Kaye, M. J. Saks and J. Sanders (eds), *Modern Scientific Evidence: The law and science of expert testimony*. St Paul, MN: West.

National Academies of Science (2002) *The Polygraph and Lie Detection*. Washington DC: National Academies Press (also on www.books.nap.edu).

Thornton, D. (2002) 'Constructing and Testing a Framework for Dynamic Risk Assessment', *Sexual Abuse* 14, pp. 139–53.

Chapter 9

Adolescents who sexually abuse

Rowland Coombes

We know what we are,
But not what we may become.

William Shakespeare

Introduction

About 20 years ago practitioners in the field of sexual abuse began to become aware of abuse *by*, and not just *of*, children and young people. It has been estimated that between a quarter and a third of alleged sexual abuse is committed by young people under 21, mainly adolescents (National Children's Homes 1992; Grubin 1998; Graham et al. 1998). At first it was thought that, unlike other juvenile delinquents who typically desist from their offending as they grow up, young sex abusers were more likely to continue in their abusive behaviour. Findings from North America, however, suggest that the large majority of such adolescents do not become adult abusers (ATSA 1997). Rasmussen (1999) estimates that perhaps 10 to 15 per cent of adolescent sex offenders continue to offend sexually. The aim therefore must be to complete accurate assessments in order to concentrate scarce resources upon those young people whose abusive behaviour appears to be at greatest risk of becoming entrenched.

Urgent responses by those treatment providers who first became aware of this phenomenon tended to borrow models of assessment and intervention from work with adults who sexually abuse. This chapter seeks to endorse and expand upon more recent developments, which emphasise that the population in question comprises young people in need first and foremost; their abusive behaviour, though illegal and harmful, is secondary to that (Chaffin and Bonner 1998). They are not necessarily embryonic adult sex offenders. Such approaches to work with young people who sexually abuse are characterised by being developmentally sensitive and holistically orientated, paying attention to the emotional life of the individual as well as addressing thoughts and behaviour.

Notwithstanding a desire to be holistic and developmentally sensitive, treatment providers must retain credibility by accounting for their recommendations about intervention and supervision on the basis of 'defensible decisions' (Kemshall 2001). This means addressing issues of risk, but doing so in a way that reflects knowledge of adolescent development, closely allied with an assessment of treatment needs.

Context

Adolescence

We should be wary of transplanting theories developed to explain deviant sexual behaviour by adults onto adolescents. This leaves us free to draw upon research into normal development in young people. First, adolescence needs to be appreciated in all its complexities. Adolescence is a time of transition from childhood to adulthood. It is characterised by a number of changes such as physiological development, increased questioning of identity, and importance of peer relationships as an alternative to the family. Researchers such as Robert Havighurst have described these changes as constituting tasks that adolescents need to complete in order to develop into adults. Adolescents do not progress through these developmental tasks separately. At any given time, they may be dealing with several developmental tasks as part of normal transition. Further, the centrality of specific developmental tasks varies with early, middle, and late periods of the transition. During the early adolescent years, young people make their first attempts to leave the dependent, secure role of a child and to establish themselves as unique individuals, independent of their parents. Early adolescence is marked by rapid physical growth and maturation. The focus of adolescents' self-concepts is thus often on their physical selves and their evaluation of their physical acceptability. Early adolescence is also a period of intense conformity to peer pressure. 'Getting along', not being different, and being accepted seem pressing to the early adolescent. The worst possibility, from the view of the early adolescent, is to be seen by peers as 'different'.

Middle adolescence is marked by the emergence of new thinking skills. The mental world of the young person is suddenly greatly expanded. Abstract concepts, such as injustice, are beginning to be understood. Although peers still play an important role in the life of middle adolescents, the latter are increasingly self-directed. Adolescents' concerns about peers are more directed toward their opposite sexed peers. Epps (1999) has identified the need for guidance to help us differentiate between 'normal and 'abusive' when considering sexual behaviour in adolescence.

In each individual the onset of puberty is subject to significant variation in age. The difference between a girl experiencing early puberty and a boy experiencing late puberty can be as much as seven years. The onset of puberty appears to be shifting, with children in Western societies starting puberty earlier, possibly by as much as four years compared to the last century. Recent research by Moore and Rosenthal (1993) states that 'young people are not mere slaves to hormonal changes, but there is no doubt that these changes can have complex emotional and behavioural effects. The strength of these depends in part on the social context in which the adolescent finds themselves.' In our society, in which there are very few clear markers to symbolise the transition from child to adult, acts such as sexual intercourse can assume great significance. One 13-year-old gang rapist described the backdrop to his offending as being teased about 'still being a virgin'. One advantage to him of offending in front of some 20 or so of his peer group was, 'because everyone was there to see it, you didn't have to blag about it, having sex'.

Research by Scott-Jones and White (1990, cited by Hanks 1997 in Calder et al. 2001) into the sexual activities of children between 12 and 15 shows that these individuals are more sexually active when they have poorly educated mothers and when they have lower educational expectations of themselves. More research is needed before we can say whether children in that position would become more preoccupied with sexual matters.

It is also during this period that the move to establish psychological independence from parents accelerates. Much psychological energy is directed toward preparing for adult roles and making preliminary decisions about vocational goals. Despite some delinquent behaviour, middle adolescence is a period during which young people are oriented toward what is right and proper. In fact, it can be a stage at which a sense of fairness is felt only too keenly: intellectually, adolescents grasp the idea of injustice and, emotionally, they can feel very frustrated that their child resources do not allow them to act upon adult desires. They need to develop a sense of behavioural maturity and learn to control their impulsiveness.

Late adolescence is marked by the final preparations for adult roles. The developmental demands of late adolescence often extend into the period that we think of as young adulthood; this stage has recently been described as that of the 'thresholder'. Late adolescents attempt to crystallise their vocational goals and to establish a sense of personal identity. Their needs for peer approval are diminished and they are largely psychologically independent from their parents. The shift to adulthood is nearly complete.

If the above is a description of a 'normal' path through adolescence, how can we use the therapeutic relationship to promote positive change in those whose experience has not been so smooth? Many of the adolescents referred to the Lucy Faithfull Foundation* have themselves suffered significant trauma. As a consequence, issues of attachment are extremely significant:

> The experience of loss, rejection, lack of warmth or empathy from parental figures can set a template of insecurity upon which subsequent experiences at school, in the extended family and with friends can be superimposed ... Research has focused on understanding the possible links between disruptive attachment, intimacy deficits and sex offending. Generally, such investigations have found a prevalence of insecure attachments, high levels of anxiety and social isolation in young male sex offenders.
>
> (Harris and Staunton 2000, quoted in Clarke 2002)

The containing environment of the therapeutic relationship, characterised by openness and safety, offers an opportunity to experience more secure forms of attachment with safer adults and therefore facilitates the reconstruction of healthier emotional structures within the internal working model of the young person's mind.

In the group setting it has been found that the therapeutic climate is a significant indicator of treatment effectiveness. Beech and Fordham (1997) found that groups rating highest for negative environment and leader control scored lowest on the level of positive change. Groups that are able to form cohesively and generate a sense of support and interdependence created the most positive change in members.

Adolescents who offend

There is a clear justification for drawing upon research into generic offending by adolescents because there has been a consistent finding that adolescents who sexually offend are more likely to re-offend non-sexually than sexually (Weinrott 1996; Elliot 1994, quoted in Beckett 1999). Ryan et al. (1996) found that 63 per cent of a large sample of more than 1,600 adolescent sex offenders had also committed non-sexual offences, 28 per cent having more than three such offences. Various studies have established retrospectively that sexual re-offending rates for young sex offenders during follow-up periods of up to six years were 7.5 per cent to 14 per cent. Corresponding figures for their general criminal recidivism were 40 per cent to 60 per cent (Sipe et al. 1998). This supports a view that programmes cannot work on sexual offending issues in isolation from other high-risk factors and problematic behaviours.

There are two types of adolescents who show anti-social behaviour: those whose behaviour is temporary and limited to adolescence, and those whose anti-social behaviour starts in childhood as conduct disorder and persists through adolescence and into adulthood. Moffitt's (1993) developmental theory of delinquency and crime distinguishes between 'life-course persistent anti-social behaviour' and 'adolescence-limited deviance'. She contended that life-course persistent individuals:

> Exhibit changing manifestations of anti-social behaviour: biting and hitting at four, shoplifting and truancy at ten, selling drugs and stealing cars at 16, robbery and rape at 22, and fraud and child abuse at 30 – the underlying disposition remains the same, but its expression changes form as new social opportunities arise at different points in development.
>
> (Moffitt 1994)

Given the phenomenon of 'adolescence-limited deviance' it is not surprising that offending has been shown to peak in the teenage years. The most popular explanation for this focuses on social influence:

> From birth children are under the influence of parents, who generally have control of their offending. However, during their teenage years, juveniles gradually break away from the control of their parents and become influenced by their peers, who may encourage offending in many cases. After age twenty, offending declines again as peer influence gives way to a new set of family influences hostile to offending, originating in spouses and co-habitees.
>
> (Farrington 1996)

For the individual who does not desist from crime there have been various concepts similar to Moffitt's life-course persistent delinquent. Hare (1993) described the psychopath as characterised by impulsivity, a need for excitement (sensation seeking), a lack of responsibility or remorse and childhood problem behaviour that develops into adult anti-social behaviour. He described psychopathic behaviour as including proneness to substance misuse, criminal misconduct and sexual promiscuity. Gottfredson and Hirschi (1990) have theorised that there is a single latent variable, namely low self-control, which is stable through life and serves as an explanation for all types of crime. They identified poor socialisation in early childhood as the cause of weak self-control.

In their review, France and Hudson (1993) suggested that approximately 50 per cent of adolescent sex offenders have a history of non-sexual arrests and that a majority can be described as conduct-disordered. Those with more serious sexual offences had higher rates of non-sexual offending. Recognising that work with this group generally (see below) has more similarities than differences with work with other young people who have significant behavioural and emotional disorders does not make up for the lack of outcome and evaluation research specific to young people who sexually abuse. It does, however, provide us with important signposts to service development.

Adolescents who sexually offend

Factors associated with long-term sexual offending are difficult to discern because there are not yet adequate prospective studies that would enable us to identify which adolescents will continue their sexually abusive behaviour into adulthood. However, on the basis of clinical experience and existing studies, a general picture of male adolescent sexual abusers has developed. Marshall (1989) suggested that problems of early emotional attachment contribute to a failure to establish intimate relationships in later life and to subsequent low self-esteem and emotional loneliness. In a chapter that brought together several research findings, Erooga and Masson (1999) identified that young male sexual abusers seem to lack social skills including dating skills and sexual knowledge. They are also often socially isolated and experience high levels of social anxiety. 'These problems may exist in addition to general social skills problems, for example in relation to initiating and maintaining conversations with peers they find attractive, and ensuring that sexual relationships are mutual and consenting' (ibid.).

To identify those adolescent sexual abusers who are at higher risk of persisting in sexual, violent and general anti-social behaviour Beckett (1999) recommends that we concentrate on individuals with the following risk factors:

1. A history of frequent physical abuse (in adolescent child abusers) and for adolescent rapists, a history of childhood neglect;

2. Childhood conduct disorder as defined by verbal and physical assault on peers at school and aggression against teachers, cruelty to animals and other people, severe destructiveness, fire setting, stealing, repeated lying, truancy and running away from home;

3. In adolescence, anti-social behaviour, delinquency, vandalism, aggression and high impulsivity; high scores on the adolescent version of the Psychopathy Checklist (Hare 1991, quoted in Beckett 1999);

4. For adolescent sex offenders, low social competence as shown by poor social skills, assertiveness deficits and isolation from peers.

In the quest for what Hanson (2000) called 'empirically-guided clinical judgement', Worling (2002) has categorised four types of risk factors according to their degree of support in research:

1. *Well-supported risk factors* are: deviant sexual interests; attitudes supportive of sexual offending; numerous past sexual offences; selection of a stranger victim; lack of intimate peer relationships or social isolation; high-stress family environment; problematic parent-offender relationships or parental rejection; incomplete offence-specific treatment.

2. *Promising risk factors*, which have been found to be predictive of adult rather than adolescent male sexual re-offending and so need more research, are: obsessive sexual interests; impulsivity; an environment supporting opportunities to re-offend.

3. *Possible risk factors* which are speculative and need further research before determining whether they should be further supported or deleted altogether, are: selection of a male victim; threats of, or use of, excessive violence/weapons during sexual offence; interpersonal aggression.

4. *Unlikely risk factors*, which should not be used for adolescents given the lack of empirical support, are: denial of the sexual offence; lack of victim empathy; history of non-sexual crimes; penetrative sexual assaults; offender's own history of child sexual abuse.

In a study that compared adolescent sex offenders with a history of non-sexual offences and those without such a history Butler and Seto (2002) found that 'sex-only' offenders had significantly fewer current behaviour problems, more pro-social attitudes and beliefs, and a lower expected risk for future delinquency than did 'sex-plus' offenders. However, they may be more likely to have deviant sexual interests (Becker 1988; Hunter et al. 1994; Butler and Seto 2002). Similarly, Langström and Grann (2000) discovered that the factors that predict general recidivism are not the same as those associated with sexual recidivism. In a retrospective follow-up study they examined 46 Swedish young sex offenders (aged 15–20) to identify which of 22 putative risk factors were associated with sexual and general recidivism over a mean time at risk of five years. Previous sex offences, poor social skills, male victim choice and two or more victims in index offence were all factors associated with sexual recidivism. In contrast, predictors of recidivism for general criminality were early conduct disorder, previous convictions, psychopathy and the use of death threats or weapons at the index sex offence.

Since deviant sexual interest has been found to be such a strong predictor of sexual recidivism, there is an obvious benefit in measuring this characteristic more carefully. Amongst adult offenders against children, paedophilic interests are associated with sexual offence history and a greater likelihood of sexual re-offending: having more than one victim, having a male victim, having younger victims and having extra-familial victims. Seto et al. (2000) completed a phallometric study comparing adolescent sex offenders with a suitable group of non-sex offenders or non-offenders, with results suggesting that paedophilic interests can be validly detected, and interpreted as such, among adolescent offenders with any male victim (i.e. even when they had female victims as well). They suggest that paedophilic interests can be detected in offenders as young as 14 years old.

Various arguments have been cited to explain how paedophilia could arise in adolescents. The discovery of paedophilic interests in early adolescence has led some researchers to suggest that such development could begin *in utero* (Quinsey and Lalumière 1995). Another model to explain the aetiology of deviant sexual arousal is that of classical conditioning. The idea is that sexual deviation is a conditioned behaviour that can become a pattern established relatively early in life (Abel et al. 1987), especially when that deviation is male rather than female paedophilia (Abel et al. 1988). However, whilst the majority of juvenile offenders in the study by Hunter et al. (1994) reported having engaged in deviant sexual fantasising before offending, the correlation between such fantasising and the frequency of masturbatory behaviour was low. Before the conditioning model can be proven, more research is needed on the links between fantasising and masturbatory behaviour especially as self-report of the latter is likely to be minimised owing to shame and/or embarrassment.

For a long time it has been thought that there is an association between deviant arousal and a reported history of being sexually or physically abused. The problem with research that tried to establish a causal link between involvement in sexual activity with an older person and subsequently becoming an adult who sexually abuses children, is that it relied upon retrospective recall of childhood risk factors. In fact, most male victims of child sexual abuse do not become paedophiles, but particular experiences and patterns of childhood behaviour are associated with an increased risk of victims becoming abusers in later life. Salter et al. (2002) found that 12 per cent of 224 formerly abused boys became abusers themselves, beginning their offending at an average age of 14 years. In almost all cases the sexual offences were against children, mainly outside their families. In a catch-up prospective study they compared risk factors during childhood between those victims who went on to abuse into adulthood and those who did not. The results reinforce the importance of witnessing and experiencing intra-familial violence as a potential mediator between becoming a victim and perpetrator of sexual abuse. Other risk factors for later offending included material neglect, lack of supervision, and sexual abuse by a female relative.

The effects of childhood and adolescent antecedents on sexual coerciveness have been analysed by Johnson and Knight (2000) using simultaneous multiple regression path analyses. The method was used to explore developmental pathways among childhood abuse, juvenile delinquency and personality dimensions: 'Children enmeshed in violent family structures often interact with delinquent peers and engage in anti-social behaviours. These delinquent experiences may in turn promote the further development of negative cognitions and subsequent aggression toward women' (ibid.). A retrospective self-report inventory was completed by 122 juvenile sex offenders (average age 16 years) who had victims of any age. Having experienced sexual abuse affected sexual coercion directly and, indirectly, through sexual compulsivity, the latter being defined as an inability to resist the urge to perform sexual acts, a component that correlates highly with sexual preoccupation and the strength of sexual drive. Physical abuse, in contrast, directly affected peer aggression and adolescent alcohol abuse, which in turn directly affected sexual coercion and hypermasculinity. This construct was defined as having attitudes supporting male dominance and relying on violence as a means of resolving conflict. It equates with the extent to which an individual holds 'macho' attitudes (e.g. risk taking, power taking, overly competitive). The channel through which sexual compulsivity and hypermasculinity influenced sexual coercion was a misogynistic fantasies factor, consisting of variables measuring aggressive fantasies against women and cognitive biases. It constituted the strongest predictor of sexual coercion. This points to the importance of modelling pro-social attitudes and behaviours towards women by male staff involved in working with this group.

Interestingly, alcohol abuse was the second strongest predictor of sexual coercion in this study, which may lead treatment providers to adapt educational interventions to try to reduce its influence.

Responses

In the absence of a national review of resources it is very hard to build a clear picture of what is currently available for this group. Despite a developing agreement about the importance of this work there has been little systematic attempt to chart who is being offered services, on what basis, using what methods, where and by whom (Morrison 1999; Bridge Childcare Development Service 2001). This should be remedied soon by the mapping project being undertaken by Helen Masson (University of Huddersfield), and Simon Hackett and Sarah Phillips (both from the University of Durham). The National Society for the Prevention of Cruelty to Children (NSPCC), the National Organisation for the Treatment of Abusers and the Youth Justice Board are jointly funding this investigation into current developments in the UK and Eire. It aims to discover the organisational, theoretical and policy bases of services for young people who sexually abuse.

In the last ten years progress has been made in establishing a network of projects around the UK. Many of these new services are run by the NSPCC and other voluntary societies with links to the National Health Service, such as the Young Abusers Project in London and to other agencies dealing with children including the new Youth Offending Teams (YOTs), such as G-MAP in Manchester.

The Lucy Faithfull Foundation is an independent provider from the charitable sector, which has been funded by the Probation Directorate to pilot an assessment, treatment and consultation service for young people aged 15 to 21 who sexually harm others. This service is currently being delivered in two young offender institutions, the Carlford Unit at Her Majesty's Youth Offending Institution (HMYOI) Warren Hill (formerly known, prior to the creation of the juvenile estate, as HMYOI Holleseley Bay) and HMYOI Stoke Heath. The service will also be available in the community through YOTs and Probation Services. A programme is being developed which will be submitted to the Home Office for accreditation. Although still in draft form it currently consists of eight stages:

1. Referrals are taken from the sentence planning board in YOIs. In the community, they come predominately from YOTs and Probation Services.

2. An initial assessment meeting, including the referrer or their representative, a family member or partner, will cover risk management and environmental assessment issues. If regarded as suitable the individual can then undergo an extended assessment over 10 to 12 sessions.

3. This leads to an initial formulation, which identifies factors that predisposed the individual to abuse and those that precipitated the abuse. Factors that maintain the abuse and those, by contrast, that protect against it are also identified. In each of the predisposing, maintaining and protective factors we examine evidence from two dimensions, personal and contextual.

4. A pre-intervention stage attempts to identify and overcome obstacles to motivation and engagement. This may include work on managing blocks relating to own abuse or arousal and this may continue alongside the main programme themes. If necessary, behaviour modification would be available to help control deviant fantasy.

5. The intervention programme consists of six core elements, which are selected in accordance with the treatment needs of the individual. The elements, not in sequential order, are: offence specific; self concept and social functioning; sexuality, healthy sexual relationships and sexual knowledge; emotional self-regulation; behavioural self-regulation; family/carer relationships and attachments.

6. At the end of intervention the young person will be helped to put together a new life plan that addresses features both internal and external to the individual.

7. Follow-up reviews aim to sustain any positive treatment outcomes through meeting with young people and their significant others. This includes attendance, where appropriate, at Multi-Agency Public Protection Panels (MAPPPs) or at information-gathering meetings leading up to MAPPPs.

8. Evaluation is based upon psychometric measures taken before and after treatment, re-offence rates, user views and our ability to identify demonstrable new skills relating to therapeutic goals.

The main theoretical foundations of the intervention programme are cognitive-behavioural and psycho-educational. However, in the light of recent advice on the use of cognitive-behavioural programmes in prison, the service is keen to 'take account of the social environments in which offenders are taking decisions' (Rex 2000). Hollin (1999) identifies effective treatment responses to offending as trying to change both the individual's personal functioning and their social system.

One model of treatment whose primary purpose is to understand the relationship between an individual's identified problems and their broader systemic context is multi-systemic therapy (MST). It aims to 'promote change at the level of the young person's social ecology and thus engage the young person's network in the task of managing negative behaviours and promoting positive adaptations' (O'Callaghan 2002). A randomised control trial conducted by Borduin et al. (1990) found that MST was more effective than individual therapy at three-year follow-up. Additionally the frequency of non-sexual re-offending was significantly lower amongst the MST group. Another, more recent, evaluation study has been completed by Worling and Curwen (2000). The treatment sample was provided with a programme of specific group-work and interventions aimed at promoting family strength and social functioning. The comparison group received no treatment or dropped out at an early stage. They found that the treatment group had a five per cent sexual recidivism rate compared with 18 per cent for the non-treated sample. Non-sexual offences, both violent and non-violent, were significantly lower for the treated sample.

The importance of working with the family, as evidenced in the research mentioned above, is also confirmed by the fact that young offenders are frequently in denial because of fear of family rejection if they admit the offence. One young man who was convicted of rape on the basis of DNA evidence continues to deny his offending, but was able to respond to a hypothetical question about factors underlying a generalised offender's denial: 'If he's lost everything he wouldn't want to lose his family as well.' Barnes and Hughes (2002) cite an unpublished paper by Kalsy (1997) whose study of 40 young sex offenders at Feltham YOI found that 62.5 per cent were in denial to their families for fear of losing emotional support.

It is usually a tremendous shock for families to be confronted with the allegations of sexual assault by their child. Smith and Trepper (1992, cited by Barnes and Hughes 2002) suggest that parental reactions to their child's sexually offending may follow a common pattern, not unlike the stages of bereavement. One parent (quoted in Hackett 2001) said she felt that she had lost her son the day he was arrested for a sexual crime: 'At the beginning I thought I had lost everything, my son, my whole life came tumbling down around me.' The stages identified by Smith and Trepper are as follows: pervasiveness of the problem; helplessness; active involvement; return to relative normality. As with the grieving process, fear of precipitating negative emotions frequently stifles good communication between people who could otherwise support each other.

It should be remembered that 'active involvement' by the carers could be in the wrong direction by actively discouraging the young person from taking responsibility for their behaviour. For example, there is the grandfather who promised to pay 'whatever it takes' to clear his 16-year-old grandson's name by winning an appeal against conviction for an incestuous rape. It later transpired that similar allegations had been made against the grandfather, throwing up several areas of concern in child protection. Does the grandfather currently have contact with children or vulnerable people? Is he implicated, either directly or indirectly, in the reasons behind his grandson's offending behaviour? What happens about the young person's plan to live with his grandparents on release? In this case, the offer of support by the family had a counter-productive effect upon treatment because previously the young man had admitted his offending but, with the prospect of his grandparents' and wider family support contingent upon denial, he chose the option of returning to a state of denial plus family 'support'. The window of opportunity to be explored in therapy with the young man is his personal commitment to the truth and his respect for himself. He expressed this by referring to the dilemma facing him and his grandfather: 'He doesn't know if I'm innocent and I don't know if he's innocent'.

Another factor that can underlie a family's defensive denial of the young person's offending is when the mother has been abused. Bentovim and Williams (1998) found that maternal own abuse was not uncommon amongst mothers of young sexual abusers. I have found that reactions by these mothers can be placed upon a continuum. At one extreme is the mother who denies her own experience of abuse and therefore is reluctant to engage with the issue in relation to her son's offending. At the other extreme I have experienced mothers whose unresolved feelings about their abuse may not lead to denial but instead may manifest as hypersensitivity and excessive caution. The ideal is an abused mother who comes to terms with her own experiences and is able to support her son in taking responsibility for his sexually abusive behaviour.

There are common themes to work with parents: they need reassurance that they are not to blame for their child's abusive behaviour; they frequently expect criticism; they feel ashamed; they are searching for an explanation. Jerry Thomas (1997 and 2001, personal communication) has described how appropriate self-disclosure by workers can help families to see them as allies rather than people whose judgement is a threat to be defended against. Research suggests that if the parents of these young people feel more supported, this may enable them to be more emotionally available to their children (Santry and McCarthy 1999). The definition of caregivers can be expanded to include parents, foster carers, extended family members, residential care workers, youth workers, teachers and police. Jenkins (1998) describes their role as follows: 'The young person's task is to accept full responsibility for the abusive behaviour. However it is the responsibility of caregivers to make this task accessible and to provide the extensive support that young men require to undertake it. Caregivers must assist the young man to discover, name, and attribute meaning to the steps he takes toward responsibility and respect.' This is crucial if the young person is to generate any positive treatment outcomes from the programme.

Motivating and engaging young people to accept full responsibility for their abusive behaviour depends heavily upon the style and approach taken by the therapeutic practitioners (Miller and Rollnick 1991). Young people are likely to feel embarrassed, defensive and ashamed of their sexually abusive behaviour. Their initial motivation for involvement in treatment is likely to be minimal, or to be related more to fear of consequences than to any desire to change. The central theme of our approach is one of collaboration. It is strongly influenced by the work of Alan Jenkins who draws upon narrative therapy to explore the social construction that has developed around the young person and their family. The dominant story of identity is likely to have been one of deficit, limitation, being problematic and abusive, devious and deviant, manipulative, uncontrolled. By contrast:

A model of engagement by invitation aims to promote the discovery and construction of an alternative story of identity: one that is informed by qualities and practices of responsibility and respect. It proposes that the young man may have preferences and a capacity for responsible, equitable, and respectful behaviour; preferences, and a capacity that are likely to have been overlooked or ignored by others and by the young man himself.

(Jenkins 1998)

These positive personal qualities can provide the basis for exploring more deeply the young person's ability to cope with not having had his needs met. This fits with the research, detailed above, that identifies how much trauma such young people are likely to have experienced. It also makes use of the nascent understanding of concepts of fairness and justice that, according to research into human development, are likely to be emerging in normal adolescence. The young person is helped to see that he has the following qualities: strengths, such as courage, gained in coping with adversity; the wish to protect others; a willingness to face up to problems; the ability to protect himself; concern for others; a sense of justice or injustice. By approaching the early stages of the work from this perspective, rather than from a focus on abusive or offending behaviour, we aim to increase the likelihood of successful engagement. Also, by examining the effects upon the young person of significant others failing to take responsibility, we lay the groundwork for helping the young person see the importance of their taking responsibility for their abusive actions. Rather than confronting resistance (Sheath 1990), this interviewing style seeks to elicit self-confrontational statements from the young person. In such a model, young people are invited to establish their own intervention goals and develop their own motivation to achieve them.

Challenges

Successful programmes for anti-social youths have consistently found social skills training to be an integral component (Rutter et al. 1998). Meta-analyses such as that of Lipsey and Wilson (1998), in which they examined 200 programmes, have found that those programmes targeting behavioural change demonstrate the most significant treatment effects. The aim of a programme should therefore be to promote both cognitive and behavioural change and develop new skills and competences. However, we should give some careful consideration as to whether all of the cognitive models currently used with adults are suitable for young people.

It is important to identify the erroneous thoughts, attitudes and beliefs that led to the offending and maintained any repetition of the behaviour. An influential approach adapted from work with adults has been the 'cycle of sexually abusive behaviour'. When using this model with young people, however, it is important to emphasise 'escape routes' (Way and Spieker 1997) to avoid the potentially demoralising effects of a belief that abusive behaviour is a self-perpetuating vicious circle. Practitioners managing risk can be aided by using such a model to analyse patterns of behaviour, but with adolescents it is far more likely that such a pattern does not exist and that their index offence is indeed their first (Chaffin 2000). They are also less likely to have persistent sexual fantasies or to have engaged in elaborate planning. On a practical level, care needs to be taken when using such a complex model with young people as they are likely to have difficulties remembering it and may struggle to adapt it to their own learning needs. Worling (1998) recommends that the offence process needs to be simplified to: situation – strong feelings – sexual thoughts – thinking errors – planning – high-risk situations – sexual assault – strong feelings.

It is possible to approach the treatment needs of adolescents through a framework of human emotional development, with attachment issues forming a helpful starting point. Ward, Hudson and McCormack (1997) have used the model of attachment style developed by Bartholomew and Horowitz to identify four different categories that may be applicable to adult sex offenders, as follows: those who are securely attached have a positive view of themselves and others; the preoccupied have a negative view of themselves but a positive view of others; dismissing individuals have a positive view of themselves but a negative view of others; the fearful have a negative view of both themselves and others. Ward, Hudson and McCormack found that the connection between attachment and problems such as fear of intimacy, affective deregulation, and negative attitudes towards women seem to be more fundamental than offender type. Secure and dismissing types reported the lowest loneliness score, while preoccupied and fearfully attached men reported significantly higher levels of loneliness. Attachment and intimacy could perhaps be used to provide a framework to approach the loneliness experienced by young people who sexually abuse and allow professionals some awareness of the 'self' and 'other' concepts held by them. Treatment could then challenge specific attitudes and beliefs related to intimacy avoidance, such as fear of intimacy, vulnerability and rejection. To do this it may be necessary to include as part of assessment a full account of their attachment history along with any maltreatment or traumatic events experienced in childhood. It is likely that young people who sexually abuse have had very few opportunities to develop secure relationships in the past. For example, a young man who frequently expressed hostility to prison staff and experienced them as antagonistic was able to acknowledge that he preferred that there not be 'bad vibes' between himself and others. When asked what 'good vibes times' he could remember as a child he could not do so. For this man and others, we need to devise an individual treatment plan that is specifically tailored to the emotional needs of the adolescent. Through their relationships with members of staff, the adolescents should have the opportunity to develop trusting relationships. One young man (probably of a 'dismissive' attachment style) described his view of fellow inmates as 'faces, not friends'. This requires the co-workers who are treating this man to model important interpersonal skills such as effective communicating, perspective taking and adaptive ways of dealing with feelings. It is also important that attempts are made whenever possible to improve the quality of the adolescents' close relationships and social support in their natural environment.

Just as the individual needs to be placed in the context of their family, so their family's functioning is highly dependent upon being embedded in the wider community and this social support needs to be encouraged if intervention is to be successful. Such an approach militates against the 'responsibility overload', where the young person bears an excessive load, which Jenkins (1998) has identified as making it very difficult for adolescent sex abusers to face up to their offending. The work with the family should identify some of the problems that may underlie the offending behaviour. This underlines the importance of carefully re-integrating the individual into society through encouraging problem solving, self-care and interdependence, education and vocational goals, social and leisure activities. The resource implications of this make it all the more important that we have an integrated structure and policy to respond to the needs of juvenile sex offenders.

Policy formation in this area has mirrored the fragmented nature of service provision for young people generally in the UK. There is a definite lack of effective local and inter-agency policy, guidance and procedures that integrate child protection and youth justice systems. Inter-agency protocols need to be established on a national basis in order to promote greater consistency of response, particularly in determining when child protection processes should be entered or exited, and how the interface with the criminal justice system should be managed. The NSPCC has recently recommended that the Children and Young People's Unit should take responsibility for ensuring a joined-up government approach to this issue by the Treasury, Home Office, Department of Health, Department for Education and Skills and the Youth Justice Board (Lovell 2002).

A serious challenge exists to find ways to encourage and evaluate beneficial change in the environment. One YOT in Pembrokeshire, Wales, helped young people 'at risk' of offending with the task of creating a video about healthy sexuality and relationships. The group were going to show the video to local schools as part of an attempt to prevent sexual crime by young people. Gene Abel, who said that 'There has never been a public health problem successfully reduced by treating individuals after they have developed the problem', has voiced an argument in favour of prevention (Abel and Rouleau 1990). Educating communities about this problem is likely to be more successful in the long term than efforts at sex offender registration and community notification, which threaten to alienate young people and their families from the very services that can help to reduce risk.

Conclusion

The quotation at the beginning of this chapter is intended to underline the fact that within every individual there is a potential for change and this motivates us to work with people. For these efforts to have the best chance of success, it is imperative that interventions are developmentally appropriate and fit the developmental needs of the young person.

We need to use the evidence emerging from research into typologies and recidivism without losing sight of the particular needs of the individual. For example, we should try to distinguish between the adolescent who offends sexually as part of a pattern of general anti-social behaviour and the young person who offends specifically in a sexual manner in the fulfilment of deviant sexual interests. Since the former are at higher risk for general offending, they may be more likely to benefit from treatment targeting general delinquency factors. For the latter group, the focus of treatment might more usefully be upon individualised and situational factors that increase the risk of sexual offending.

Not all theories and materials are transferable between adults and young people who sexually abuse. In light of research into adolescence, adolescent delinquency and characteristics of adolescents who sexually abuse, we can conclude that programmes should aim to integrate an individual's treatment goals into their community and social systems. This is essential if any treatment gains are to be maintained after intervention and follow-up.

Note

*The author is a senior clinical therapist at the Lucy Faithfull Foundation.

References

Abel, G. G., Becker, J. V., Cunningham-Rathner, J., Mittelman, M. S., Murphy, W. D. and Rouleau, J. L. (1987), 'Self-reported Sex Crimes of Non-incarcerated Paraphiliacs', *Journal of Interpersonal Violence* 2, pp. 3–25.

Abel, G. G., Becker, J. V., Cunningham-Rathner, J., Mittelman, M. S. and Rouleau, J. L. (1988), 'Multiple Paraphilic Diagnosis Among Sex Offenders', *Bulletin of the American Academy of Psychiatry and the Law* 16, pp. 153–68.

Abel, G. G. and Rouleau, J. (1990) 'The Nature and Extent of Sexual Assault', in W. L. Marshall, D. R. Laws and H. E. Barbaree (eds) *Handbook of Sexual Assault: issues, theories and treatment of the offender*. New York: Plenum.

ATSA (1997) *Position on the Effective Legal Management of Juvenile Sex Offenders*. Beaverton: Oregon.

Barnes, C. and Hughes, G. (2002) 'Family Work with Adolescent Sex Offenders', in M. C. Calder (ed) *Young People Who Sexually Abuse: building the evidence base for your practice*. Dorset: Russell House Publishing.

Becker, J. V. (1988). 'Adolescent Sex Offenders', *The Behaviour Therapist* 11, pp. 185–7.

Beckett, R. (1999) 'Evaluation of Adolescent Sexual Abusers', in M. Erooga and H. Masson (eds) *Children and Young People Who Sexually Abuse Others: challenges and responses*. London: Routledge.

Beech, A. and Fordham, A. (1997) 'Therapeutic Climate of Sexual Offender Treatment Programs', *Sexual Abuse* 9, pp. 219–37.

Bentovim, A. and Williams, B. (1998) 'Children and Adolescents: victims who become perpetrators', *Advances in Psychiatric Treatment* 4, pp. 101–7.

Borduin, C. M., Hengeller, S. W., Blaske, D. M. and Stein, R. J. (1990) 'Multisystemic Treatment of Adolescent Sex Offenders', *International Journal of Offender Therapy and Comparative Criminology* 34:2, pp. 105–13.

Bowlby, J. (1988) *A Secure Base: parent-child attachment and healthy human development*. New York: Basic Books.

Bridge Childcare Development Service (2001) *Childhood Lost: Part 8 case review report DM*. Hay on Wye: Bridge Publishing.

Butler, S. M., and Seto, M. C. (2002) 'Distinguishing Two Types of Juvenile Sex Offenders', *Journal of the American Academy of Child and Adolescent Psychiatry* 41, pp. 83–90.

Calder, M. C., Hanks, H., Epps, K. J., Print, B., Morrison, T. and Henniker, J. (2001) *Juveniles and Children who Sexually Abuse: frameworks for assessment*. Dorset: Russell House Publishing.

Chaffin, M. (2000) 'Family and Ecological Emphasis in Interventions: a developmental perspective in working with children, adolescents and adults with sexually abusive behaviours' (Keynote address to the 10th Annual Conference of the National Organisation for the Treatment of Abusers, Dublin).

Chaffin, M. and Bonner, B. (1998) '"Don't Shoot, We're Your Children": have we gone too far in our response to adolescent sexual abusers and children with sexual behaviour problems?', *Child Maltreatment* 3, pp. 314–16.

Clarke, P. (2002) 'Therapeutic Communities: a model for effective intervention with teenagers known to have perpetrated sexual abuse', in M. C. Calder (ed) *Young People Who Sexually Abuse: building the evidence base for your practice*. Dorset: Russell House Publishing.

Epps, K. J. (1999) 'Causal Explanations: filling the theoretical reservoir', in M. C. Calder (ed) *Working with Young People Who Sexually Abuse: new pieces of the jigsaw puzzle*. Dorset: Russell House Publishing.

Erooga, M. and Masson, H. (eds) (1999) *Children and Young People Who Sexually Abuse Others: challenges and responses*. London: Routledge.

France, K. G. and Hudson, S. M. (1993) 'The Conduct Disorders and the Juvenile Sex Offender', in H. E. Barbaree, W. L. Marshall, S. M. Hudson (eds) *The Juvenile Sex Offender*. New York: Guilford Press.

Gottfredson, M. R. and Hirschi, T. (1990) *A General Theory of Crime*. Stanford, California: Stanford University Press.

Graham, F., Richardson, G. and Bhate, S. R. (1998) 'Development of a Service for Sexually Abusive Adolescents in the Northeast of England', in W. L. Marshall, Y. M. Fernandez, S. M. Hudson and T. Ward (eds) *Sourcebook of Treatment Programmes for Sex Offenders*. New York: Plenum.

Grubin, D. (1998) *Sex Offending Against Children: understanding the risk*. London: Home Office.

Hackett, S. (2001) *Facing the Future: a guide for parents of young people who have sexually abused*. Dorset: Russell House Publishing.

Hanson, R. K. and Bussière, M. T. (1998) 'Predicting Relapse: a meta-analysis of sexual offender recidivism studies', *Journal of Consulting and Clinical Psychology* 66, pp. 348–62.

Hare, R. D. (1993) *Without Conscience: the disturbing world of the psychopaths among us*. New York: Simon & Schuster.

Harris, V. and Staunton, C. (2000) 'The Antecedents of Young Male Sex Offenders', in G. Boswell (ed) *Violent Children and Adolescents: asking the question why*. London: Whurr Publishers.

Havighurst, R. J. (1972) *Developmental Tasks and Education*. McKay.

Hoghughi, M. S., Bhate, S.R. and Graham, F. (eds) (1997) *Working with Sexually Abusive Adolescents*. California: Sage.

Hollin, C. R. (1999) 'Treatment Programs for Offenders: meta-analysis, "what works", and beyond', *International Journal of Law and Psychiatry* 22:3–4, pp. 361–72.

Hunter, J. A., Goodwin, D. W. and Becker, J. V. (1994) 'The Relationship between Phallometrically Measured Deviant Sexual Arousal and Clinical Characteristics in Juvenile Sexual Offenders', *Behaviour Research and Therapy* 32, pp. 533–8.

Jenkins, A. (1990) *Invitations to Responsibility: the therapeutic engagement of men who are violent and abusive*. Adelaide: Dulwich Centre Publications.

Jenkins, A. (1998) 'Invitations to Responsibility: engaging adolescent and young men who have sexually abused', in W. L. Marshall, Y. M. Fernandez, S. M. Hudson and T. Ward (eds) *Sourcebook of Treatment Programmes for Sex Offenders*. New York: Plenum.

Johnson, G. M. and Knight, R. A. (2000) 'Developmental Antecedents of Sexual Coercion in Juvenile Sex Offenders', *Sexual Abuse* 7, pp. 165–78.

Kemshall, H. (2001) 'Risk Assessment and Management of Known Sexual and Violent Offenders: a review of current issues', *Police Research Series*, Paper 140. London: Home Office, Policing and Reducing Crime Unit.

Langström, N. and Grann, M. (2000) 'Risk for Criminal Recidivism Among Young Sex Offenders', *Journal of Interpersonal Violence* 15, pp. 855–71.

Lipsey, M. and Wilson, D. B. (1998) 'Effective Intervention for Serious Juvenile Offenders', in R. L. Loeber and D. P. Farrington (eds) *Serious and Violent Juvenile Offenders: risk factors and successful interventions*. California: Sage.

Lovell, E. (2002) 'I think I might need some more help with this problem . . .', *Responding to Children and Young People Who Display Sexually Harmful Behaviour*. London: NSPCC.

Marshall, W. L. (1989) 'Invited Essay: intimacy, loneliness and sexual offenders', *Behaviour Research and Therapy* 27, pp. 491–503.

Miller, W. R. and Rollnick, S. (1991) *Motivational Interviewing: preparing people to change addictive behaviours*. New York: Guilford Press.

Moffitt, T. E. (1993) 'Adolescence-Limited and Life-Course Persistent Antisocial Behaviour: a developmental taxonomy', *Psychological Review* 100, pp. 674–701.

Moore, S. and Rosenthal, D. (1993) *Sexuality in Adolescence*. London: Routledge.

Morrison, T. (1999) 'Is There a Strategy Out There?' in M. Erooga and H. Masson (eds) (1999) *Children and Young People Who Sexually Abuse Others: challenges and responses*. London: Routledge.

National Children's Homes (1992) *Report of the Committee of Enquiry into Children and Young People Who Sexually Abuse Other Children*. London: NCH.

O' Callaghan, D. (2002) 'Providing a Research Informed Service for Young People Who Sexually Abuse', in M. C. Calder (ed) *Young People Who Sexually Abuse: building the evidence base for your practice*. Dorset: Russell House Publishing.

Quinsey, V. L. and Lalumière, M. L. (1995) 'Evolutionary Perspectives on Sexual Offending', *Sexual Abuse* 7, pp 301–15.

Rasmussen, L. A. (1999) 'Factors Related to Recidivism Among Juvenile Sexual Offenders', *Sexual Abuse* 11:1, pp. 69–85.

Rex, S. A. (2000) 'Beyond Cognitive-Behaviouralism? Reflections on the Effectiveness Literature', in A. Bottoms, L. Gelsthorpe and S. Rex (eds) *Community Penalties, Change and Challenges*. Devon: Willan Publishing.

Rutter, M., Giller, H. and Hagel, A. (1998) *Antisocial Behaviour by Young People*. Cambridge: Cambridge University Press.

Ryan, G., Miyoshi T. J., Mezner J. L., Krugman R. D. and Fryer G. E. (1996) 'Trends in a National Sample of Sexually Abusive Youths', *Journal of American Academy of Child Adolescent Psychiatry* 35, pp. 17–25.

Salter, D., McMillan, D, Richards, M., Talbot, T., Hodges, J., Bentovim, A., Hastings, R., Stevenson, J. and Skuse, D. (2003) 'Development of Sexually Abusive Behaviour in Sexually Abused Males: a longitudinal study', *The Lancet* 361:9356 (8 February).

Santry, S. and McCarthy, G. (1999) 'Attachment and intimacy in young people who sexually abuse', in M. C. Calder (ed.) *Working with Young People who Sexually Abuse: new pieces of the jigsaw puzzle*. Dorset: Russell House Publishing.

Seto, M. C., Lalumière, M. L. and Blanchard, R. (2000) 'The Discriminative Validity of a Phallometric Test for Pedophilic Interests Among Adolescent Sex Offenders Against Children', *Psychological Assessment* 12, pp. 319–27.

Sheath, M. (1990) 'Confrontative Work with Sex Offenders: legitimised nonce-bashing?' *Probation Journal* 37:4, pp. 159–62.

Sipe, R., Jensen, E. L. and Everett, R. S. (1998) 'Adolescent Sexual Offenders Grown Up: Recidivism in Young Adulthood', *Criminal Justice and Behaviour* 25, pp. 109–24.

Thomas, J. (1997) 'The Family in Treatment', in G. Ryan and S. Lane (eds), *Juvenile Sex Offending – Causes, Consequences and Corrections*. Sussex: Wiley.

Ward, T., Hudson, S. M. and McCormack J. (1997) 'Attachment Style, Intimacy Deficits, and Sexual Offending', in B. K. Schwartz and H. R. Cellini (eds) *The Sex Offender: new insights, treatment innovations, and legal developments*. Kingston, New Jersey: Civic Research Institute.

Way, I. F. and Spieker, S. D. (1997) *The Cycle of Offence: a framework for treating adolescent sex offenders*. Notre Dame, Indiana: Jace Publications.

Weinrott, M. R. (1996) *Juvenile Sexual Aggression: a critical review*. Colorado: Institute of Behavioural Science.

Worling, J. R. (1998) 'Adolescent Sexual Offender Treatment at the SAFE-T Program', in W. L. Marshall, Y. M. Fernandez, S. M. Hudson and T. Ward (eds) *Sourcebook of Treatment Programmes for Sex Offenders*. New York: Plenum.

Worling, J. R. (2002) 'Assessing Risk of Sexual Assault Recidivism with Adolescent Sex Offenders', in M. C. Calder (ed) *Young People Who Sexually Abuse: building the evidence base for your practice*. Dorset: Russell House Publishing.

Worling, J. R. and Curwen, T. (2000) 'Adolescent Sexual Offenders Recidivism: success of specialized treatment and implications for risk prediction', *Child Abuse and Neglect* 24:7, pp. 965–82.

Chapter 10

Developing Multi-Agency Public Protection Arrangements

Tim Bryan and Paddy Doyle

Introduction

This chapter is written from the perspective of the authors, two criminal justice practitioners who had the opportunity of using their professional experience to help shape the creation and early development of these arrangements. The fact that we were secondees from the police service and the probation service into the Public Protection Unit (PPU) of the National Probation Directorate (NPD) allowed us to experience directly the creative tension that can develop from inter-disciplinary work as well as to model the critical relationship that now exists between the police and probation in the arena of public protection. Our experiences, many of them undertaken jointly, of writing the *Initial Guidance*, co-ordinating the production of the first year's annual Multi-Agency Public Protection Arrangements (MAPPA) reports, facilitating successive years of regional seminars and contributing substantially to the publication of *The MAPPA Guidance* in March 2003, have given us an invaluable insight into the work already achieved across the 42 areas of England and Wales. In particular, it has given us an appreciation of the potential for further development as well as the challenges of reaching that potential.

The views expressed here are those of the authors and do not necessarily reflect a government perspective.

Creation of responsible authorities

Sections 67 and 68 of the Criminal Justice and Court Services Act 2000 stand as a watershed in the development of multi-agency arrangements for public protection. Indeed, many would consider they represent the

189

birth of MAPPA both legally and organisationally for the police and probation services. However, without detracting from the general importance of this legislation, it would be wrong to attribute everything to it. The MAPPA legislation confirmed and consolidated what was already good and emerging practice: it did not create something entirely new. This is part of the nature of English law-making: essentially empirical and cautious (witness the need for further legislation to strengthen the MAPPA now before Parliament).

The MAPPA legislation was implemented in April 2001 and established a number of legal responsibilities for the police and probation services of England and Wales to be discharged jointly as the Responsible Authority. The Act defined the Responsible Authority as being the chief officer of police and the local probation board for each area, and their responsibilities comprised the following:

- establishing arrangements for assessing and managing the risk of serious harm posed by certain sexual, violent and other dangerous offenders

- reviewing these arrangements with a view to monitoring their effectiveness

- preparing and publishing an annual report on the discharge of these arrangements within the area.

While the Act stopped short of formalising public protection arrangements with other agencies, the *Initial Guidance* noted that a number of statutory and voluntary agencies, in addition to the police and probation, had an important role to play in effective public protection. This was a theme that the Responsible Authority was encouraged to develop and to which most positively responded. (Importantly, this element of partnership will be strengthened and formalised in the current Criminal Justice Bill through provision for certain agencies to be under a 'duty to co-operate' with the arrangements.)

The purpose of the MAPPA was to assess and manage the risks posed by certain sexual and violent offenders in order to prevent re-offending and to minimise the risk of serious harm to the public. From the outset the intention was for this to be achieved by the 'consolidation and development of existing public protection work and to promote best practice across England and Wales'. This initial consolidation required the Responsible Authority to:

- establish strategic management for reviewing and monitoring the effectiveness of the arrangements made and for revising them as necessary or expedient

- establish and agree systems and processes for sharing information and for inter-agency working on all the relevant offenders

- establish and agree systems and processes for a Multi-Agency Public Protection Panel (MAPPP) for the highest risk cases, including young offenders

- establish and agree systems and processes to ensure that only those 'critical few' who require that additional consideration are referred to a MAPPP

- consider resource allocation, multi-agency training, and community and media communications

- agree the Annual Report and statistics.

The context of MAPPA development

This initial development of MAPPA, and indeed its subsequent progress, occur within a broader professional and political context that is significant in determining the shape of that development. Take, for instance, the Responsible Authority: the probation service and the police service in each area. Prior to 1991 the probation service had very little contact with or influence over many of those dangerous or potentially dangerous offenders who are subject to MAPPA after their release from prison. Such offenders tended not to be granted parole because of the risk of harm they posed and so were not subject to any form of post-release supervision. The 1991 Criminal Justice Act changed that by requiring all offenders serving 12 months' imprisonment or more to be subject to supervision on release. Importantly, for the first time it also made public protection a permanent item on the agenda of the probation service, and one that has grown in significance. Hence the first objective in the National Probation Service's first strategy document 'A New Choreography': 'more accurate and effective assessment and management of risk and dangerousness'.

Within a similar period the police have also experienced significant organisational and cultural change in respect of their response to serious sexual offending. During the early 1990s it was increasingly recognised that the police alone were not able to deal effectively with all sexual offending, and that there needed to be a greater emphasis on victim care. In relation to child victims in particular, the formation of child protection teams highlighted the invaluable support that other agencies such as social services provide for the ongoing needs of victims and their families, as well as the important information held by other agencies about perpetrators or potential perpetrators. Energy and resources were therefore directed at improved care and treatment of victims, not just at the point of initial contact with the police but throughout the criminal justice process. However, the attitude of the police remained essentially reactive to the investigation of serious sexual offending until the Sex Offender Act 1997 made the implicit requirement for the police to join with the Probation Service and others in proactively assessing and managing future risk. This presented two challenges to the police: the first, to develop an intelligence-led approach to sex offenders and sexual offending and to accord it significance among the numerous policing priorities; and secondly, to establish an effective partnership with the probation service, a criminal justice agency with which, stereotypically, most police officers would consider they had little in common.

There has been positive progress on the first in some areas of England and Wales, and this will be discussed later. However, the second has been unequivocally successful. Indeed, one of the really exciting aspects of public protection development has been the growth in trust and co-operation between the police and probation services, adding enormous value to the way each agency is able to conduct its statutory responsibilities. While this has been primarily focused around sex offenders and their offending, this new relationship has opened up opportunities for development into other areas of criminality (such as persistent offenders, domestic violence and gun crime), and strengthened some of the new inter-agency organisational structures such as crime and disorder partnerships, Youth Offending Teams (YOTs) and drug action teams. For example, good practice now sees the police more commonly taking on a role in sentence supervision and support, which belies the image of the police as merely an enforcement agency. Conversely, good practice among probation officers has seen a shift from what has been perceived as 'welfare' to a more sharply focused approach combining treatment intervention and enforcement. While these cultural changes have taken several years, it would not have been possible for the MAPPA legislation to have been enacted successfully unless that process had already begun.

In addition to these organisational and cultural changes, the professional environment in which such offenders are managed has become increasingly complex and demanding. This is witnessed by recent and intended legislative provisions; measures that have increased the power of the state to impose conditions, restrictions and tougher penalties on those offenders thought to pose risks to public safety. Such measures include:

- The Sex Offenders Act 1997, which explicitly required certain sex offenders to register their addresses with the police and implicitly expected the police to work with the probation service and others in respect of those offenders. This is now widely seen as a watershed in the establishment of effective working relationships between police, probation and, increasingly over time, with a range of other agencies such as health, housing and social services.

- The Crime and Disorder Act 1998, which established a duty on local authorities, police, probation and health authorities to work together to address local crime problems as informed by a public crime audit. It also established a new hybrid order, the Sex Offender Order, which strengthened the controls that could be placed on sex offenders who were reasonably considered to pose a risk of harm to the public. Additionally this Order placed a registration requirement on offenders who were convicted prior to the Sex Offenders Act 1997.

- The Crime Sentences Act 1998, which enabled the courts to impose discretionary life sentences for second serious violent or sexual offences or extended periods of supervision where continuing harm was posed.

- The Criminal Justice Bill, which proposes the extension of the Responsible Authority in each area of England and Wales to include the prison service, and will also establish for a number of agencies a 'duty to co-operate' with the Responsible Authority in the assessment and management of risk posed by those offenders falling within MAPPA. These agencies currently include local authority social services, housing and education, registered social landlords, various elements of the health service, YOTs, social security and electronic monitoring providers. It also proposes formalising the role of lay advisers in the strategic management of MAPPA.

- The Sexual Offences Bill, a comprehensive review of sex offences which provides for a number of new offences that clearly set out what is and what is not acceptable sexual behaviour. In particular it creates a new offence of meeting a child following sexual grooming, and makes provision for a number of new orders including risk of sexual harm orders, notification orders and sexual offences prevention orders.[1]

- Proposed mental health legislation for the assessment, treatment and detention of those suffering from dangerous and severe personality disorders.

In this challenging environment there are a number of factors which support the argument for a phased development of MAPPA. For instance, in public protection terms we have in fact already come a long way in a very short space of time. During this period the balance between the rights of individuals and the degree to which the state seeks to intervene in individuals' lives for the purpose of protecting the public from potentially dangerous offenders has changed significantly. Over the past decade, although human rights and data protection legislation have been implemented, the balance has shifted, and continues to shift, in favour of greater public protection. However, because the focus of MAPPA is on this risk of harm caused by dangerous offenders, there are a number of factors that lead to a sense of urgency when people approach this subject. The public perception, informed as it often is by the distorted presentation of the issues in much of the media, is dominated by images of predatory strangers waiting to abduct and sexually abuse children. The system is seen as 'too soft' on such offenders and if the public is offered MAPPA as a solution rather than the often-voiced preferred alternatives of castration and imprisonment, then MAPPA had better be demonstrably foolproof – nothing short of total protection will do. We have become a risk-averse society. However, the reality is that even if MAPPA were to operate perfectly, serious sexual and violent offences would still occur. The unpalatable reality is that research indicates that a significant proportion of such offences are committed by people with no criminal antecedents.

This reflects a key feature of the context in which public protection takes place. The fact that public protection is based on a number of complex processes and interactions with the offender and between agencies does not accord with the media's desire for simple messages and straightforward solutions to problems. But their shaping of the context may raise unrealistic expectations that the police and probation services can never deliver. And the inevitable failure to meet these expectations whips up public hysteria about the effectiveness of public protection, generating a great deal of anxiety but little objectivity. This is not to suggest that 'success' is never achieved but, because it is measured by the negative proxy of no re-offending, it wins no plaudits and is inevitably overshadowed by the sensationalism of the failures.

The political response to this understandable public pressure is to seek to make the MAPPA as good as the public would wish them to be – right now. It is of little comfort for a politician facing public outrage about some real or potential threat to its members to be required to counsel patience on the promise that every effort is being made to improve an admittedly fallible system. All of this is further exacerbated by the unrealistic expectation which has arisen that as a society we have the right to be protected from all risk. This is repeatedly articulated in the phrase seemingly compulsorily employed by all local or national political spokespersons asked to respond to any tragedy, be it a transport, public health or child protection issue, vis, 'We must make sure that this never happens again', as if with sufficient effort and determination such future risks could be eliminated entirely. As Hazel Kemshall has commented:

> The desirable outcome of MAPPA is effective risk management. However this should not be understood as a 'zero risk' as this position can never be achieved ... Risk management should be understood as harm reduction either through the reduction of the likelihood of a risk occurring or the reduction of its impact should it occur.
>
> (Kemshall 2003)

Professionals, too, are often caught up in this impatience for improved systems that reduce the onus placed on their professional judgement, faced as they are on a daily basis with the challenge of managing the risks posed to the public by difficult and complex offenders.

Against this background the work to develop MAPPA has importantly needed to hold the tension between this impatience and the firm belief that only well-grounded and solidly-developed systems will ultimately offer the best practice that we all desire for our public protection arrangements. Solutions produced in haste often fail to deliver the intended outcomes, and this would clearly be unacceptable. Similarly, for the solutions to be effective requires more than just the imposition of new procedures. We therefore have come to describe MAPPA development as something which falls into three phases, each of which is essential if we are to reach the shared objective of establishing systems that prevent re-offending and minimise the risk of serious harm to the public caused by certain known offenders. The phases are:

- Phase One – the establishment of MAPPA to some common basic minimum standards across England and Wales.

- Phase Two – the establishment of a national framework for MAPPA, including strategic management arrangements, with agreed national standards and performance indicators.

- Phase Three – the establishment of 'What Works'[2] evidence-based practice and possibly accreditation of approved systems for MAPPA.

The first year, 2001/2

Although the *Initial Guidance* set out the minimum requirements for each Responsible Authority, it was clear that areas were beginning from very different places with regard to existing structures, a position well illustrated by the research of Maguire et al. It was therefore necessary not only to publish guidance but also to develop mechanisms for supporting and encouraging the implementation of it. So, with the agreement of Terry Grange, Chief Constable of Dyfed Powys and the lead officer for the Association of Chief Police Officers (ACPO), and using the newly appointed National Probation Service regional managers, the Public Protection Unit (PPU) arranged ten regional seminars during October/ November 2001. These events hosted over 600 representatives from agencies locally involved in MAPPP and were positively received. Not surprisingly, police and probation were in the majority, but a number of areas had made considerable efforts to involve colleagues from social services, housing, YOTs and health as key partners.

The aim of each seminar was to assist areas in their development of the work of MAPPPs by informing them of emerging political concerns, the agenda for proposed national development and, in a series of workshops, to engage practitioners and managers in shaping a national MAPPA perspective on key issues. The issues for discussion included lay involvement, offender involvement, the management of lower-risk offenders, the responsibilities of lead agencies, costs and effective resourcing, joint and multi-agency training, community notification and designing performance indicators. Although the variety of views expressed during these workshops was a reflection of the diversity of the audience and each area's experience of MAPPP, it did provide some very strong messages that have informed subsequent policy development. In particular, the role of lay people as members of the strategic management boards, currently being piloted in eight areas of England and Wales, and the development of a framework for the assessment and management of risk posed by all offenders within MAPPA, and not just the 'critical few', owe much to the strength of views expressed during these workshops.

The regional seminars also provided an invaluable opportunity for the trialing of guidance for the first Annual Reports for 2001/2. This guidance, published in February 2002, prescribed a basic structure for the reports describing the area's arrangements for risk assessment and management, the agencies involved, the strategic management arrangements, reference to the use of disclosure as an aspect of risk management and the engagement with victims through the statutory responsibility of the probation service under s.69 of the Criminal Justice and Court Services Act 2000. Importantly, it determined the statistical information areas were required to publish in their Annual Reports, and for this inaugural year explained how a central MAPPA report, published by the NPD and ACPO, would provide a national perspective that was supportive of local reports. While the seminars gave opportunity for areas to describe what was being achieved, they also raised a series of questions about the capacity of agencies to progress centrally driven initiatives in the absence of additional resources and the need for an agreed national framework for MAPPA.

However, encouraged by the enthusiasm and professionalism with which areas were tackling public protection issues, even in the absence of comprehensive guidance, it was clear that the PPU, at the strategic direction of ACPO and the NPD, needed to progress the development of a national framework for MAPPA. So, in March 2002, a series of meetings was convened with key practitioners and senior managers from across England and Wales who represented the breadth of agencies engaged in MAPPA. Representatives from housing, health, YOTs, social services and prisons joined with police and probation officers and the PPU to talk about process and procedures, risk assessment and management, and outputs and outcomes. Their deliberations were to form the basis of draft MAPPA guidance which the second round of regional seminars, in October and November 2002, were to use as a springboard for informing and involving areas in this iterative process.

In the midst of this policy development, the reality of sexual and violent offending continued. In August 2002, as many areas were publishing their annual MAPPA reports, the tragedy of Soham – the abduction and murder of Jessica Chapman and Holly Wells – began to unfold. We were reminded of the tragedy two years previously when Sarah Payne was murdered, and similar emotions of horror and sadness were generated. Yet the predicted outburst of violence towards sex offenders and paedophiles in the summer of 2000 did not occur, even though the Annual Reports were putting the number of registered sex offenders in each area into the public domain for the first time. While there were lessons to be learnt regarding the central co-ordination of the publication of the Annual Reports, the fact that potentially sensitive information could be placed in the public domain without major public disorder was an indication that the debate in respect of public safety issues has the potential to progress. The decision to release the Annual Reports over an eight-week period, staggering the dissemination of data, was taken by ministers so that media interest in the statistics did not detract attention from the excellent work being undertaken through MAPPA. This was successful: local interest in the Area Reports was generally positive. Inevitably, however, when all the figures were available a number of newspapers ran articles seeking to establish 'league tables' or find explanations for the variable distribution of registered sex offenders in particular areas. 'Sex offenders move home to "hotspots" close to jail', was the headline of an article which purported to establish a link between the areas of the country with the highest

Table 10.1 The total number of sexual, violent and other offenders included within MAPPA 2001/2

Registered sex offenders	18,513
RSOs per 100,000	35
Sex offenders cautioned/convicted for breach of registration requirement	682
Total Sex Offender Orders granted	81
Violent and other sex offenders	27,477
Other offenders	1,219
Total MAPPA offenders	47,209

proportion of registered sex offenders and the prisons which hold the highest number of sex offenders.

Table 10.1 shows the cumulative totals of the information included within the Area Reports. The relatively small number of Sex Offender Orders confirmed research undertaken by the Home Office that there was variable uptake across areas of this risk management option. In part this was due to some areas placing higher thresholds on their use or using other methods for the management and containment of offenders. Generally, the reports and the statistical information they contained highlighted the complexity of MAPPA and reinforced the need for the *Further Guidance* – issued to areas in respect of the second Annual MAPPA Reports for 2002/3 – to provide consistent mechanisms for focusing attention on those offenders who pose the highest risk of serious harm to the public.

The *Further Guidance* built on this statistical base but extended it in two important aspects. First, it required areas to identify the number of offenders within MAPPA who were considered to represent the 'critical few' and had therefore been managed at some point during the reporting year through the MAPPP. Second, it required identification of this 'critical few' to determine the number against whom either some form of enforcement action had been undertaken (such as breach of licence or breach of Restraining/Sex Offender Orders) or who, while managed through the MAPPP, had been charged with a serious sexual or violent offence. This broadening of information disclosed to the public was not merely about more detailed quantitative data. Importantly, it began to focus on the outcome of MAPPA for the highest-risk offenders, those considered within the MAPPP, with regard to their serious re-offending or the pre-emptive enforcement action taken by agencies. This process of evaluation and performance measurement is fundamental to the development of best practice within MAPPA and has been assisted by the publication in March 2003 of a national MAPPA framework.

MAPPA Guidance 2003

This *Guidance* establishes the MAPPA framework that seeks to achieve two objectives through the Responsible Authorities of England and Wales: to improve the consistency and quality of the MAPPA and to strengthen the strategic management within areas. The first will be achieved through the implementation of the MAPPA operational 'framework' or model; the second by developing the Strategic Management Board (SMB) in each area so that it is more challenging of the quality of its own arrangements.

The *operational framework* as set out in the simplified linear form in Figure 10.1 recognises four core functions for MAPPA:

1. The identification of all MAPPA offenders.

2. The sharing of information among those agencies involved in the assessment of risk.

3. The assessment of the risk of serious harm.

4. The management of that risk.

An essential feature of this framework is the dynamic and overlapping nature of these functions, meaning that risk management meetings, for instance, are not simply about formulating and reviewing risk management plans, but will also necessitate information sharing and a review of risk assessments. The framework reflects what is already occurring within many areas of England and Wales, and for the first time clarifies the functions of MAPPA and introduces agreed principles and terminology within it.

MAPPA properly starts with the identification of the relevant offenders who fall under the requirements of the legislation. Although more complex than many appreciate, accurate identification will be the basis of the legality of subsequent action and ensure that finite resources are properly targeted. The circumstances in which offenders enter and leave the arrangements must be clear. Put simply, there are three categories of offenders: *registered sex offenders* (as defined by s. 68(2) CJCS Act), *violent and other sexual offenders* who receive a sentence of imprisonment of 12 months or more (as defined by s. 68(3)-(5)CJCS Act), and *other offenders* who are considered by the Responsible Authority to pose a risk of harm to the public (as defined by s. 67(2)(b) CJCS Act). For the first two categories, offenders enter the arrangements at the point of sentence or caution where appropriate, and leave at the end of their registration requirement or licence

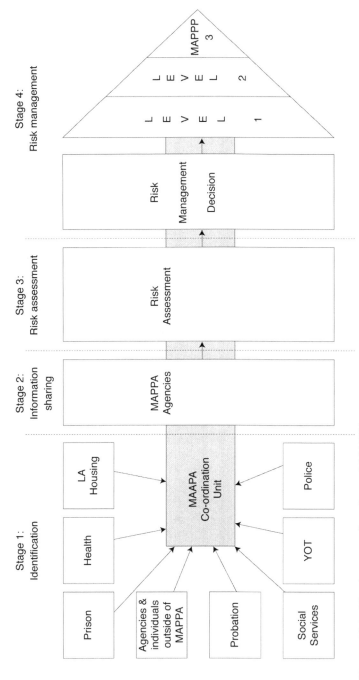

Figure 10.1 The four core functions of MAPPA

supervision, whichever is the longer. The statutory nature of supervision on release from custody with these two categories means that the primary managing agencies are the probation service, YOTs and/or the police service. While MAPPA is frequently framed only within a community context, significant benefits will accrue when the development of assessment and management plans is made in conjunction with the prison service, or other custodial institution, throughout the period of sentence and not just immediately prior to release. (The inclusion of the prison service in the Responsible Authority will greatly facilitate this.) In contrast to this, the last category, 'other offenders', can be identified by a variety of agencies involved in MAPPA, without necessary reference to a current offence. These individuals often pose the most intractable of problems to social care agencies as the majority are not under any statutory supervision or mental health control. As Table 10.1 indicates, 'other offenders' were only a small proportion of more than 47,000 offenders who were considered by MAPPA in the first year. If, as many predict, the numbers in each category increase significantly in the next five to ten years, the accuracy of identification will acquire added importance.

In addition, the *Guidance* addresses other important issues, some of which have been a source of confusion. These include determining which Responsible Authority is responsible for an offender, the protocol for transferring that responsibility, and acknowledging that not all people who pose a risk of serious harm to the public fall within the remit of MAPPA. Importantly, the *Guidance* also highlights the need for areas to continue to recognise the vital role that many offenders play in regulating their own behaviour, and that through the managing agencies offenders should be aware of MAPPA. MAPPA rightly focuses on the risks posed by the offender but the *Guidance* emphasises the need for clearer recognition of the position of victims; a point made eloquently to us during the regional seminars of 2002. The vehicle for this in the first instance is clearly the probation victim contact service, although a number of areas have also developed effective communication through Victim Support and other similar agencies.

The concepts of rigorous risk assessment and robust risk management are central to best practice in public protection, and the *Guidance* recognises that both are heavily dependent on the quality of information-sharing arrangements. Without the right information being shared and analysed by those undertaking assessment and management decisions, public protection may be compromised. The *Guidance* therefore reiterates the principles governing those arrangements, with reference to the common law duty of confidence, the Data Protection Act 1998 and the European Convention on Human Rights (ECHR). While acknowledging that these principles and the development of local information sharing protocols have been part of the initial development of MAPPA, and importantly the basis of growing trust between agencies, the *Guidance* also anticipates the provisions of the Criminal Justice Bill regarding the duty to co-operate

As Figure 10.1 illustrates, a vital component of the framework that enables the effective integration of the four functions is what is referred to as MAPPA co-ordination. This term reflects a role currently undertaken in areas by a variety of individuals and agencies but which the Responsible Authority must ensure operates effectively. The role of MAPPA co-ordination includes:

- providing, on behalf of the Responsible Authority, the central point(s) of contact within an area for the initial notification of and subsequent receipt and dissemination of relevant information about all MAPPA offenders

- maintaining a record of the level to which each offender is being referred and managed

- co-ordinating the meetings of level 2 risk management and the MAPPP

- collating and analysing data for the SMB on the operation of MAPPA.

Many areas have already made significant progress in establishing this co-ordination through MAPPP managers and police intelligence units; and the development of the ViSOR (Violent and Sex Offender Register) database, as a jointly owned national network for MAPPA offenders, offers the exciting prospect for the rapid collation, analysis and exchange of relevant information, by 2004.

As to risk assessment, the *Guidance* acknowledges the considerable progress made in developing reliable assessment, at the same time recognising that it is not a precise science and will always require the combination of reliable assessment methods and informed professional judgement. However, the development of the Offender Assessment System (OASys) across the probation and prison services of England and Wales offers enormous potential for consistency of practice and terminology within MAPPA. Therefore, the OASys definitions for levels of risk of harm (low, medium, high and very high) and the categorisation of the people to whom that harm is posed (the public, prisoners, a known adult, children, staff and self) are usefully incorporated in the *Guidance*. However, OASys cannot provide an in-depth assessment on all aspects of risk for all offenders, and important reference is made to other assessment methods such as Risk Matrix 2000 for sex offenders and ASSET for young offenders, and to the contribution that other agencies will make to the risk assessment process, either through their own approved methods or by their professional judgement.

With regard to risk management, the *Guidance* identifies both principles and terminology that should underpin the MAPPA development. Figure 10.1 shows the three levels of risk management: level 1 – ordinary risk management, level 2 – active inter-agency risk management and level 3 – MAPPP. This connected structure is intended to enable resources to be deployed to manage identified risk in the most efficient and effective manner, and is based on three principles. First, the strength of this management lies in co-ordinating the way each agency fulfils its respective responsibilities and thereby makes the co-ordinated outcome greater than the sum of the parts. The second is that effective risk management should aim to integrate both internal and external controls; that is, those that promote the offender's self management as well as those that are designed principally to constrain risk. Finally, effective management should ensure that each case is managed at the lowest appropriate level consistent with providing a defensible management plan. The decision is therefore based on both the risk of harm assessment and a judgement about the risk management needs of the case. This latter point is well illustrated in the following example.

John is a sex offender of middle age with a history of offending against children outside the family, and his risk assessment indicates a high risk of serious harm. He has completed the SOTP in prison with good results. He will be living in a probation-approved premises on release in a different area to that in which he offended and in which the victims of his most recent offences still live. He gives every indication of being fully co-operative with supervision and he will be attending the probation sex offender relapse prevention programme. The decision taken by probation is that his risk is appropriately managed by ordinary risk management (Level 1) and this continues without any concerns for some months.

As the time when John will need to leave the approved premises approaches, no certain move-on housing option is identified and the normal probation officer requests of the housing providers are not proving fruitful. John has been getting depressed and this is worrying staff at the approved premises, who wonder whether some form of medical assessment may be needed. The probation service refer the case to Level 2 – active inter-agency risk management – in order to try to get a collective approach to these problems.

Multi-agency work progresses as above but soon afterwards a new resident at the premises recognises John as a high-profile offender who had hit the headlines in the press in the former home area they shared. The media respond in a manner that leads to concerns about John's safety and the security of the approved premises in the light of public interest generated by the media reports. The case is referred to MAPPP (Level 3).

What this example illustrates is that, while John's risk of harm does not change during this period, there is a significant change in the risk management needs of the case. Indeed those needs could be appropriately met only by the case being transferred through the three levels of MAPPA risk management and the access to the different services and resources necessary to provide a defensible risk management plan.

The implementation and development of this operational framework will clearly require strong and consistent strategic management, and this is the second limb of the *Guidance* that emphasises the critical role of the SMB. Although sub-section (3) of Section 67 of the Criminal Justice and Court Services Act (2000) requires that the Responsible Authority in each area must 'keep the arrangements [i.e. the MAPPA] established by it under review with a view to monitoring their effectiveness and making any changes to them that appear necessary or expedient', the *Guidance* recognises that this role is best undertaken by a multi-agency SMB. While some margin of discretion in defining the role has been left with areas, the following core features will be common to all SMBs:

- monitoring (on at least a quarterly basis) and evaluating the operation of the MAPPA, particularly that of the MAPPPs

- establishing connections which support effective operational work with other public protection arrangements, such as Area Child Protection Committees, local Crime and Disorder Partnerships and local Criminal Justice Boards

- preparing and publishing the Annual Report (as required by Section 67 (4) and (5)) and promoting the work of the MAPPA in the area

- planning the longer-term development of the MAPPA in the light of regular (at least annual) reviews of the arrangements, and with respect to legislative and wider criminal justice changes

- identifying and planning how to meet common training and developmental needs of those working in the MAPPA.

Conclusions

With the MAPPA *Guidance* issued only recently it is premature to comment on its effectiveness in addressing some of the shortcomings in the first phase of MAPPA development. However, from our current experience of policy and practice, it is possible to identify three challenges that will shape that continued development over the next two years. The first relates to change management, the second to resourcing, and the third to critical cases and effective public communication.

The speed and expectation of change within public protection are considerable, and the ability of areas to respond will be critical to continued development of MAPPA. The MAPPA *Guidance* is just part of that change but presents a considerable amount that the Responsible Authority must act upon, shaping existing practice or adding to it. The creation of a robust SMB is central to this. In addition, by the end of 2003 it is anticipated that the requirements of the Sex Offences Bill and the Criminal Justice Bill will be determined and these, together with recommendations flowing from public inquiries – such as Lord Laming's report on the Victoria Climbié Inquiry and inspectorate reports such as *Safeguarding Children* – will place additional pressures on the Responsible Authority to effect change. The PPU recognises that it has a role to play advising and disseminating best practice.

Mention has been made of the *Guidance* being the basis upon which a more effective evaluation of MAPPA will occur and from which national standards and evidenced-based best practice will be identified. This work is essential if the true costs of MAPPA, including both the costs incurred through risk management and the costs saved through crime reduction, are to be identified. Only with such costing can MAPPA begin to be prioritised within agency business plans and properly resourced at both a local and a national level.

Finally, MAPPA, despite all that has been said, is likely to remain a small yet at times highly significant and emotive area of public interest. Such interest will undoubtedly be shaped by critical cases and influenced by how the SMB undertakes its communication with the media and the general public. The opportunity, through the vehicle of MAPPA, of moving the public debate about sex offenders forward is a real one, but will be achieved only if Responsible Authorities, and SMBs in particular, engage with the challenge of extending public information into public education. Then members of the public will begin to understand the real nature of risk in the community and what protective and preventative actions are possible, both by themselves and from public agencies. This is an ambitious challenge but one that from our perspective appears to be within the capability of those agencies that are forming an increasingly effective partnership through MAPPA.

Notes

1 Home Office (2001) *Initial Guidance*. London: National Probation Directorate.
2 Home Office (2003) *The MAPPA Guidance*. London: National Probation Directorate.
3 Home Office (2001) *A New Choreography. Strategic Framework 2001–2004*. London: National Probation Service.
4 Details can be found at the Home Office website: www.sexualoffencesbill. homeoffice.gov.uk
5 Soothill, K., Francis, B., Ackerley, E. and Fligelstone, R. (2002) *Murder and Serious Sexual Assault: what criminal histories can reveal about future serious offending*, Police Research Series Paper 144. London: Home Office.
6 Kemshall, H. (2003) *The Community Management of High-Risk Offenders. Prison Service Journal*, March 2003.
7 'What Works' was part of the government's Crime Reduction Strategy, introduced in 1998, which aims to ensure that all probation and prison treatment programmes are based on evidence of success and are therefore evaluated, accredited and, as appropriate, adopted nationally.
8 Maguire, M., Kemshall, H., Noakes, L. and Wincup. E. (2001) *Risk Management of Sexual and Violent Offenders: the Work of Public Protection Panels*, Police Research Series Paper 139. London: Home Office.
9 National Probation Directorate (2002) *Regional Seminars on Managing Sex, Violent and Other Dangerous Offenders* (unpublished).
10 Kennedy, D., Frean, A. and Ford, R. *The Times*, 14 September 2002.
11 Knock, K. (2002) *The Police Perspective on Sex Offender Orders: a preliminary review of policy and practice*, Police Research Series Paper 155. London: Home Office.
12 Home Office (2003) *Further Guidance (2) MAPPA Annual Report 2002/3*. London: National Probation Directorate.
13 Department of Health (2002) *Safeguarding Children*. London: Department of Health.

Chapter 11

Joined-up worrying: the Multi-Agency Public Protection Panels

Roxanne Lieb*

The Home Office's publication, *Protection through Partnership*, describes the purposes and accomplishments of the 40 plus Multi-Agency Public Protection Panels (MAPPPs) across the UK (Home Office 2002). These local bodies, mandated by the Criminal Justice and Court Services Act 2000,[1] combine the efforts of police and probation services to manage the 'risks posed in that area by ... relevant sexual and violent offenders, and other persons who are considered by them to be persons who may cause serious harm to the public' (Criminal Justice and Court Services Act 2000).

The document communicates a strong tone of confidence, leaving the impression that local government officials are working hard to manage violent and sexual offenders. Readers learn that the police and probation services are collaborating to accomplish this ambitious goal, working with other social service agencies. Risk assessment is 'rigorous' and followed by 'robust' management of that risk. The result of this new government policy? As described in the document, the public's protection from violent and sexual offenders has been improved. This type of communications strategy, known as 'public reassurance', has been adopted as a 'key plank of the government's programme to reform and modernise policing' (Povey 2001). Minister Hilary Benn's forward to the MAPPP report concludes with his hopes that the reader 'finds the report useful, informative, and reassuring'.

The political history of MAPPPs helps explain this communication strategy. Following the high-profile murder of a young girl, Sarah Payne, in 2000, a Sunday newspaper published the names and addresses of known and suspected 'paedophiles'. Vigilante activity followed, as did revelations of errors in the identifications. The newspaper withdrew its pledge to continue the exposures, switching to a demand that the government adopt a version of the US laws that allow public officials to warn citizens about sex offenders released from prison who are moving to a community (Hall 2001). These laws, known under the umbrella term 'Megan's Law', were first introduced in the US in 1990 and by 1994 were required by federal law if states wanted their full allocation of block grant funds for anti-crime activities (Matson and Lieb 1997). The Home Office resisted this pressure to adopt Megan's Law, arguing that it would create vigilante activity and result in 'paedophiles going underground' (Home Office News Release, 15 September 2000).

The Home Office chose instead to expand features of the Sex Offender's Act 1997 and to expand the police/probation collaborations that had emerged in several jurisdictions. In 2002, legislation was passed to require police and probation officials in local jurisdictions to assess jointly the risks posed by individuals convicted of a sexual or violent offence, and then rely on inter-agency collaboration to manage those risks. To accomplish these tasks, MAPPPs were established as a 'significant development in public protection' (Home Office July 2002: 4). Annual reports to the public are required by these bodies; the first set was published in September 2002.[2] In addition, each MAPPP has produced protocols defining their operating policies and operations; these documents are confidential.

This chapter relies on the MAPPPs' Annual Reports and protocols to examine the decisions made by these bodies regarding structure, focus, and decision-making. In order to respect confidentiality, the originating jurisdictions are not identified.[3] Since this chapter reviews the initial documents from MAPPPs, it represents an early stage in these evolving organisations.

Statutory direction and guidance

Initial guidance from the Home Office defined the MAPPPs' key tasks as follows:[4]

- Share information on highest risk offenders and determine risk.

- Recommend actions to manage risk.

- Monitor and implement agreed actions.

- Review decisions when circumstances change.

- Manage resources.

The 2001–2 Annual Report summarises the purposes of MAPPPs, offering examples of local decisions and actions. Additionally, the Report further defines the MAPPP roles and purposes and sets new expectations for consultation and notification of victims. The document indicates that over 47,000 offenders were under the organisations' jurisdiction, of whom 18,513 were registered sex offenders, and another 27,477 were violent and other sexual offenders (covered by the registration law), and 1,219 were other offenders (Home Office 2002: 9).

The document also clarifies and further defines the day-to-day operations of the body. The MAPPP is expected to handle only the 'very high risk' cases. The National Probation Service has created a Public Protection Unit for the country's highest risk cases; this body can provide short-term additional resources. In 2001–2, 173 cases were referred to the group (Home Office 2002, v11).

In 2002, the Home Office held regional meetings with MAPPP representatives across the country and afterwards produced further guidance to the groups (National Probation Service 2001). This document concentrated on the expected content and format for the MAPPPs' annual reports (Home Office 2002).

Because the Home Office documents are designed to communicate reassurance, readers may lose sight of the tremendous responsibility assigned to MAPPPs. It is one thing to utter the phrase, 'management of high risk individuals in the community'; it is altogether different to undertake the accomplishment of this goal. The enormity of their charge can be underestimated as a result of the 'reassuring' tone of the Home Office documents. The task is daunting: MAPPPs are to assess the risk of violent and sexual offenders coming to their area (primarily from prison and mental hospitals); identify those who pose the highest risk; develop individualised plans to mitigate this risk and, for the indefinite future, monitor the person and anticipate how life changes may alter their risk.

Considering this scope, it is no surprise that the MAPPPs have chosen a wide variety of structures, decision-making apparatuses and priorities. The protocols reveal a fascinating variety of decisions, variety obviously influenced by factors such as geography, history of high-profile offenders in that area, local personalities, and variable comfort levels with police-probation collaboration. The next section will explore the approaches MAPPPs have taken to key decisions.

Who should be watched?

The Home Office publications related to the MAPPPs stress the central role of risk assessment in deciding which people may pose the highest

risks. Several references are made to actuarial risk assessment instruments that estimate the risk that persons with certain backgrounds
will recidivate. The focus on risk issues fits into a 'risk culture' emphasis
that concerns many criminologists. Kemshall and Maguire (2001) artfully
reviewed this debate from its inception in the 1970s, when it was termed
the 'dangerousness debate', to the present, where 'risk penalty' is often
the key phrase.

The risk penalty literature leads one to clear expectations about how
groups like the MAPPPs will approach their task. The centrepiece of all
work should be an actuarial assessment that calculates risk in a scientific
manner. As the 'touchstone', this assessment will supersede judgement
calls, instincts, and whim. Persons rated as high risk will remain of
concern, even when they appear to be stabilised or to have turned their
life around; similarly, those rated as low risk will be 'off the list' even if
they act hostile and challenging when encountered by a police or
probation officer.

When Kemshall and Maguire examined six MAPPPs in their first stage
of functioning, they discovered that risk assessment did not meet this
pattern (2001). In their words, 'risk management had something of an
"old-fashioned" feel about it, relying mainly on visits and conversations
with offenders and people who knew them' (p. 253). The MAPPP
documents reinforce this impression. If actuarial assessments were the
central core of the MAPPP strategy, one would expect detailed instruc-
tions on scoring, sources of documentation, and procedures for exceptions (if any). The descriptions might evoke an insurance company's
rules about setting premium levels.

In contrast, the MAPPP protocols describe the actuarial risk assessment as a starting point for group decisions. In no case does the process
end there, nor does the actuarial determination appear to carry particular
weight, certainly not in comparison to judgement. In many instances, the
protocols call for a series of risk assessments, typically some combination
of Risk Matrix 2000, the Offender Assessment System developed by the
Prison and National Probation Services (OASys), and Offender Group
Reconviction Scale (OGRS). Some protocols call for the MAPPP to
consider all of these, in addition to unspecified 'other factors.' The
perspective embedded in these documents is explicitly stated by one
MAPPP: 'Professional judgement will remain an essential ingredient in
all risk assessments.'

Clearly, there was debate within the groups about how to categorise
the risk levels, and what the particular focus should be. Is the MAPPP,
for example, concerned about the risk identified individuals pose to
themselves, the risk of self-harm? How about their risk to current and
former partners? Their children? Or is the focus more on people likely

to harm strangers or even a large number of people? Presumably someone suspected of being a terrorist would not be under the purview of a MAPPP, but the definition clearly covers this possibility.

Many MAPPPs also take responsibility for more than potential violent and sexual crime. One describes their task as 'assessing whether or not, in what way, to whom and in what circumstances, a person may harm others', specifically referencing not only the public, but the probation and police staff, as well as the individual's potential for self-harm.

Many MAPPP documents reference the fluctuating nature of risk in individuals. As one document notes, 'risk can be accelerated if certain dynamic factors are present and thus reviewing of risk on low and medium risk offenders is paramount.' With this approach, those of concern are not restricted to the 'high risk list' but every individual meeting the broad parameters of the law.

What happens to the people on the list?

Once someone is listed as high risk, what happens next? What options are available to the MAPPPs? The Multi-Agency Public Protection Arrangements (MAPPA) Annual Report for 2001–2 advises that MAPPPs are likely to focus on the following conditions:

- requirement to live at a specific address and obey a curfew (electronically monitored)
- prohibition from entering certain localities and making contact with certain people (victims)
- restrictions on type of employment.

Very little space in the individual MAPPP protocols is concerned with the question of what is to be done; typically, the documents reference a 'risk management plan' without any specifics. For those MAPPPs that identified activities, the examples included:

- informing the victim
- restricting the individual's employment
- rehousing the person
- visiting the person
- prompt follow-up in the event of failed visits to the probation officer
- setting treatment requirements.

For many people, the MAPPP's assignment to manage dangerous people in the community evokes images of 24-hour surveillance. Television and movies, as well as news reports about high-profile cases, create and reinforce this impression. Obviously, tracking someone's movements at this intense level requires a team of police officers; but such resources are rarely available and, if so, only for a short duration. Most individuals on the high-risk lists are likely to remain there for some time, while new offenders released from prison will be continually added. Thus, the total number of people on the MAPPP's high-risk list will increase exponentially over time, while resources remain relatively stable.

Putting these dimensions together, we have MAPPPs setting very ambitious goals for their work, often with a vague description of actions that will be used to accomplish these expansive responsibilities. The list of dangerous people is ever expanding, with resources likely to be stable at best. With this combination of elements, the list starts to take on characteristics of a 'List of People to Worry About', with collaboration resulting in 'joined-up worrying'.

As the MAPPPs evolve, their choices and strategies may set stricter parameters on their responsibilities. Otherwise, the result could be expectations and promises to the public regarding high-profile incidents that are later uncovered as ideals, not reality.

What information should organisations share and how should they share it?

As the starting point for a collaborative activity involving sensitive information, the rules for information sharing are of paramount concern to MAPPPs. Many MAPPPs have dedicated extensive efforts to defining how and when this sharing will occur and creating safeguards for transmission.

Many MAPPPs begin each meeting with a recitation of confidentiality rules, followed by each participant signing a document attesting to his or her willingness to abide by these rules. Several MAPPPs have set precise rules about what information will be covered in the meeting minutes, with requirements that each member sign the minutes and attest to their accuracy, then return them to the meeting organiser. Frequently, members are directed that minutes cannot be photocopied, and each member organisation must designate a secure filing cabinet in which they will be stored.

The confidentiality sections of the protocols are at present the 'heart and soul' of the MAPPPs. The 'risk penalty' debate in criminological literature did not anticipate this first stage, perhaps because inter-agency collaboration was not envisioned. In many ways, the protocols reveal a group of people in a community wrestling with a very difficult question: how can we look out for the overall safety of the community and not simultaneously create threats to that safety?

One set of protocols provides specific guidance to members about how and what information to share. Members are advised to consider the following questions:

- Is the information you are sharing relevant to managing the risks posed by the potentially dangerous person? Remember there is a difference between need to know and nice to know. The Data Protection Act only allows you to share relevant information.

- Before sharing information are you clear in your own mind what are facts and what is opinion? Only share *facts* in the information sharing section of the meeting. There is time later to discuss the implications and judgements of all the facts shared in the meeting.

- Don't take your own notes. The minutes will be circulated to all organisations that have attended the meeting (having been checked for accuracy). Only note down any actions you need to take.

- The security of the information held in the minutes is your responsibility in line with your own organisation's data protection policy.

Reading the protocols, it becomes clear that the MAPPP members view confidentiality as the essential first building block for collaboration. As one MAPPP document indicated, 'The intention is to build trust between the agencies/organisations who are signatories to these protocols through a better understanding of the implications of disclosure and confidence in the ways others will not abuse information given to them.'

The literature on alliances among business partners suggests that trust between organisations evolves with identifiable stages. The partners begin with 'uncertainty about partners' motives', coupled with a 'lack of detailed knowledge about how they operate'. For trust to evolve, Child and Faulkner (1998) have identified specific stages that include the following:

- realistic commitments that are subject to 'careful calculation and scrutiny' and therefore can be tested as either accomplished or not

- agreement in 'writing, in detail, with the minimum of ambiguity'.

With protocols, the MAPPPs have taken this first step; Child and Faulkner's analysis identifies a significant role for sharing of information. Over time, they assert, this exchange of information helps break down barriers between people, and in doing so, helps 'generate the mutual confidence that takes trust forward beyond a basis of calculation onto one of shared understanding and predictability' (p. 59).

Who goes on the list?

The initial guidance directs that the MAPPP concern itself with the highest risk cases, 'including young offenders' (Home Office 2001: 3). MAPPPs appear to have interpreted this direction in several ways. A few specifically decided not to handle young offenders; 'the majority of young people do not pose a serious risk of harm to the public'. One body designated that responsibility exclusively to the Youth Offending Team. Another set a minimum age of 16 for consideration by the group.

What role will services and treatment serve in MAPPP management?

Most protocols do not address whether and how persons on the list are to receive services and treatment. For one MAPPP, however, the individual's access to services is identified as an integral part of the management strategy: 'ensuring that the individual assessed as posing high risk of serious harm can, by agreement or requirement, relevantly access services that might reduce future risks of causing harm'.

Where will offenders live?

Housing is often the centrepiece of MAPPP management strategies. Some MAPPPs include a major section on accommodation issues in their protocols, summarising detailed agreements reached with housing authorities. In one MAPPP, the police and probation representatives have agreed to inform the housing agents fully about the person's history and situation, committing themselves to specific agreements about the frequency of their visits to the person. Another protocol specifically allows housing authorities to refuse to take a high-risk individual after learning about their background. These agreements represent sharing of power, as well as responsibility, with housing officials.

Will the MAPPP inform the listed individual?

Again, one finds contrasts in the choices that MAPPPs have made. Some groups chose explicitly not to inform individuals about their listing on the high-risk register; others consider the interaction with the person about the listing decision and its consequences as one basis for effective management of their risk. One protocol states that the individual is a key part of accurate risk assessment and 'unless there are compelling reasons not to do so', the person will be approached and offered an opportunity to comment on the assessment. Another body intends that the individual be 'left with no doubt as to the focus of work and expectations of the body'. Some groups have chosen to mail the individual a notice regarding their decision.

How will MAPPP decisions be made?

A variety of organisational structures have been created to accomplish MAPPP goals. The two designated partners in the statute are the police and probation service and, in all cases, leadership is provided by one or both of these groups. Some MAPPPS have elected to have the police provide leadership, others have selected probation, and others have established shared leadership, sometimes hiring a manager who reports to both organisations. Most MAPPPs have established two entities to implement the law: a policy-making management body and an operations body. Called by various names (MAPPP Management Panel, Risk Assessment Management Panel, MAPPP Strategy Group), the policy group meets less frequently and includes more senior staff. The other entity is an operations body, reviewing individual cases and planning actions. In some jurisdictions, several operations groups exist, dividing the jurisdictions into smaller units.

In terms of decision-making, a few protocols define precise rules. For example, one indicates that for someone to be put on the register, a 'clear majority' of the panel must agree. Another MAPPP specifies that cases not considered suitable for registration will not be referred again unless a revised risk assessment occurs. One protocol allows members to record their dissent to decisions in the minutes.

What role is appropriate for victims?

The Home Office's further guidance to the MAPPPs directs that the groups pay particular attention to victim issues, with sections of the

Annual Report devoted to the work undertaken with victims 'to minimise re-victimisation' and keep victims 'properly apprised of the release of offenders' (Home Office Issue No. 2, 2002 v2). This emphasis recalls the Home Secretary's 1999 statements that 'for too long victims of crime have not been given the proper support and protection they deserve. This must change. I am determined to ensure that their needs are placed at the very heart of the criminal justice system' (Straw 1999: 8).

The first group of protocols contain only a few references to victim issues. They are referenced as a 'key audience for protection' from high-risk individuals by one group. Another identified them as important informants, particularly about their partners. A premise statement from one body's protocols indicates that 'well planned and timely meetings should allow the victim perspective to be fully integrated into public protection considerations. The feelings of the victim(s) and any risk or fear of revictimisation should be fully considered at MAPPPS. The victim perspective may well influence the risk management plan that emerges from the meeting.'

Contrast with the US

As stated earlier, the Home Office elected not to take the US path with community notification about individual released sex offenders. In the US, public officials sift through information about those sex offenders about to leave prison, deciding which individuals present particular dangers to citizens. Categorising these offenders into three levels of risk – low, medium, and high – the officials provide information to the public about those grouped into the highest risk level. Notification methods in the US vary and include news releases, door-to-door flyers, information posted on the Internet, or posters in local law enforcement premises (Matson and Lieb 1997; Lovell 2001). In 2003, some jurisdictions began contacting residences through automated calling systems with taped messages about a high-risk sex offender living in the vicinity (Hartman 2003).

For the US, the key governmental activity related to Megan's Law is the identification and notification process. The assumption is that members of the public can use this information to avoid contact with these individuals, and ensure that their children are kept away from them. Presumably, the cautions are also extended to employers who are careful about employing these individuals, landlords about renting to them, and so forth. Undoubtedly, law enforcement uses knowledge about high-risk individuals in its intelligence operations, but this use is not required by federal law.

Challenges to the constitutionality of two states' notification law reached the US Supreme Court in late 2002 and may influence practices in the US, particularly the use of the Internet to post names of high-risk individuals (Greenhouse 2002).

Conclusions

The first set of MAPPP protocols reveals significant variety in the arrangements and decision-making by the 42 entities. The legislation outlined ambitious goals for these groups, and the documents reveal that the local groups have approached this responsibility with ambition and creativity. The enormity of their task – management of sexual and violent persons in the community – cannot be overstated. Early and important steps in forging alliances have taken place as police and probation services, as well as a variety of other entities, have established confidentiality agreements and decision-making apparatuses.

In terms of the day-to-day work of the MAPPPs, it becomes clear that the MAPPP members have taken on significant responsibility for their community's safety. Limited resources are attached to this responsibility, and the list of identified dangerous persons will only increase.

The next phases of MAPPP's evolution are likely to take individual groups in even more diverse directions as they try to meet the government's directives. This diversity offers a great opportunity for learning about management of dangerous people, and multi-agency collaborations in sensitive governmental areas. Systematic examinations of MAPPPs could help chart the next set of policies on this topic.

Notes

*Roxanne Lieb was an Atlantic Fellow in Public Policy in 2002, based at the Institute of Criminology at the University of Cambridge.
1 Sections 67 and 68.
2 See www.onlinemappa.info/
3 Letters from Amanda Matravers and the author requesting the protocols from probation agencies and police departments were sent in the autumn of 2002. The letters indicated the nature of the research efforts and requested copies of the documents. The letter pledged that the documents would remain confidential.
4 Multi-Agency Public Protection Arrangements, 13 September 2002.

References

Child, J. and Faulkner, D. (1998) *Strategies of Cooperation*. New York: Oxford University Press.

Criminal Justice and Court Services Act 2000 (2000) Chapter 43, Section 67. London: HMSO.

Greenhouse, L. (2002) 'Court Looks at Sex Offender Lists' *New York Times* 14 November 2002.

Hall, S. (2001) 'Argument rages over Sarah's law: Why parents' key demand is rejected by police', *Guardian Unlimited*, 13 December 2001.

Hartman, D. (2003) *Notification system may announce sex offenders*, in email from Alisa Klein to the Association for the Treatment of Sexual Abusers Listserve, *Automated Phone Calls to Be Used for Community Notification*.

Home Office (2001) *NPD Regional Seminars on Managing Sex, Violent and other Dangerous Offenders*. London: HMSO.

Home Office, Further Guidance (1) to police and probation services on the Criminal Justice and Court Services Act 2000, Sections 67 & 68, *Guidance on Production of Annual Report 2002–2003*, Issue No. 1. London: HMSO.

Home Office, Further Guidance (2) to police and probation services on the Criminal Justice and Court Services Act 2000, Sections 67 & 68 (Multi-Agency Public Protection Arrangements – MAPPA), *Guidance on Production of Annual Report 2002–2003*, Issue No. 2. London: HMSO.

Home Office (2002) *Protection Through Partnership: Multi-Agency Public Protection Arrangements, Annual Report 2001–2*. London: Home Office Communications Directorate.

Home Office News Release (2000) *Government Proposals Better to Protect Children From Sex and Violent Offenders*. London: HMSO.

Kemshall, H. and Maguire, M. (2001) 'Public Protection, Partnership and Risk Penalty', *Punishment and Society* 3.2, pp. 237–64.

Lovell, E. (2001) *Megan's Law: does it protect children?*. London: National Society for the Prevention of Cruelty to Children.

Maguire, M., Kemshall, H., Noaks, L., Wincup, E., and Sharpe, K. (2001) *Risk Management of Sexual and Violent Offenders: the work of public protection panels*. London: Home Office.

Matson, S. and Lieb, R (1997) *Megan's Law: a review of state and federal legislation*. Olympia, WA: Washington State Institute for Public Policy.

National Probation Service (2001) *NPD Regional Seminars on Managing Sex, Violent, and Other Dangerous Offenders*. London: Home Office.

Povey, Sir K. (2001) *Open All Hours: a thematic inspection report on the role of police visibility and accessibility in public reassurance*. London: HMIC.

Straw, J. (1999) 'Partners Against Crime', *Victim Support Magazine* Summer 71, p. 8.

Chapter 12

Challenges for the police service

Terence Grange

Introduction

Other chapters in this volume discuss the issues involved in managing sex offenders from academic, policy making and pragmatic perspectives. This chapter concentrates upon the pragmatic consequences of legislative change and media pressures to the police service as one of the 'responsible authorities' for the management of sex offenders.

In setting out the history of police involvement in this area and the changes brought to police culture by the requirement to proactively monitor and manage the behaviour and activities of sex offenders, I discuss the inception of the Sex Offenders Act 1997. Using the example of the release of Sidney Cooke upon an outraged public in 1998, I will seek to show the pressures the presence of such offenders in the community place upon police and probation staff. Other less notorious examples will demonstrate the resistance of communities to the presence of offenders and how police resources and time can be consumed by the management not just of the offender but also the resistant local community.

I then discuss the challenges presented to the police by the changed legislation, by pressures upon politicians from the media and the public, and by the behaviour of the media. How we react to and manage these pressures and, in particular, how we seek to interact with the public on the housing of sex offenders and community notifications on those considered dangerous, will present the reality of the situation as we seek to balance our accountabilities under the Human Rights Act and the Sex Offenders Act.

Finally, I discuss the future and reach some broad conclusions as to where we are being led by the legislation and reactions to it from the public, the media and the offenders.

Current legislation

The current position is that the Sex Offenders Act has permitted the police service to enforce a requirement for sex offenders to register with the police, provide photographs and fingerprints, state a home address, and inform the police of any absence of more than seven days. It encourages, but does not legally support, police monitoring, visiting and surveillance of offenders. It permits breaches of Articles within the Human Rights Act regarding the offender's right to privacy and family life, right to go to and stay where he wishes and to associate with others. Sex Offender Orders (introduced under the Crime and Disorder Act of 1998) allow the judiciary to issue edicts forbidding an offender to visit certain places, such as leisure centres or parks, and there are criminal penalties for non-compliance.

In isolation the legislation appears effective. However, pending requirements for other authorities (housing, health, and social services) to assist police and probation, it is at present less effective than it could be. In the face of an unsupportive media, particularly the tabloid newspapers, the measure struggles to gain public support. Given the willingness of the offenders and the legal profession to use the Human Rights Act and other legislation to deter police/probation management regimes, the police are unsure as to how demanding they can be. The legislation does not meet the public's wish to know more about who is in their midst.

The current proposals to tighten up on the registration of offenders and to enforce greater involvement and compliance by other authorities in support of police and probation are to be welcomed. As will be discussed later in this chapter, there are developing issues as to the ability of the police to monitor registered sex offenders effectively. The speed with which some offenders have sought to use the Human Rights Act to avoid monitoring brings into question the issue of whether or not the police should have powers to enter their premises and to ensure that they respond both to questions and to monitoring. The Human Rights Act may be used to counter police activity and the balance between that Act and the Sex Offenders Act, together with the forthcoming changes to it, will be fought out in the courts. The concept of making those convicted of sex offences register, whether they be British nationals or foreign nationals who are registered on arrival in the United Kingdom, appears sound. However, the reality is that unless foreign governments have bilateral arrangements with the United Kingdom, there is no effective means for our immigration service and the police to know that people entering the country are offenders. Therefore, the government will need to create bilateral arrangements with foreign governments. That will be a very long and complex process. Meanwhile, people about whom we know very little continue to enter the country.

The presence on the register of people convicted of offences associated with watching children being sexually abused on the Internet presents further complexities. Many argue that these people are not dangerous, but the fact remains that when convicted they are placed on the register. It may be that the government should explore the possibility of using Sex Offender Orders to forbid such people from using Internet chat rooms and devise a means of monitoring their Internet activity so that the criminal implications of ignoring the Sex Offender Orders can be brought to bear on them. The new offence of 'sexual grooming' (introduced in the Sex Offences Bill 2003) is designed to tackle those who misuse the Internet to befriend children with a view to sexually abusing them.

Hi-tech solutions to monitoring the activities of registered offenders such as bracelets and other means of tagging will, as with other offenders, founder on the fact that the offenders rapidly work out how to counter this form of monitoring. Therefore, the relevant authorities will still need to make risk analysis the focal point of monitoring and, with all the consequent dangers of wrongly assessing someone, rely upon that analysis and conduct their monitoring accordingly.

How they will improve on the current position and how a single sex offender database and risk analysis process adopted nationally will work will be the stuff of future analysis by academics. For the pragmatist, how we came to be where we are and the reality of sex offender management is the context in which this chapter is set.

Child protection: marginalisation and partnership

Sex offenders have been with us always. It is only recently that their presence and activities have excited major governmental, media and public interest. There has always been concern over the occasional outrage committed by a stranger, but the dramatic rise in levels of interest over the past five years and the subsequent activities of politicians, the mass media and a concerned public have produced radical changes in both the legislative approach and in the deployment of staff and the activities of the police service. These changes have taken place against a backdrop of persistent and intense media pressure and a radically more demanding and unforgiving public.

Prior to the Sex Offenders Act 1997, the police service had not viewed the management of sex offenders and the proactive monitoring of people on a sex offenders register as a core police activity. Indeed, the concept of proactive approaches to the management of criminals and crime was only slowly taking hold.

Child protection work has never been a major priority for government and police forces. It has a history of marginalisation within police forces, with the officers conducting it traditionally seen as more akin to social workers than real police officers. The reality is that the people engaged in child protection are investigating some of the most serious crimes committed against children. Their work is crucial to the development of the children they safeguard and, to an extent, the future stability of those individuals and the families they may create. However, neither senior management team support, nor funding, nor cultural approval has, until very recently, been given to the function and to the officers engaged in it. The Laming Report into the death of Victoria Climbié demonstrates this only too clearly. Until the prevailing organisational and cultural approach is overtaken by one which acknowledges just how serious the crimes being committed against children are, and just how complicated the investigatory regime is, the management of sex offenders is likely to remain equally marginalised. The two go together and both need to be seen as priorities by government and police authorities. Until this occurs, I have reservations as to the likelihood of child protection and the management of sex offenders being managed effectively by police forces.

Though the Crime and Disorder Act 1994 mandated partnership between local police commanders and local authority chief executives working to reduce crime and disorder, its impact upon police culture was not great. Arguably, even now it is marginal in many places. Similarly, working in partnership with the probation service was a marginal activity conducted by crime reduction and community safety departments, themselves on the extremities of both police activity and cultural thinking.

The culture of the detective as a hero investigating crime, and patrolling officers enforcing public peace were the predominant features of traditional policing. Small, tightly knit groups worked to their own ethics and culture, almost in isolation from the outside world, and in part dismissive of the crime reduction agenda. Investigation, arrest and prosecution, linked to a high detection rate, prevailed. Engagement with other organisations was viewed as necessary to the pursuit of detection rather than to crime reduction. In-depth engagement with probation and social services on this or any other subject was unusual and the services, whose cultures were and are markedly different, co-existed with little partnership dimension.

The incidents that brought about the Sex Offenders Act 1997 also initiated major media interest on the issue of sex offending and more precisely of paedophilia and paedophiles. That interest and the 'monsterisation' of sex offenders remains to this day and is unlikely to diminish.

Community reactions to paedophiles

The urge to 'out' people and to pursue an issue to the point of recklessness was seen at its worst when the notorious paedophile Sidney Cooke was released and taken to the West Country. The *Bristol Evening Post* stated confidently that he was being looked after by police in Broadbury Road police station. A mob gathered and serious violence ensued.

The same paper then introduced its 'rumour line' inviting people to call with information or merely gossip as to Cooke's location. The local police were forced into the position of regularly commenting or refusing to comment on the rumours and gossip printed. The search for Cooke prevailed throughout the police force area. The government absented itself from the issue, with only the local MP Paddy Ashdown actively seeking to support the police approach. He was subsequently attacked in the street.

Little has changed in the following six years. Whenever the media find a 'monster' there is a public reaction. In 2002 in the west of Wales a man suspected of being a paedophile was killed; two men await trial. In the same area a local newspaper printed the name and address of a man charged with indecent assault on a child; his neighbour's windows were destroyed the same day.

In a village in north Pembrokeshire, one of Britain's quietest counties, a suspected paedophile was housed by the local authority. An informal community group promptly wrote to the Council and the chief constable threatening direct action against the man and his family unless he was removed. The direct action suggested was picketing his house and if necessary his physical removal.

In north Powys a released offender housed in a small village was located by a relative of his victim and the village plastered with his photograph. The local chief probation officer and chief police officer faced an angry village bent upon his removal. He was removed.

All these incidents occurred in the most peaceful area in England and Wales within three months. They have been mirrored across the country.

The engagement of politicians has resulted in major legislation and a desire for the government to direct and monitor more closely the activities of those engaged in the management of sex offenders. The Sex Offenders Act itself, changes to it and to other relevant legislation, and the desire to manage public perceptions have elicited contradictory responses by government. Meeting the changes introduced and managing the consequences of political action and inaction have also presented complex challenges.

The public have been warned of unseen dangerous people in their midst and have read and watched avidly the police and others' responses to outrageous acts perpetrated on children. Their reaction has been one of fear, and by some a demand to be given the names and addresses of known and convicted sex offenders. The incidents at Paulsgrove in Portsmouth in 2001 were not unique. The public's reaction to the presence of an offender has been to reject the individual via pressure upon him, the local authorities and police and probation services and by outright intimidation and violence.

Multi-agency management of sex offenders

Where are we today? We have 42 local sex offender registers and a small team attempting to create a single unified register accessible by police forces and probation services across England and Wales. Funding for this necessary system is not guaranteed.

Multi Agency Public Protection Panels (MAPPPs) have existed in diverse forms across England and Wales for three years. Their constituent members are police and probation, both named as responsible authorities. Their responsibility is to assess the relative risks posed by people on the sex offenders register and the violent offenders known to them; currently there are 18,000 registered sex offenders and 24,000 violent offenders. Violent offenders have no registration requirement. Other organisations asked, but not yet required, to assist in the management of offenders are local housing, social services and health authorities.

The MAPPPs have to assess relative risks and manage the supervision and monitoring of those considered to be high risk. To manage the process, risk analysis tools used by the Prison Service, the Offender Assessment System (OASys) and the risk analysis tool created by David Thornton, Risk Matrix 2000, have been adopted. Their use by all responsible authorities is intended to bring about consistency in the identification of risk and the subsequent management of the high risk offenders.

The reality is that dependent upon funding and staffing the assessments can be followed through with appropriate supervision and monitoring arrangements by probation and police. As no new funding was made available to support what, for the police, is a new activity, the training, development of necessary teams and growth of best practice have been hindered by inconsistencies in the government's demands upon the police.

To support MAPPPs, forces have senior officers in divisions or groups of divisions tasked to attend and manage police involvement. Public Protection Teams have been deployed to oversee police monitoring activities, and likewise surveillance teams to conduct covert watching. The numbers to be risk assessed and monitored are such that full-time deployment of personnel is becoming the norm.

The Sex Offenders Act is being amended to make the management of offenders easier and to force early notification of changing circumstances upon them (see Sex Offences Bill 2003).

Future challenges

The change in the police approach, the introduction of accountabilities and the even closer working of the agencies involved have all been positive outcomes. What then are the challenges currently facing the police service and what are those for the future?

For the present the challenges are those mentioned above: government and political activity and reaction to pressures, the media, the offenders and public perception of the offenders and their place in our society.

The politics of sex offender management

Sex offending and paedophilia are intractable and very complex issues. Managing sex offenders and paedophiles requires clear national policy and activity, political courage to make and stand by unpopular decisions, a clear statement that it is a priority issue, and long-term concentration upon it by government in its planning and interactions with policing.

At present, the government is being driven by imperatives that detract from the type of long-term thinking and unpopular decision-making necessary to the development of better management of sex offenders. The ever-present urge to present itself in a good light in the face of mounting criticism of the criminal justice system, and a heightened sense of fear, particularly over street robbery, gun crime, drugs and other issues, have led to the government seeking to engage itself in all these areas via close supervision of police activity to 'improve the situation'.

The consequences for other activities were and are profound; the less obvious but more complex issues lose resources to these immediate priorities. Governmental concerns about robbery, crack cocaine usage and gun crime are bringing about resourcing issues for the police. The management and monitoring of sex offenders, a role pressed upon the police but not funded, will suffer in the face of such short-term approaches by government.

Taking unpopular decisions is not something governments willingly do. In the face of public anger and media pressure, particularly on an issue such as the treatment of sex offenders, easy options are taken. The closing of the Wolvercote Clinic in July 2002 is one such case. Having decided upon an alternative site the government bowed to public pressure and closed the clinic without moving to the new site. The consequences are the absence of a top class facility in which offenders were able to confront their offending, and the return to their homes of offenders who have not completed the programme they volunteered to undergo.

There is still no replacement facility in sight and police forces are dealing with the consequences of this lack of political courage.

Similarly, the government's very late change of decision as to how the first MAPPA reports would be presented left local chief officers of police and probation to deal with the consequences. That they handled the situation well did not detract from the anger felt at what they perceived as central government's evasion of its responsibilities.

Engaging with government, made easier via the Dangerous Offenders Unit, remains complex and unrewarding due to the government's ever-present desires both to be seen to be in control and to remain popular, desires which in this arena are often mutually exclusive. The reluctance of members of Parliament, with a few honourable exceptions, to engage in difficult decisions adds to the difficulties faced at operational level for managing offenders.

In the environment currently surrounding the politics of crime and criminality these difficulties are unlikely to be easily managed.

Managing the media

The British media, in particular the written media, are possibly the most questioning and challenging media group in the world. Their cynicism towards public services and their search for a scapegoat produce extraordinary pressures on those upon whom they focus their ire. The right of a free press to report what it sees and to challenge those engaged in public or private service should not be constrained. However, the pressures their engagement can induce should be better understood.

The campaigning approach the newspapers take – Sarah's Law and the decriminalisation of cannabis being two examples – can and do impact greatly upon public thinking and on government. The merits of

Sarah's Law are arguable; the simple demand for controlled access by concerned parents and others to information about known/convicted or suspected paedophiles has some force. However, the making of monsters via 'name and shame' campaigns and the solemn washing of editorial hands regarding the consequences of people's photographs appearing on the front page present challenges for the police, probation and others engaged in attempting to manage the people concerned.

Controlled access is a chimera, adopting the guise of respectable parents seeking information. It suggests that a breach of confidentiality by these respectable parents could be made a crime. The concept ignores the reality of individual and group human behaviour. In an environment in which those who engage physically in inappropriate activity with children, sexually abuse them or who watch such abuse via the Internet are described in the mass media as monsters, the public are unlikely to take a rational approach to their presence. The media know this; there are major examples such as Paulsgrove and more minor examples, four forced removals from villages in the middle and west of Wales in three months in 2002, which demonstrate this.

The local media were involved in attempts to prevent the Wolvercote Clinic re-opening. Direct confrontations on the radio and on television with those engaged in managing offenders, with demands that they answer the impossible question, 'Wouldn't you want to know if a pervert or paedophile lived in your street?' create an environment in which attempts rationally to explain the debate regarding the human rights of the innocent and the human rights of the known or suspected sex offender result only in condemnation of the police officers attempting to explain their difficulties.

Both have rights; the duty of a police officer is to positively reinforce the human rights of organisations and people with whom he or she may have no sympathy. The popular media does not accept the complexity of that position. The police officer becomes the target of their wrath.

Paedophiles and the public

To the general public the idea of known sex offenders and paedophiles being placed in their midst is unacceptable. Should the individual be an outsider, who is not from their immediate locality, that feeling is reinforced. The vast majority of abusers are dangerous only to their own children or extended relatives. The public perceive them as a risk to all.

For the police and probation services, the appropriate disclosure of the names and locations of offenders and the housing of those offenders are the most complex and demanding areas of our interaction with the public.

227

Open disclosure, Sarah's Law, does not take place. The MAPPP will assess the risks posed by the presence of an offender in a given street or apartment or near a school, leisure centre or park/open space. Given all that is known from the risk assessment tools and the dynamic monitoring/supervision of the offender a decision may be made to notify suitable people of his presence.

The school headteacher, leisure centre managers or group leader will receive written notification, photograph and a full briefing as to who he is and the relevant dangers posed. Thus confidentiality and briefing only to those who need to know are assured. The offender is informed of the intent to disclose; one such individual has successfully used the Human Rights Act to prevent disclosure.

Where disclosure occurs outside the planned environment and, indeed, where wider disclosure is seen as advisable, police and probation services have to manage the process. Public meetings have taken place where the community's fears and the process of management are discussed. To the authorities this is a risk-laden environment in which their ability to prevent re-offending and to ensure public safety is openly challenged. Discussion of the risks posed by particular individuals can founder on wider public fears. People are unconvinced by the argument that offenders are, in the main, not dangerous, and if dangerous, to their own families rather than to the community at large. They have no wish to discover whether the authorities are right or wrong.

Housing offenders presents similar problems. Many housing authorities will assist, many will not. Some who will retain the right to do so only with full disclosure to local residents. An offender who is released into the wider community may live in a place of his choice or one chosen by the responsible authorities. In the absence of his own accommodation the MAPPP for the relevant area will seek, through the local authority or a housing association, to find suitable accommodation. The housing authority will be informed of the relative risks posed and the monitoring arrangements. They may choose to assist or not.

The most appropriate methods of disclosure and housing must be found. Public meetings are almost always hostile, and despite the competence of the authorities, the public almost always reject the presence of the offender. Therefore, bail hostels and other probation accommodations tend to house the individuals in groups; not the most satisfactory solution.

Seeking to overcome the current hostile atmosphere and the media's misrepresentation of risk is proving almost impossible. Despite regularly pointing out the rarity of child abduction by strangers, this continues to be perceived as the greatest risk. In the written or broadcast media discussion of the issue of sex offender management focuses on the latest alleged incident or loophole in the legislation. The will and the stamina to respond to and deal proactively with the media has to be set against other realities; the day job is managing a police force. It is an issue from which others who could assist shy away. During the Sidney Cooke incident the Home Office declared the issue an operational matter and not one for them. Persistent rebuttal of inaccurate information and a willingness to explain are the only weapons available. They have to be deployed via a sceptical media.

All these issues: the necessary meeting structures, the staffing and costs of monitoring offenders and the extra costs of managing public knowledge, suspicion and reaction to their apparent presence are neither specifically funded by government nor are they an explicit priority of government. There are no performance measures other than that there should not be another organisational failure. That will be the measure of success used by the public, the media and government.

Managing the offender

The final challenge is that of actually managing the offenders. Registration and subsequent monitoring are not welcomed by them. A few have not registered. Others have registered and appear to be compliant. However, the reality for the police service is that the register presents as many challenges as solutions.

There are some 18,000 registered sex offenders at large in our communities. The majority present only a small risk of danger to others. A very few pose a serious risk. Differentiating between the two is far more complex than the public and media understand and is a more fluid situation than is accepted. To the teams and individuals charged with monitoring them and considering the various options open, such as Sex Offender Orders, the separation of the dangerous from the less dangerous is at the heart of the monitoring process. Not all can be monitored, at least not to the extent the public would perceive as acceptable. There are 128,000 police officers and 18,000 registered sex offenders; there are in addition 24,000 violent offenders. The mathematics of full supervision do not add up.

Therefore, following risk analysis and MAPPA agreement, those considered to be higher risk receive greater attention. Many do not co-operate fully and some seek to use other government legislation to inhibit police monitoring. Restraining Orders under the Protection from Harassment Act 1997 have been sought (*Crosby v Parratt* and the Commissioner of the Metropolitan Police, 2002) to deter a detective constable from attending the home of a registered offender and actively monitoring his conduct.

The Human Rights Act has been used in an attempt to enforce the rights to privacy and a family life of a known paedophile. The judiciary has been asked to balance the offender's rights to privacy against the rights of the public to security from those who, they fear, may harm them. Formal complaints against officers have been made alleging abuse of authority and other issues.

Managing these reactions, and the consequent focus on the officers, whilst retaining an equally clear focus on securing public safety, presents the officers involved and their management with unique problems.

Others who pose a risk and are aware of their rights present other issues. Regularly moving from one place to another, at random and with minimal notice, presses police forces into escorting these individuals wherever they choose to travel. One case saw an individual escorted by police from central England to coastal resorts and then to Scotland, incidentally voiding a Sex Offender Order taken out in England in the process.

The internal management issues such activities cause, and the consequent queries from other organisations and local MPs, add to the complexities involved, as well as to the costs of the exercise.

Managing the future

What, then, of the future? There is a need for a single nationwide sex offender database, easily accessible by the police and probation services and in time by other organisations. This project, ViSOR (the Violent and Sex Offenders Register) should be complete for the police service by December 2003.

The Internet and the access it provides present further problems for the police. The hitherto unrecognised interest in watching child abuse via the Internet has come upon the police suddenly, very publicly, in large numbers and with the additional complication of the type of offender being identified.

Operation Ore, the investigation of 7,000 or more people accessing an Internet site specifically dedicated to child sexual abuse, has stretched the resources of police forces to the limit. From the date of first notification each force has had to recruit and train additional computer crime analysts and forensic people to conduct in-depth analysis of thousands of computers. In-depth research on the individual, family and working lives of all involved are being conducted, occasionally in the full glow of the media. For some 12 months so far and for 24 months to come this single operation has and is radically distorting force priorities.

Operation Ore presents a different set of issues because of the type of person being investigated: namely, police officers, teachers, judges, senior civil servants, nurses, doctors, senior prison service personnel.

The effect on public perceptions of the caring professions is yet to be clarified. The impact of this number of additions to the sex offenders register, and the issue of risk analysis of what is a different form of involvement in child abuse and a different type of offender may also need investigation.

Risk analysis and its refinement are essential to better focus the efforts of police and probation. The development of OASys and the Matrix 2000 tools and the training, another unfunded cost, are essential to the monitoring exercise.

Closer and better engagement with the authorities essential to the success of placing offenders in the community (housing, local political leaders, social services, and others) and gaining acceptance of this form of management are prerequisite to success. Obtaining such support in what clearly is an adverse environment remains one of the greatest challenges. Confronting a public unwilling to accept offenders in their midst remains an issue. The openness and willingness of the police and probation services in these circumstances does not matter; the outcome remains almost inevitable – the offender is moved.

Communicating with the public in the heat of the outing of an offender remains the most immediate and difficult challenge. Engaging in a considered debate with the public via the media and the political body on the problems surrounding the managing of sex offenders remains an intractable issue.

How that is to be managed – and other contributions to this debate argue that full public access to information is the most likely outcome – will bear heavily on the practical issues of managing offenders and the relationship between the police and the local community. In the absence of some form of understanding of the present approach, the cycle of placement of offenders and public dissatisfaction and threatened action will continue.

A more thoughtful long-term approach by government is also necessary for the proactive management of offenders inside and outside prison. The development of enforced treatment regimes within prisons will make for difficult choices for those convicted and sent to prison. Unless it is supported by a similar regime for those not serving sentences the future of treatment appears bleak. For the police the need is obvious; the Wolvercote Clinic and other such centres are essential to proper offender management and the ability of the police to contribute to this. In the absence of such facilities and the inevitability of even longer registers, the police simply will not have the capacity to match the demand for monitoring.

Police forces need to accept that this area of work requires greater funding and greater prominence in both strategic and tactical thinking.

The use of offender registers for sex, violence and possibly domestic violence presents a double-edged sword.

The targets for attention will be clearly identifiable. There will, however, be large numbers of them. Analysing the risks posed by each separate individual and recording that analysis and the decision-making that accompanies it will be essential to the 'defensible decision-making' approach that will underpin the process. For the public and the media there will be one simple question should an incident occur: 'Was the offender on the register?' If so, the involvement of all agencies and the actions and decisions that were taken will be subject to the most intense scrutiny. Chief police officers will need to acknowledge the pressures of the role and organise their resources, staff the activities and provide other emotional and practical support, despite the pressures to meet other governmental priorities. Whether, when under pressure to improve detection rates elsewhere, they have the fortitude to do so will be a crucial issue in the improvement of police performance in this area.

Index